american
cookie

american cookie

THE SNAPS, DROPS, JUMBLES, TEA CAKES, BARS & BROWNIES
That We Have Loved for Generations

anne byrn

PHOTOGRAPHY BY TINA RUPP

RODALE

Published in the United States by Rodale Books, an imprint of the Crown Publishing Group,
a division of Penguin Random House LLC, New York.

crownpublishing.com

rodalebooks.com

RODALE and the Plant colophon are registered trademarks of Penguin Random House LLC.

Library of Congress Cataloging-in-Publication Data is available.

ISBN 978-1-62336-545-5

Ebook ISBN 978-1-62336-546-2

Printed in China

Book design by Amy C. King

Photographs by Tina Rupp

Food styling by Paul Grimes

Prop styling by Stephanie Hanes

10 9 8 7 6 5 4 3 2 1

First Edition

For everyone who bakes cookies and memories.

CONTENTS

Introduction

If you stop between bites to think about it, the little cakes, cookies, and candies that have given Americans so much pleasure through the years are fascinating morsels of history. They are expressions of love, small squares of a nostalgic place in time, stains in a beloved old family cookbook, remembrances of cookie jars and a childhood past, little dots connecting the holidays in our lives. And they are timeless, every one of them, as suitable to bake today as they were generations ago.

Molasses thins baked to a crisp in a wood-fired oven, honey drops served by the hundreds in the Roosevelt White House, a beloved chocolate meringue cookie first sold in a Savannah Jewish deli, Mexican wedding cookies dredged in confectioners' sugar in San Antonio, ginger-spicy Creole stage planks, oatmeal lace cookies so thin you can see through them, chewy butterscotch blondies, the anise-flavored bizcochitos of New Mexico and their rich history, all-American brownies, Kentucky bourbon balls, tea cakes and sugar cookies, peanut butter cookies first baked for children in the school lunch program, the mysterious snickerdoodles, and, of course, the iconic Toll House cookie. These are all small American bites that tell a big story.

In fact, the first cakes baked in early America were more small than large. Patterned after the tea cakes served in England, these new American cakes went by names such as queen cakes and were flavored with lemon, lavender, or caraway. They were dainties on a plate, served in small portions at a time when sugar was prohibitively expensive and you had to be wealthy to carry on the British custom of serving tea and cakes in early America.

Early colonists brought their cookie recipes

with them, and we can thank the Dutch for the word *cookie*. A recipe called "Cookies" was included in the first US cookbook, *American Cookery* by Amelia Simmons, in 1796. It contained just sugar, pearlash (an early leavener) as well as milk, flour, butter, and pounded coriander seeds. The English, too, brought their recipes for "jumbals" or "jumbles," sugar cookies that took on many forms once they settled into American kitchens.

In the South, with the addition of leavening, those sugar cookies transformed into leavened tea cakes, first called Jackson Jumbles in the early 1800s after President Andrew Jackson. After the Civil War was over, these tea cakes became a diaspora food dear to African Americans. Many freed slaves and their families resettled outside the South and took their tea cake recipes with them.

In fact, the whole wonderful melting pot of countries that have shaped the soul of America is present in the small bites we pop into our mouth. The French petits fours; Dutch New Year cookies; Italian fig cookies; Spanish cookies of lard and anise; Moravian gingersnaps; African benne wafers; Scottish shortbread; Creole beignets, calas, and pralines; Mexican sopaipillas; and German lebkuchen, or what Americans know as gingerbread cookies—they all belong to us.

These little cookies, cakes, and candies from distant lands are now a part of our American foodways, appearing slightly different in our land. As early American settlers adapted their recipes to new ingredients, ovens, religious practices, life on the farm or in the city, new jobs or no job, and the American way of living and baking, it is only natural that their recipes morphed into something new.

When researching my book *American Cake*, I quickly learned that the cakes America loves were not always stacked, frosted, and sliced. They were not always served at momentous occasions, nor their ingredients imported, precious, and carefully measured. These small bites were everyday recipes, baked spontaneously, beloved by children, packed into lunch boxes and stuffed into pockets, and crafted from ingredients you had on hand. And just like the larger American cakes, these smaller bites—be they soft nutmeg and currant cake, buttery vanilla cookie, gingerbread, chewy almond macaroon, deep chocolate chip cookie, salty peanut brittle, or crisp ricotta doughnut—have intriguing stories to tell. They may be small, but they speak volumes about what was going in America when they were first baked.

Take something as simple as a snickerdoodle cookie. Baking them might take you back to the day in your grandmother's kitchen when you were young and hungry. You can smell the vanilla, butter, cinnamon, and the magical aroma coming from the oven as those cookies baked until golden brown. You remember not being able to wait long enough for the cookies to cool, and how you ate them so quickly. That was decades ago, and yet that nostalgic image remains with you, much like Marcel Proust experienced with his storied madeleine more than 100 years ago.

Think more deeply about those snicker-doodles: Did your grandmother bake them with butter or vegetable shortening? Did she live in the Midwest, where snickerdoodles have long

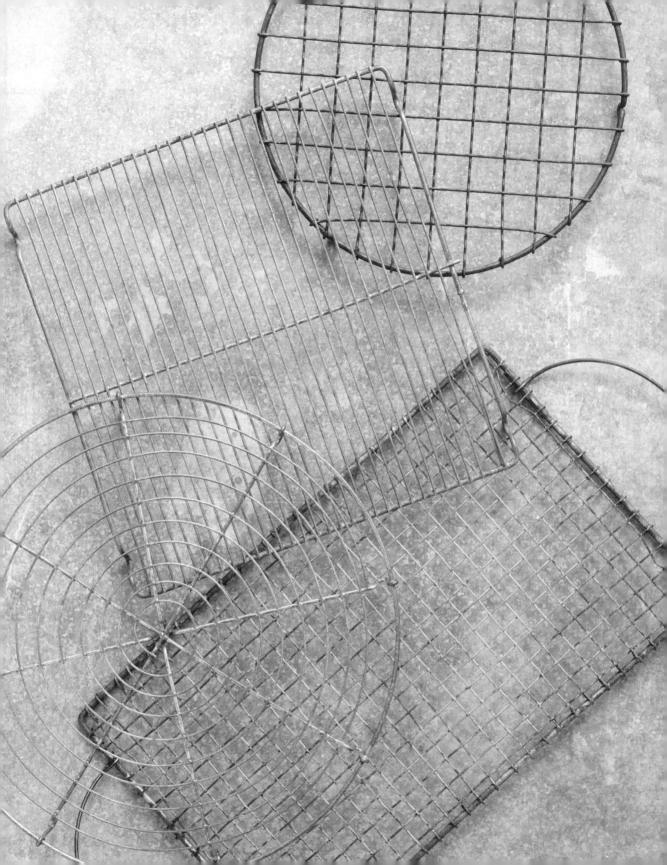

been popular? Did she make them small enough for children's hands, which was how cookies were originally baked? How did your grandmother affect your life as a child? These are deep questions that most of us can answer—and all because of a home-baked cookie.

Before the days of oversize dark chocolate bakery cookies, before Mrs. Fields and David's, even before Rice Krispies squares and the 13" × 9" pan took over the American fascination, in the heartland of America, small cookies, bars, dainty cakes, fried doughnuts, and butterscotch candies were assembled with whatever was on hand.

Once again, I ask you to bake along with me and travel back in time to explore the sweet bites of America's history. These recipes may be new discoveries altogether or they may bring back a flood of memories from your past. Put the kettle on for tea, and let's get baking.

A Baker's Dozen Cookie-Baking Tips

1. **MAKE THE DOUGH FIRST.** Sometimes it needs to rest an hour or overnight before baking to improve the cookies' texture.

2. **READ THE RECIPE** through before you begin. With cookies, it's easy to substitute ingredients or use slightly less or more of an add-in than the recipe instructs. But you must have flour, sugar, sometimes eggs, and some type of fat, whether it's butter, shortening, lard, or oil.

3. **PREHEAT THE OVEN** to 350° or 375°F for 10 to 15 minutes before you plan to bake. These are the most common cookie-baking temps. Position the rack in the center of the oven, or a notch up from the center position, as the recipe suggests.

4. **THE COOKIE RECIPES** in this book call for a conventional oven, where you will need to bake one pan at a time. If you want to bake cookies in a convection oven, you will need to decrease the oven temperature by 25°F and also decrease the baking time by 25 percent. Then you can bake multiple pans of cookies on different racks all at once. For example, a cookie recipe at 350°F for 12 minutes in a conventional oven would be baked at 325°F for 9 minutes in a convection oven.

5. **MEASURE FLOUR BY SPOONING** it into the dry-ingredient measuring cups and leveling off the top with a knife.

6. **MEASURE GRANULATED SUGAR BY POURING** it into the measuring cup. When you measure brown sugar, pack it into the cup before leveling it off.

7. **BUTTER SHOULD BE AT ROOM TEMPERATURE** for cookie baking. A couple of hours ahead of baking, place it on the kitchen counter to soften. Or, if you are working with cold butter, place it in the microwave on high power for 8 to 10 seconds, or until soft.

8. **EGGS SHOULD BE LARGE** and ideally at room temperature. But baking with eggs straight from the fridge is okay and not going to ruin your recipe. If, however, you are

THE AMERICAN COOKIE LARDER: *Stocking the Pantry to Bake*

THE KEY INGREDIENTS for cookies and small cakes are much the same as larger cakes, but with a few differences. First, without the frosting or filling found with cake assembly, these cookies are on their own when it comes to flavor and texture. So you'd better use the best ingredients you've got. Second, you're not as worried about the rise or the leavening of cookies as you are with cake. But you need to be concerned about texture—the crispness or softness—because that sort of thing sets one cookie apart from another. And those textural differences can be achieved with ingredients. Brown sugar, for example, will make a softer and chewier cookie than white granulated sugar, which makes cookies crisp. Unbleached flour

baking meringue cookies or macaroons—cookies that call for beaten egg whites—you will achieve more volume if you beat room temperature egg whites.

9. **LESS IS MORE** when it comes to blending ingredients and beating cookies. You can use an electric hand mixer when creaming butter and sugar, and many recipes can be made using a wooden spoon.

10. **CHOOSE THE RIGHT PAN.** Shiny aluminum pans are the best, as they bake cookies that are crisp and evenly browned. Darker tin pans are fine for oatmeal and chocolate chip cookies where you want more browning, caramelizing, and flavor. But beware of dark nonstick pans when baking sugar cookies and other light-colored doughs because they will quickly darken your cookies. If in doubt of your pan, line it first with parchment paper to keep the cookies baking evenly and also to make cookie removal a snap. Either restaurant-style half sheet pans with 1" sides or the completely flat cookie sheet pans are fine for baking these recipes.

11. **CHECK FOR COOKIE DONENESS** at the first baking time listed in the recipe. Turn on the oven light to watch for signs of doneness—browning around the edges, mostly. Or with chocolate cookies, a change in the appearance, from shiny to opaque. Remove the first batch and let it rest on the pan for 1 minute, then transfer with a metal spatula to a wire rack to cool. Once you have the correct time for baking the cookies, and you are using the same size cookie each time you bake, then you can continue baking all the dough.

12. **LET COOKIES COOL COMPLETELY** before storing. To keep cookies crisp, store them in metal containers with tight-fitting lids. To keep them soft, store in ceramic, wooden, glass, or plastic containers. Cookies freeze well, stored in zipper-lock plastic bags, in the freezer.

And the 13th tip: **BAKE A TEST COOKIE!** You can always adjust the salt or cinnamon or seasoning if you bake one cookie first and try it.

gives cookies a more solid bite, a heft to them, which works in chocolate chip cookies and other sturdy cookies where you want a big, powerful cookie. And salt is a critical ingredient in keeping sweet cookies in a flavor balance. It is especially important when you are baking chocolate cookies. So you might want to bake one test cookie first, sample it, and then adjust the salt or cinnamon or other spices in the bowl before baking the whole recipe.

Flour

Unlike cakes that make it or break it depending on the type of flour used, cookies and bars are much more adaptable and laid-back. As long as you don't substitute self-rising flour for all-purpose (which would add too much leavening and salt for a recipe that might also call for baking soda, salt, or baking powder), you will be fine. So bake with what you have in your pantry—all-purpose bleached or unbleached. The latter makes a heftier cookie with a nice chewiness to it. Bleached all-purpose and cake flour are softer and will make a more fragile cookie. When baking chocolate chip cookies, you can try different types of all-purpose flour to get the texture you like—whether rounded and firm or a crispier cookie that spreads more on the pan. It's really personal preference. Of course, you can substitute half whole wheat flour in these recipes. I have not tested these recipes using a gluten-free flour substitute.

Sugar

It's critical to cookie baking and candy making. Sugar provides sweetness and also tenderness and encourages browning in cakes. White granulated sugar makes cookies crisp, whereas brown sugar makes them chewy and brings in a deeper flavor. Sweetness can also come from honey, sorghum, or molasses, but these are not a one-for-one swap for white sugar because they are liquid ingredients. If you are using them for some of the white sugar in a recipe, you need to compensate for this added liquid by reducing liquid or slightly increasing flour. Sweetness can also be achieved by add-ins like raisins, dates, and cherries. Throughout history, cooks have made all sorts of substitutions in baking—experimentation is allowed! And when sugar was rationed and unavailable during wartimes in our history, cooks got creative. Molasses subbed for white sugar, and during the Civil

The Easiest Cookie Cutter Is a Juice Glass

Today we have access to all sizes of round and shaped cookie cutters. But before there was this vast assortment, people just used a juice glass, an empty can, or a baking powder tin to stamp out cookies. And you can, too! Choose the glass or empty can size you like best, and dip it into flour before stamping out the cookies. That way the cutter doesn't stick to the dough.

How to Bake Bars and Brownies Like a Pro

All brownie recipes are not made alike, and it's easy—believe it or not—to mess up homemade brownies. Here are five suggestions for successful brownies every time.

1. **WATCH THE FLOUR**—as in, don't add too much. Spoon it into the measuring cup and level off the top with a knife. This sage advice from the late actress Katharine Hepburn was the secret to her fudgy brownies. Flour adds structure, but it can dry out cake and brownie batters. And when adding chocolate, as in the case of brownies, this is especially true because chocolate acts as a "flour" in baking, giving structure to a recipe but also increasing the likelihood of dryness.

2. **THE BETTER CHOCOLATE**, the better brownie. Use the best cocoa or unsweetened chocolate you can afford.

3. **CHANGE UP THE SUGAR** from white to brown for a brownie that is deeper in color and flavor and has a slight chewiness to it. The first "brownie" baked by Fannie Farmer, by the way, was baked with brown sugar.

4. **KNOW THE METHOD** for the type of brownie you love. If you love cakey brownies, go with the method of creaming butter and sugar, adding eggs one at a time, adding chocolate and finally flour. However, if you love fudgy brownies, use the saucepan method of melting butter first, then creaming sugar, adding eggs, chocolate, and finally dry ingredients. Be careful not to overbeat the batter for fudgy brownies.

5. **AND FINALLY,** two tips in one. Don't overbake. Watch the baking time and pull the brownies or bars from the oven when the sides and corners are crisp and the center has just set. You can test this with your finger or with a toothpick. Brownies and bar cookies continue to bake a bit as they cool. And once they are cool, freeze them before slicing and serving. It doesn't matter how long—could be 1 hour or 1 day. This makes for chewier bars and fudgier brownies.

War, hard-pressed cooks sweetened baked goods with boiled-down watermelon juice. In the Northeast, maple syrup was cooked down to create a maple sugar for baking.

Butter

Most of the recipes in this book call for unsalted butter. I prefer to bake cookies and little cakes with it because that way I can better control the salt content of the recipe. If you love sea salt or kosher salt in cooking, by all means use it in baking. And when paired with chocolate, especially chocolate chips, salt really brings out the flavor of the chocolate. A few recipes call for lightly salted butter, and if that's the case, then no other salt is needed in the recipe. As for European-style or cultured butter, use it if you have it in these recipes. It is not essential. Some pastry experts believe its slightly higher butterfat content makes pastries flakier.

Eggs

The recipes in this book call for large eggs. When baking with an old family recipe, remember that the eggs of yesterday—1 ounce—were smaller than they are today—from 1.75 to 2 ounces each. Take a little time to test out an old recipe to get it right before spending a lot of money on ingredients.

Flavorings

Salt, cinnamon, nutmeg, ginger, vanilla, etc., are important additions to your cookie and cake pantry. If you love spices, keep an up-to-date spice cabinet with ground ginger, nutmeg, allspice, cardamom, coriander, and cinnamon. Ground spices keep 2 to 3 years, and whole spices keep up to 4 years. If you love more subtle sugar cookies, have a lemon on hand so you can grate the zest into the dough. Or be adventurous and add rose water (found at Middle Eastern markets), caraway seeds, or ground anise seeds. Vanilla extract complements chocolate batters and pretty much any cookie dough. But look back through historical recipes and you will see vanilla extract wasn't used in cake baking until the late 1800s, and it wasn't until the early 1900s that vanilla was used to bake cookies. We get lazy and toss in vanilla—and it is delicious in sugar cookies!—but open your mind to other flavorings as you read this book.

Add-Ins

If butter, sugar, flour, and eggs are the hardware of a cookie recipe, then the add-ins are the software. They are what make cookies, bars, little cakes, and fried things fun and interesting and seasonal and adaptable to the occasion or personality. If you love coconut, add it! If you love dark chocolate, splurge on bittersweet chips for baking chocolate chip cookies. If you love cherries, stock up on dried cherries or cranberries and use them instead of raisins in oatmeal cookies. If pecan trees come into harvest near you, stock your freezer with pecan pieces and add them to your favorite cookies and bars. Or when you find almonds or walnuts in the market, freeze them for baking days ahead. As a rule, nuts taste best in cookies when they are finely chopped and/or toasted. And if finely chopped, they have a greater chance of toasting while the cookies bake. Don't forget oats—rolled or old-fashioned oats seem to work the best—for adding heft and health to drop cookies, too.

THE RIGHT PAN FOR THE JOB

PANS HAVE ALWAYS been dictated by the oven. If the oven was small, you baked on small pans. As ovens got larger after World War II, pans got bigger, too. It does make you wonder if the popularity of small cakes in early America had to do with the fact that the wood-fired oven was cooling down, and you still had a little time left to bake something small.

Even when we moved on from wood to coal to gas ovens in the 1930s, the pans were still small because the ovens were smaller than they are today. Baking a batch of cookies took time to put in pan after pan. Those early pans were made of cast iron or tin.

Today, the pan on which you bake cookies matters. You can get by using the restaurant-quality half sheet pans sold in cooking stores and Costco, but if you have a tin metal sheet, the darker ones that are thin and hard to clean, all the better for your cookies: These bake extra-crispy cookies because they bake the cookies quickly. Don't rush out and buy one—use what you have—but know if you are baking cookies on dark, thin cookie sheets, you will need to keep the oven light on and check for early browning around the edges.

For prepping those pans for cookie baking, follow the recipe instructions. Most recipes call for the cookies to be dropped onto ungreased pans. Some call for greased pans. One or two call for aluminum foil. All cookies will come off the pan easily if you line the baking pan with parchment paper first. That one sheet of paper can be reused throughout the recipe.

A Quick Cookie Snapshot

Here are some of the favorite American cookies and when they were first created.

CHOCOLATE CHIP. Ruth Wakefield baked them in the Toll House Inn in Whitman, Massachusetts, in 1933 and changed our cookie world forever by adding chocolate chunks to vanilla cookie dough.

OREO. In 1912 in New York, the National Biscuit Company (Nabisco) rolled out a nationwide sales campaign for this chocolate sandwich cookie that was a copy of the earlier Hydrox cookie from Sunshine Biscuits.

VANILLA WAFER. An extremely popular homemade cookie throughout history, it was commercialized by Nabisco in 1929.

FIG NEWTON. In 1891, people believed figs were good for health. Fig cookies had long been baked by Italian immigrants to the United States. But Charles Roser of Kenton, Ohio, developed the machinery needed to mass-produce them, and Fig Newtons were eventually sold to Nabisco.

GIRL SCOUT COOKIES. First baked for fund-raising in 1917 by a Girl Scout troop in Muskogee, Oklahoma.

PEPPERIDGE FARM MILANO. From the Pepperidge Farm bread company founded by Margaret Rudkin in Fairfield, Connecticut, in 1937, these cookies came along in the 1950s for sheer practicality. The sandwiching of chocolate filling between two buttery wafers kept the chocolate from melting during shipping.

FROM PAST TO PRESENT: *Baking Little Cakes and Cookies Today*

UNLIKE THE GRAND LAYER CAKES, our cookies have had some crazy names. They've been described by their shape and appearance. They've been named for real and imaginary people. And often the names are for phrases and words used in the past but not so much anymore. Candies, too. Divinity? Fudge? There is so much to love about the names of American small bites. Just don't take them too seriously!

The first jumbles were British sugar cookies shaped in a ring. Hermits were loved in the Northeast and full of spices and raisins. Snaps were originally Dutch, contained no egg, and they were best stored in a metal tin to stay crisp. Wafers have been baked through the years and describe a thin cookie, most often sliced from a log of refrigerated cookie dough.

Rocks and Billy Goats are those fruitcake-like cookies, heavy and dense from ingredients. Kisses were the opposite—sweet meringue cookies often with coconut or chocolate. Macaroons were similar, just a bit chewier and heavier. And cry babies were spice cookies said to soothe even a crying baby.

Through the years, the cookie names have changed. Baking methods have streamlined. We've got better equipment and larger ovens. But it's likely that the recipes being baked in kitchens today are the same as they were 100 years ago. American cookies, candies, and sweet bites are simple ways to hang on to the traditions and recipes baked by our ancestors. They have evolved, and yet they haven't changed that much. They are still loved by children. They are still tucked into lunch boxes. They are still baked at the holidays. And they are still longed for and remembered. Enjoy!

The Importance of the Cookie Jar

Pulitzer Prize–winning author Marjorie Kinnan Rawlings is best known for her novel *The Yearling* and the memoir called *Cross Creek* that describes her life in rural north Florida in the 1930s. Her cookbook, *Cross Creek Cookery*, followed and shared the recipes of the local people as well as her food memories as a child. On the subject of a cookie jar, Rawlings was opinionated:

> Any child who does not have a country grandmother who keeps a cooky jar is as much to be pitied as one who grows up with protruding teeth. If it is impossible for a grandmother to live in or move to the country, solely to insure the proper spiritual start for coming generations, at least it is possible to have a cooky jar.

Rawlings's grandmother lived in a Michigan farmhouse where there were two cookie jars on a shelf just inside the door that led from the kitchen to a downstairs cellar where butter was churned and crocks of pickles, preserves, and fruit butters "gave off a thin cool scent of mingled spices." The cookie jars held sugar, molasses, and hickory-nut cookies. And the rules of the house were as follows: Children did not need to ask permission to grab a cookie. Grandmother considered this "piecing," what Rawlings's mother looked down on as snacking. But as this was Grandmother's house, and Grandmother said she had successfully raised seven children "on the theory that one should have food when one was hungry," cookies were free for the taking most any time of the day for grandchildren. And Rawlings remembered those cookies assuaged hunger and didn't spoil a meal.

The cookie jar is not only a vessel in which to store freshly baked cookies, but it is a symbol of life well lived. It is a sign that the kitchen is the heart of the home, that the oven is turned on, and that family cookie recipes are being baked. According to Harva Hachten and Terese Allen in their book, *The Flavor of Wisconsin*, the "two most universal food memories of childhood in old Wisconsin were the smell of cookies baking and the filled cookie jar always at the ready for snacking." That jar might have been a wedding gift, it might have been passed down from one family member to another, and if so symbolized continuity and the security of tradition. And it might have been a part of a collection of cookie jars, especially if you were the late artist Andy Warhol. He loved cookie jars and collected about 175 of them that were auctioned at Sotheby's galleries in 1988 for nearly $250,000.

Nearly everyone I interviewed for this book had fond memories of a cookie jar in their past. Ours was a wooden bucket with top and handle. It held mostly oatmeal or chocolate chip cookies when I was growing up in Tennessee. It also held biscuits when my mother baked them to serve with fried chicken. We didn't have the Scandinavian or German ancestry that brings cookie memories and cookie jar necessity with it. Ours was a warm southern climate where sweets like cakes and pies were left on the kitchen counter. But when the weather turned cool, and school was in full swing, I remember the smell of chocolate chip cookies baking and how they filled up that cookie bucket. To a child, this was satiety, sustenance, and love.

1

DROP COOKIES
PAST & PRESENT

Dropping cookie dough onto pans *has been an act of love throughout history. This chapter of favorite drop cookie recipes brings together kitchen favorites from all regions, spans the centuries, and satisfies every craving. These cookies might be familiar to you or yet to be discovered. And they range from simple to sinful, from no-frills to special occasion, from ginger-spiced to fruit-studded to just about the best chocolate chip cookie on this planet.*

I begin with the ginger-spiced Grandma Hartman's Molasses Cookies and the fabled Joe Froggers and follow with sugar cookies like the old Dutch Tea Cookies and a slightly more modern Cousin Irene's Sugar Cookies. Then come chocolate cookies, oats, peanut butter, and those cookies crammed with nuts, fruits, and goodies—some people call them "kitchen sink," but in Texas they call them "cowboys."

Throughout history we have baked drop cookies with what we had on hand. These cookies have varied from a recipe more than they have followed it. And their magic comes not from chemistry and getting all the measurements just right but in their ability to pull together effortlessly at the last minute and taste great!

The earliest drop cookies were mostly likely spoonfuls of sweetened, beaten egg whites dropped onto hot cast-iron pans and placed in the oven. Or they were drops of pound cake or fruitcake batter baked in small portions to save time and feed many. The earliest cookies in this chapter weren't even called cookies when people first baked them. They were known as snickerdoodles, wafers, drops, kisses, or rocks. As the pans changed, the ovens improved, and more ingredients became accessible and available, cookies as we know them were born. Drop cookies remain popular because they are dead-easy to bake by any of us—grandmothers, moms, dads, even first-time cooks.

What you get today with a drop cookie is the same as it was years ago—a modest cookie that symbolizes childhood, simpler times, seasonal ingredients, and a last-minute desire to bake something for those you love.

GRANDMA HARTMAN'S MOLASSES COOKIES

1¼ cups granulated sugar, divided use

¾ cup vegetable shortening (see Baking Tips) or ½ cup (1 stick) unsalted butter, at room temperature

¼ cup molasses or sorghum

1 large egg

2 cups all-purpose flour

2 teaspoons baking soda

1 teaspoon ground cinnamon

½ teaspoon ground ginger

½ teaspoon salt

MAKES: About 4 dozen (2½" to 3") cookies

MARY REBECCA OGBURN HARTMAN was born in 1915 in Kenmare, North Dakota. Her family was Amish, and they moved to Gettysburg, Pennsylvania, when she was a teenager. Here Mary Rebecca would marry, raise five children, farm the land, and live as a Mennonite. This cookie was one of the treasures from her kitchen, says great-granddaughter Stephanie Golding. "Bean Grandma"—as her great-grandchildren called her because she and "Bean Grandpa" were always tending to their green beans in the garden—was a gifted cook. "As a young girl, I can still remember going over to her house in the summer and getting a whiff of what she was cooking or baking. . . . They didn't have air-conditioning," Golding says, "so the smells burst through the windows and open doors."

In the middle of the kitchen was a table, and Golding remembers sitting at that table, "with my eye level being barely over the table top," and watching Bean Grandma move back and forth between the refrigerator and stove baking these molasses cookies. Golding says the combination of warm weather and the salty, sweet cookies left a permanent imprint in her mind.

I first tasted this molasses cookie at the Josephine restaurant opening in Nashville. Golding and her husband, Brent, who live in Columbia, a small south-central Pennsylvania town in the heart of Amish country, were living in Nashville at the time and helped open the restaurant. Everyone in the Josephine kitchen loved Golding's family cookie recipe so much that they gave away cookies and the recipe on opening nights.

This recipe explains why cookies have been an important contribution to American family life. It has a story that continues to unfold with new generations of cookie bakers, and it works today as it did yesterday because it's easy to bake with what you have on hand. You just roll balls of dough in granulated sugar and flatten them with the bottom of a glass on a pan before baking. Bean Grandma let her cookies cool 2 minutes before serving—I hope you can wait that long!

PREP: 20 TO 25 MINUTES   CHILL: 1 TO 2 HOURS   BAKE: 7 TO 9 MINUTES

1. Place 1 cup of the sugar and the shortening or soft butter in a large mixing bowl. Beat with an electric mixer on medium speed until creamy, about 2 minutes. Add the molasses and egg, and beat on low until just combined.

2. In a separate bowl, sift together the flour, baking soda, cinnamon, ginger, and salt. Fold into the creamed mixture, and mix on low speed until just combined, 30 seconds. Remove the beaters, cover the bowl with plastic wrap, and chill for 1 to 2 hours.

3. Place a rack in the center of the oven, and preheat the oven to 350°F.

4. Remove the dough from the refrigerator. Drop the dough in 1" pieces onto ungreased baking sheets. Space each piece about 3" apart. Roll the pieces in the remaining $\frac{1}{4}$ cup granulated sugar to form balls. Flatten the cookies with the bottom of a juice glass. Place the pan in the oven.

5. Bake the cookies until lightly browned around the edges, 7 to 9 minutes. (Grandma Hartman would pull her cookies out of the oven between $6\frac{1}{2}$ and $7\frac{1}{2}$ minutes, just to make sure. She liked the cookies to be soft when they came out of the oven. But you can bake them slightly longer.) Remove the cookies with a metal spatula and transfer to a wire rack to cool for 2 minutes before serving. Repeat with the remaining dough. Store the cookies in an airtight container.

BAKING TIPS: *The Hartman family says the recipe tastes best with Crisco shortening and Grandma's molasses with the green label. This makes these cookies uniquely Grandma Hartman's, although you can certainly use butter instead of shortening and substitute sorghum for the molasses, as they did at Josephine restaurant on opening nights.*

JOE FROGGERS

Butter or vegetable shortening for prepping the pans

2 cups all-purpose flour (see Baking Tip)

1 teaspoon ground ginger

$\frac{1}{2}$ teaspoon salt

$\frac{1}{4}$ teaspoon ground cloves

$\frac{1}{4}$ teaspoon ground nutmeg

$\frac{1}{4}$ teaspoon ground allspice

$\frac{1}{2}$ cup unsulfured molasses

$\frac{1}{2}$ teaspoon baking soda

5 tablespoons unsalted butter, at room temperature

$\frac{1}{2}$ cup granulated sugar

$\frac{1}{2}$ cup dark rum

MAKES: 20 to 22 (2$\frac{1}{2}$" to 3") cookies

THIS SOFT AND MEMORABLE cookie born in Marblehead, Massachusetts, after the Revolutionary War was called a Joe Frogger. It was supposedly named for a freed slave named Joseph Brown who ran a tavern called Black Joe's on the edge of a millpond with his wife, Lucretia. The tavern was the scene of much revelry, according to Smithsonian researcher Julia Blakely, and known for its ginger cookie baked in an iron skillet. This cookie was unlike other ginger cookies of its time because it was large and fat—almost pancakelike, and laden with rum, a plentiful ingredient in early New England. Ginger has long been valued as a stomach settler, and local fishermen who went out to sea in search of cod took along Joe Froggers to ward off seasickness.

Another story behind the moniker of this old cookie stated that Joe Froggers were named for the fat frogs and lily pads present in the pond behind Joe's tavern. And another is that the name is a corruption of the term "Joe Flogger." According to Blakely, this is what fishermen called their provisions while at sea.

Regardless, these cookies are delicious and easy to bake. And they stay fresh for a week because the rum keeps them moist and flavorful. Adding rum to this cookie dough wasn't new—so-called "tavern biscuits" in early 19th-century American cookbooks called for a little brandy, sweet wine, or rum.

PREP: 15 TO 20 MINUTES   CHILL: 3 HOURS OR OVERNIGHT   BAKE: 9 TO 11 MINUTES

1. Place the flour, ginger, salt, cloves, nutmeg, and allspice in a medium-size bowl and sift or whisk to combine well. Set aside. Pour the molasses into a measuring cup, and stir in the baking soda to combine. Set aside.

2. Place the soft butter and sugar in a large bowl, and beat with an electric mixer on medium speed until creamy and fluffy, about 1 minute. Pour in the molasses and soda mixture and blend on low. Add the rum and blend on low until combined. Remove the beaters.

(continued on next page)

TOP TO BOTTOM: *Grandma Hartman's Molasses Cookies, Joe Froggers, and Cry Babies*

3. Stir the flour mixture ½ cup at a time into the butter mixture with a wooden spoon until smooth. Cover the bowl with plastic wrap and place in the refrigerator at least 3 hours.

4. Place a rack in the center of the oven, and preheat the oven to 375°F. Pinch off large pieces of dough and drop them, spaced 6 to a pan, on lightly greased baking sheets. Press down on each piece until it is 3" in diameter and about ⅓" thick. Place a pan in the oven.

5. Bake the cookies until they slightly deepen in color and are set in texture, 9 to 11 minutes. Immediately transfer the cookies to a wire rack to cool. Let the baking sheet cool to room temperature, then repeat with the remaining dough.

6. Store the cookies in an airtight container for up to a week.

BAKING TIP: *You can bake these cookies with unbleached or bleached flour. The latter results in slightly softer cookies.*

Chill Dough for Easy Rolling

When making Joe Froggers, allow enough time to chill the dough— 3 hours in advance, or overnight—so the cookies don't spread as much while baking.

CRY BABIES

Butter or vegetable shortening for prepping the pans

2 cups all-purpose flour

1 teaspoon baking soda

1 teaspoon ground cinnamon

$\frac{1}{2}$ teaspoon ground nutmeg

$\frac{1}{4}$ teaspoon salt

$\frac{1}{2}$ cup light brown sugar, firmly packed

$\frac{1}{4}$ cup (4 tablespoons) unsalted butter, at room temperature

$\frac{1}{4}$ cup vegetable shortening

$\frac{1}{2}$ cup molasses

1 large egg

$\frac{1}{2}$ cup water

MAKES: About 4 dozen 2" cookies

WHEN CHILDREN CRY, DO you soothe them, distract them, or possibly bake them molasses spice cookies? An old spice cookie recipe that dates from 1885 was called the cry baby. It was early comfort food, and just the smell of these aromatic cookies baking makes you feel better, no matter your age.

Cry babies were popular in many states—Delaware, West Virginia, and much of the Midwest. They remained a favorite well into the 1960s and were placed on school lunch programs in Minnesota and Vermont. They were also a true war cookie. New York food historian Joanne Lamb Hayes, who has researched the foods of the World War II years, says cry babies have simple ingredients, an easy method, and could be baked during rationing, using lard or shortening if butter was scarce. Here is the cry babies cookie recipe adapted from Hayes's *Grandma's Wartime Baking Book*.

PREP: 15 TO 20 MINUTES   BAKE: 7 TO 9 MINUTES

---

1. Place a rack in the center of the oven, and preheat the oven to 375°F. Lightly grease 2 baking sheets. Stir together the flour, baking soda, cinnamon, nutmeg, and salt in a small bowl. Set aside.

2. In a medium-size bowl, beat the brown sugar, soft butter, and shortening with an electric mixer on medium-high speed until fluffy, 1 to 2 minutes. Beat in the molasses, then beat in the egg, until well combined, about 30 seconds each. Scrape the bowl with a rubber spatula. Add the flour mixture and water alternately in 2 batches and beat on low speed just to combine the ingredients.

3. Dollop the dough onto the prepared baking sheets using a teaspoon, placing them 2" to 3" apart. Place a pan in the oven.

4. Bake the cookies until just firm at the center, 7 to 9 minutes. Remove the sheets from the oven and allow the cookies to cool on the sheets for 1 to 2 minutes, then use a metal spatula to transfer the cookies to a wire rack. Repeat with the remaining dough. Store up to a week in an airtight container.

Wartime Cookies Tell a Story

If your favorite cookie contains oats, prunes, coconut, dates, or is made without eggs—like a gingersnap—it's probably a wartime cookie. If it contains vegetable shortening instead of butter, uses "baking syrup" (corn syrup) to save sugar, or contains peanuts, it's a war cookie. Shortening was cheaper than butter and had a longer shelf life for cookies shipped overseas. Corn syrup as a sweetener enjoyed a wartime heyday due to sugar rationing. Peanuts were promoted as being a good source of protein and B vitamins. And if your favorite cookie has a name like "cry babies" or "war cookie" or "war shortbread," then yes, it was popular for baking during the two world wars.

According to author and historian Joanne Lamb Hayes in *Grandma's Wartime Baking Book*, a cookie jar was a fixture in the early 1940s American home. But World War II put a strain on cookie baking because sugar and butter were rationed. What was available were molasses, brown sugar, corn syrup, honey, margarine, and vegetable shortening. And dried fruit. This fruit, says Hayes, made the dough go further. And it made the cookies taste sweeter and kept them moist for shipping to troops stationed overseas.

At the time, margarine was promoted as a nutritious food because it was "vitaminized" and "fortified." Wartime margarine was packaged with a separate container of yellow coloring so you could color it at home. Prior to the war, butter manufacturers had lobbied lawmakers to make it illegal to sell colored margarine, Hayes says. In her book research, she talked to people who remembered being children during the war and fighting with siblings for the right to knead the color into the margarine.

Vegetable shortening was used in lieu of butter and made nice sugar cookie dough that easily could be rolled and cut into shapes. And if the wartime cook wanted to get creative, Gold Medal flour magazine advertisements included the patterns of a battleship, sailor, field gun, and plane to lay over your cookie dough like a stencil and cut into shapes. But cookies made with shortening lacked butter flavor, Hayes says, so war cooks spread the top of cookies or bars with a little butter when they came out of the oven.

Time was at a shortage, too, in the war kitchen because many women worked outside the home. Perfectly rolled and stamped-out cookies were too much trouble for these times, so busy cooks opted for drop cookies and icebox cookies, which could be ready to bake when they were. Or they saved even more time and pressed the cookie dough into a pan and baked bars.

But when it was time for a treat—a holiday or birthday—the cookie everyone longed for and appreciated was the sugar cookie. Its simple ingredients—sugar, butter, eggs, flour—tasted even sweeter when you didn't have them often.

DUTCH TEA COOKIES

1 cup (2 sticks) butter, at room temperature (see Baking Tip)

1½ cups granulated sugar

3½ cups unbleached all-purpose flour

¾ cup water, chilled in the refrigerator

MAKES: About 8 dozen (1½") cookies

WITHOUT EGG OR LEAVENING, these tea cookies bake up crispy every time. And they are delicious no matter how long you bake them. If left in the oven until pale golden brown around the edges, they have a softness to them resembling tea cakes. But bake them a bit longer and the cookies develop more flavor and crunch and are oddly reminiscent of a buttery biscotti—perfect for serving with tea.

Dutch historian Peter G. Rose says this recipe may be one of the oldest cookies in America. She found the recipe in the handwritten cookbook of Maria Sanders van Rensselaer (1749–1830) and adapted it for the modern kitchen in her book *Matters of Taste: Food and Drink in Seventeenth-Century Dutch Art and Life*. Maria was a Dutch wife and mother who managed the prosperous Albany, New York, home and farm called Cherry Hill after her husband's death. Rose says Maria called these "Tea Cookjes," which was a half-English, half-Dutch phonetic spelling of the word cookies.

PREP: 15 TO 20 MINUTES   CHILL: 1 HOUR TO OVERNIGHT   BAKE: 16 TO 20 MINUTES

---

1. Place the soft butter (and ¼ teaspoon salt, if using unsalted butter) in the bowl of an electric mixer fitted with a paddle and beat on low speed until the butter has creamed well, about 1 minute. With the mixer running, gradually pour in the sugar, stopping once to scrape down the sides of the bowl with a rubber spatula. Resume adding the sugar and beat until smooth and creamy, about 3 minutes total time. Set aside.

2. Measure the flour into a medium-size mixing bowl. Spoon a third of the flour into the butter and sugar mixture and beat on low speed to combine. Add half of the water, then beat until smooth. Add another third of the flour, then the remaining water, and finally the last third of the flour, beating only until just incorporated. Cover the top of the bowl with plastic wrap and place in the refrigerator to chill at least 1 hour and as long as overnight.

(continued on next page)

3. Place a rack in the center of the oven, and preheat the oven to 350°F.

4. Scoop or spoon about ½" balls of dough onto baking sheets, spacing them at least 1" apart. These cookies do not spread much in baking. You can get 12 to 15 cookies per baking sheet. Place the baking sheets in the oven.

5. Bake the cookies unitl golden brown around the edges and underneath, 16 to 20 minutes, depending on your oven and how browned and crispy you like the cookies.

6. Transfer the cookies at once to a wire rack to completely cool. Repeat with the remaining dough, giving the baking sheets time to cool down between batches. Once cool, serve with tea. Or place in storage containers and freeze for up to 6 months.

BAKING TIP: *Use lightly salted butter in this recipe or use unsalted butter and ¼ teaspoon salt. Bake these with either regular butter or the European-style higher butterfat butter found in many supermarkets.*

The Dutch Pioneered Cookie Baking in America

In the 55 years—between 1609 and 1664—that the Netherlands controlled the Hudson River Valley, the Dutch were able to establish trading posts and towns along the river that would eventually become the towns that exist today. To the north was Fort Orange (known today as Albany); in the middle, Wiltwyck (now Kingston); and to the south, New Amsterdam (now New York City). When the Dutch East India Company and its English sailor Henry Hudson wanted to find a northeast passage to India for trading spices, the ship was unsuccessful and turned west across the Atlantic hoping to find a northwest passage via the Pacific Ocean. But again they were unsuccessful, and after traveling as far north up what is now the Hudson River as they could go, these voyagers claimed the Hudson River Valley for the Dutch. The early Dutch in America were entrepreneurs and fur traders, and they brought their culture with them from the Netherlands. In fact, the Dutch bakers traded cookies with the native Americans for beaver skins, according to historian Peter G. Rose. In each Dutch settlement, there was a town bakery, where there was a central oven where the baker baked bread for home consumption. But some bakers couldn't resist the trade of cookies for skins as viable early commerce and were arrested, Rose learned from her research. Regardless, the Dutch foodways were established in America, and its deep imprint can be found today not only in tea cookies but also in doughnuts—*ollykoeks*.

1908 ROCKS

2½ cups all-purpose flour

1 teaspoon ground allspice

1 teaspoon ground cinnamon

2¼ cups (12 ounces) chopped dates

2¼ cups (12 ounces) chopped walnuts

1½ cups granulated sugar

1 cup (2 sticks) lightly salted butter, melted

3 large eggs

1 teaspoon baking soda (see Baking Tip)

3 tablespoons boiling water

MAKES: About 9 dozen (1½") cookies

LONG BEFORE AMERICAN COOKIES were called cookies, we named these recipes for what they looked like. "Rocks" might not have been the most glamorous sounding cookie, but boy, were they popular. Countless rock cookie recipes fill the cookbooks of the early 1900s. They were a fruitcake cookie—thick batter mixed with nuts, spices, and dried fruit. Rocks were pretty much the same cookie as Billy Goats, a fanciful name for a rock cookie.

What you added to this cookie said much about the time period—chopped dates were popular in baking in the early 1900s, for example. And it said something about where you lived: whether you were baking with walnuts or pecans, for example, showed you lived in either the North or South. This recipe was attributed to the state of Illinois and was printed in the *Courier-Journal* in Louisville, Kentucky, in 1908. It makes more than 100 small cookies, which is a little labor intensive, but back then cookies were smaller than they are today. And there was seldom an empty cookie jar.

PREP: 20 TO 25 MINUTES   BAKE: 9 TO 11 MINUTES

---

1. Place a rack in the center of the oven, and preheat the oven to 350°F.

2. Whisk together the flour, allspice, and cinnamon in a medium-size mixing bowl. Fold the dates and walnuts into the flour mixture. Set aside.

3. Place the sugar and melted butter in a large mixing bowl and beat with an electric mixer on low speed to combine, 1 minute. Add the eggs one at a time, mixing on medium-high speed until incorporated, about 10 seconds for each egg. Scrape down the sides of the bowl with a rubber spatula.

4. In a small bowl, stir together the baking soda and boiling water until dissolved. Pour it into the butter and sugar mixture, and mix on medium speed until combined, about 10 seconds. Scrape down the sides of the bowl. Fold in the flour mixture until just combined, about 30 seconds.

5. Drop 1" balls of dough at least 1½" apart on an ungreased cookie sheet. Place the sheet in the oven.

6. Bake the cookies until the bottom edges are golden, 9 to 11 minutes. Remove the pan from the oven and let it cool on the rack for 1 minute. Transfer the cookies to a wire rack to completely cool. The cookies will seem pale at first but will become more golden as they cool.

BAKING TIP: *Baking soda was often dissolved in hot water because it was more coarse in texture then and needed dissolving before adding to the recipe. This is not necessarily a step you need to follow nowadays with modern baking soda.*

Old Recipes Didn't Chill Dough

In 1908, cooks didn't pop pans of cookie dough into the fridge to keep cool before baking. So cookies were baked right after the dough was mixed. Baking 1" balls of room-temperature dough dropped from a spoon resulted in flatter (about 1½") cookies if you were baking in a warm kitchen or during the summer. Whereas if your kitchen was cold, and the batter was cold, the chilled 1" drops of dough didn't spread in baking and appeared smaller and more rocklike in appearance.

COUSIN IRENE'S SUGAR COOKIES

1 cup (2 sticks) unsalted butter, at room temperature

1 cup confectioners' sugar

1 large egg, at room temperature (see Baking Tips)

½ teaspoon vanilla extract

2¼ cups sifted all-purpose flour

½ teaspoon baking soda

½ teaspoon cream of tartar

¼ to ½ teaspoon salt (see Baking Tips)

⅓ cup granulated sugar, for pressing into cookies

MAKES: About 32 (2¾" to 3") cookies

LOVED BY YOUNG AND old, sugar cookies need no explanation or excuse for baking. They are appropriate dusted with white sugar, glammed up with sugar sprinkles, or just baked "as is."

The secret is a great family recipe and attention to detail. Connie Carter, following in the footsteps of her late mother Gladys Carter, recommends European-style or cultured butter when baking these cookies. "You want more butterfat in this cookie," says Carter, a retired librarian at the Library of Congress in Washington, DC. Those butters have a higher butterfat content and less water. This makes the cookies taste better and bake up crispy, too.

The recipe comes from Carter's Cousin Irene, but Carter likes to think her mother improved on the recipe by sheer mistake. "Somehow my mother copied the original recipe as 1 cup powdered sugar," she says, even though the original had ½ cup powdered and ½ cup granulated sugar.

Cream of tartar is a little-known secret ingredient that keeps the cookies white, Carter adds. And to give these cookies their rich flavor, Carter uses Madagascar vanilla. For perfect dough, she begins with room-temperature butter and egg, and she sifts her flour before measuring. Then she uses a cookie scoop to measure out perfectly round balls, making uniform cookies. And she bakes on a silicone baking mat, such as a Silpat, to prevent the cookies from sticking to the pan.

PREP: 10 TO 15 MINUTES **CHILL: AT LEAST 2 HOURS** **BAKE: 8 TO 9 MINUTES**

1. Place the soft butter and confectioners' sugar in a large mixing bowl and beat with an electric mixer on medium-high speed until creamy, about 2 minutes. Add the egg and vanilla and beat just to combine, about 20 seconds longer. Scrape down the bowl with a rubber spatula.

2. In a sifter, combine the sifted flour, baking soda, cream of tartar, and salt. Sift about half of the flour mixture into the butter mixture. Beat on low speed just to combine, 15 seconds. Scrape down the bowl. Add the remaining flour mixture and beat just to combine. Scrape down the bowl. Cover the bowl with plastic wrap and place in the fridge until firm, at least 2 hours.

(continued on next page)

3. When ready to bake, place a rack in the center of the oven, and preheat the oven to 375°F. Line a baking sheet with a silicone baking mat or aluminum foil.

4. Remove the dough from the fridge. Using a small cookie scoop (about 1½" in diameter and 1" deep), drop dough 2¼" to 2½" apart on the pan. Dunk a flat-bottomed glass in cold water. Immediately press the glass into the granulated sugar. Press the glass onto the scoops of dough until each scoop is about a 2" round. Repeat by scooping dough and dipping the glass into sugar between each press. Place the pan in the oven.

5. Bake the cookies until the edges are golden brown, about 8 to 9 minutes. Remove at once to a wire rack to cool. Repeat with the remaining dough. Store the cookies in an airtight container.

BAKING TIPS: *If the egg is straight from the fridge, place it in a bowl of warm water for 5 minutes. Connie uses ½ teaspoon salt, but I liked slightly less—¼ teaspoon. And try to keep the dough refrigerated between batches. Cold dough doesn't stick to the bottom of glass and is easier to handle.*

SNICKERDOODLES

DOUGH

1$\frac{1}{2}$ cups granulated sugar

$\frac{1}{2}$ cup (1 stick) butter, at room temperature (see Baking Tip)

$\frac{1}{2}$ cup vegetable shortening

1 teaspoon vanilla extract

2 large eggs

2$\frac{3}{4}$ cups all-purpose flour

2 teaspoons cream of tartar

1 teaspoon baking soda

TOPPING

$\frac{1}{4}$ cup plus 1 tablespoon granulated sugar

2 teaspoons ground cinnamon

MAKES: About 4$\frac{1}{2}$ dozen (2$\frac{1}{2}$") cookies

SNICKERDOODLES ARE A CHERISHED American cookie. They have been popular within the Mennonite and Amish baking communities for decades, and one state embraces the snickerdoodle as its own: Indiana. With one of the largest Amish communities in America, Indiana is where Hoosier poet James Whitcomb Riley is said to have dubbed them his favorite cookie. Each year on his birthday—October 7—snickerdoodles are baked at the historic James Whitcomb Riley home in Indianapolis as a remembrance.

The story begins in 1891, when Cornelia Campbell Bedford, better known as "Nellie," shared a recipe for snickerdoodles. The New York City cooking teacher and newspaper columnist had been developing recipes for the Cleveland Baking Powder company, and her snickerdoodles recipe, a sugar cookie dough spread into a pan and sprinkled liberally with cinnamon and sugar before baking, went viral. Which, at the end of the 19th century, meant the bar cookie was discussed in newspaper columns daily for the next year.

Early recipes called for butter, but in 1923 Crisco marketed "Mrs. T's Snicker Doodles: the favorite recipe of an English-woman" in their advertising. There was a snickerdoodle shift from butter to vegetable shortening in the dough and from bar to cookie in the 1930s.

But the quirky name has always been the appeal. John Mariani says in *The Dictionary of American Food and Drink* that this nonsense word implied the cookie was quick to make. And it doesn't really matter where this simple cookie with the silly name was born. We love to say its name. It sounds like Yankee Doodle and characters out of a Raggedy Ann children's book—Snickersnapper, Snitznoodle, and Snarlydoodle. And it makes you smile just to think about it.

PREP: 15 TO 20 MINUTES   BAKE: 8 TO 10 MINUTES

---

1. Place a rack in the upper third of the oven, and preheat the oven to 375°F.

2. For dough, place the sugar, soft butter, and shortening in a large mixing bowl and beat with an electric mixer on medium speed until creamy, about 2 minutes, scraping down the side of the

(continued on next page)

bowl once with a rubber spatula. Add vanilla and the eggs, one at a time, continuing to beat on medium speed for about 30 seconds.

3. Place the flour, cream of tartar, and baking soda in a medium-size bowl and stir with a fork to combine. Add the flour mixture to the butter and sugar mixture, and beat on low speed until incorporated, scraping down the side of the bowl as needed.

4. For the topping, stir together the sugar and cinnamon in a shallow bowl.

5. Using a teaspoon, scoop the cookie dough into balls about 1¼" in diameter. The dough will be soft but manageable. Sprinkle the balls with the cinnamon-sugar mixture until evenly coated. Drop them about 2" apart on an ungreased baking sheet.

6. Bake the cookies until the edges are lightly golden but the centers are still a little soft to the touch, 8 to 10 minutes. Remove the baking sheet from the oven and let the cookies rest on the pan 1 minute. Using a metal spatula, transfer the cookies to wire racks to cool completely. Scrape the baking sheet, then repeat the process with the remaining cookie dough, letting the baking sheet cool first so the dough does not spread too much. Store the cookies in an airtight container.

BAKING TIP: *While some recipes call for shortening and some for butter, the mix of butter and shortening is the best of both worlds. The butter adds flavor, and the shortening helps the cookies keep a rounded shape while baking. Add a little ground nutmeg to the topping, if you like.*

SCHRAFFT'S BUTTERSCOTCH COOKIES

1 cup (2 sticks) unsalted butter, at room temperature

1½ cups dark brown sugar, firmly packed

1 large egg

2 tablespoons dry milk powder

1 tablespoon vanilla extract

2 cups all-purpose flour

½ teaspoon baking soda

½ teaspoon salt

1 cup finely chopped pecans, if desired

MAKES: 4 dozen (2") cookies

BUTTERSCOTCH WAS ORIGINALLY A Scottish candy made from butter, brown sugar, and lemon juice. In America you could buy "London Butterscotch" in 1854, and it was billed as the candy that cured what ailed you. The first recipe for making butterscotch at home was shared around 1875, according to historian John Mariani. It was during this time that W. F. Schrafft's candy shops, opening in Boston in 1861, would evolve into a chain of restaurants known for butterscotch sundaes and their legendary "butterscotch wafers," which cost 24 cents a pound in 1907.

What made Schrafft's butterscotch wafers so popular, especially with children, is that they had the butterscotch candy flavor but in a chewy cookie form. Long after Schrafft's closed and was just a memory to old-timers, James Beard called the retired president of Schrafft's and asked for the wafer recipe. That recipe would be scaled down to a much smaller yield and be improved through tinkering. But the key ingredients of these nostalgic cookies remain the same—dark brown sugar for flavor and dry milk powder for creaminess. They truly will cure what ails you!

PREP: 15 MINUTES   BAKE: 10 TO 12 MINUTES

---

1. Place a rack in the center of the oven, and preheat the oven to 375°F.

2. Place the soft butter and brown sugar in a large bowl and beat with an electric mixer on medium speed until creamy, 1 to 2 minutes. Add the egg, milk powder, and vanilla and beat just to combine the egg.

3. Stir together the flour, baking soda, and salt in a small bowl. Fold the flour mixture into the butter and sugar mixture with a rubber spatula until well combined. Fold in the pecans, if desired. Drop 1" balls of cookie dough on an ungreased baking sheet, spacing them about 2" apart.

4. Bake the cookies until they are flat and crisp, 10 to 12 minutes. Transfer to a wire rack to cool, about 15 minutes. Repeat with the remaining cookie dough. Store the cookies in an airtight container.

MRS. NESBITT'S HONEY DROPS

CANDIED ORANGE PEEL (NEED ½ CUP)

2 large oranges
(see Baking Tip)

1 cup water, divided
use

¾ cup granulated
sugar

DOUGH

½ cup (1 stick)
unsalted butter, at
room temperature

½ cup vegetable
shortening

½ cup granulated
sugar

1 cup honey

1 large egg

½ teaspoon vanilla
extract

¾ cup well-chopped
walnuts

3½ cups all-purpose
flour

2 teaspoons baking
powder

½ teaspoon salt

½ teaspoon cinnamon

MAKES: About
10 dozen (1½") cookies

WHEN HENRIETTA NESBITT, THE woman in charge of the Franklin and Eleanor Roosevelt White House kitchen, needed drop cookies for a party, this was her go-to recipe. One batch of her Honey Drops yielded more than a hundred cookies, just in time for frequent, unexpected guests. Eleanor Roosevelt is said to have been a generous host, entertaining thousands for tea.

Nesbitt was a Hyde Park, New York, friend and colleague of Mrs. Roosevelt, and the two met at the League of Women Voters meetings. She had never worked outside the home when Mrs. Roosevelt asked her to move to Washington, DC, in 1933 and supervise the cooking, cleaning, and entertaining at the White House. But Nesbitt was a skilled baker, and she was willing to try this seemingly insurmountable job as she and her husband needed the income, according to Barbara Haber in her book, *From Hardtack to Home Fries.*

And while Nesbitt was often criticized for her cooking, especially by President Roosevelt, this cookie recipe pleased most everyone. It includes walnuts, cinnamon, honey, and candied orange peel, the latter a little trouble to make from scratch today. Candied orange peel used to be an ingredient you could buy in candy shops, and it was a popular flavoring in the early 1900s. In her book the *White House Diary,* Nesbitt said she was always on the lookout for new cookies like this one to serve at teas and receptions. And she reflected, "President and Mrs. Roosevelt wanted to please their guests. They wanted to make them happy, just as, if they had been able, they would have extended that happiness to all the world."

This recipe is adapted from *The Presidential Cookbook* by Henrietta Nesbitt, and *From Hardtack to Home Fries* by Barbara Haber.

PREP: 15 TO 20 MINUTES, PLUS TIME TO MAKE CANDIED ORANGE PEEL, IF DESIRED
BAKE: 14 TO 17 MINUTES

---

1. A day ahead or overnight, prepare the candied orange peel. Wash and dry the oranges. Using a carrot peeler or curved knife, peel the zest from the oranges in thin strips or pieces, leaving the white layer on the orange. Pour ½ cup of the water into a medium-size saucepan and place on the stove. Bring to a boil

(continued on next page)

over high heat and add the peel. Boil for 1 minute, then drain and rinse with cold water. Drain and rinse again, and set aside. Next, place the remaining $\frac{1}{2}$ cup water and the sugar in the same saucepan. Heat over high heat to a boil, stirring to dissolve the sugar. Add the peel and lower the heat to a medium-low simmer. Simmer the peel for 15 to 20 minutes. Remove the peel with a slotted spoon or tongs and place on a wire rack with waxed paper underneath to catch the drips. Allow the peel to cool and dry for about 12 hours, or overnight. Chop into small bits.

2. Place a rack in the center of the oven, and preheat the oven to 325°F.

3. For the dough, place the soft butter and shortening in a large bowl, and beat with an electric mixer on medium speed until creamy, about 30 seconds. Add the sugar and honey and beat until combined well, 30 seconds. Beat in the egg until combined, 15 to 20 seconds. Scrape down the bowl with a rubber spatula. Add the vanilla, walnuts, and reserved chopped orange peel and beat until well combined, 15 to 20 seconds. Scrape the bowl.

4. Sift together the flour, baking powder, salt, and cinnamon into a medium-size bowl. Add the flour mixture in batches to the butter mixture, beating on low speed until just combined. Scrape down the bowl after each addition.

5. Drop the cookie dough in 1" balls about $1\frac{1}{2}$" to 2" apart on an ungreased baking sheet. Place the pan in the oven.

6. Bake the cookies until they are light brown on the bottom edges, about 14 to 17 minutes. Immediately remove the cookies to a wire rack to cool. Repeat with the remaining cookie dough. Store the cookies in an airtight container.

BAKING TIP: *If you are purchasing candied orange peel, you can omit the first step.*

DECORATING OPTION: Toss cooled cookies in a plastic bag containing confectioners' sugar. Or, before baking, roll dough balls in white or raw cane sugar. You can also drizzle a thin stream of honey over cooled cookies on a serving plate.

RUTH WAKEFIELD'S CHOCOLATE CRUNCH COOKIES

1 cup (2 sticks) unsalted butter, room temperature (see Baking Tips)

¾ cup dark brown sugar, firmly packed

¾ cup granulated sugar

2 large eggs

1 teaspoon baking soda

1 teaspoon hot water

1 teaspoon vanilla extract

2 to 2¼ cups all-purpose flour (see Baking Tips)

1 teaspoon salt

1 cup chopped pecans or walnuts

1 pound semisweet chocolate, chopped (see Baking Tips)

MAKES: 6 to 7 dozen (2") cookies

IF WE COULD STEP back in time to the late-1930s kitchen of the Toll House Inn in Whitman, Massachusetts, we might understand how Ruth Graves Wakefield ran out of cocoa for her chocolate jumble cookies and needed to make a quick substitution. This was the resourceful post-Depression, pre–World War II era when cooks made do and substituted what they had on hand in recipes.

Spying two chocolate bars, Wakefield chopped them and folded them into the cookie batter. She thought the chocolate would melt as the cookies baked, but it didn't. That shortcut not only would turn out to be a life-changing moment for this hardworking restaurateur, but it would turn the cookie world upside down for eternity.

Connie Carter, retired librarian at the Library of Congress, whose mother went to college with Wakefield, recalls her mother telling her the story that after Wakefield made the switch to chopped chocolate in her Chocolate Crunch Cookies, her guests liked them better. Those cookies became the Toll House cookies we all know and love, and Nestlé inked a deal with Wakefield and promised her a lifetime supply of chocolate if she would let them put the recipe on the back of the chocolate bar. It didn't take long for Nestlé to unveil chocolate chips and to rename the cookie recipe after the Toll House Inn where they were born.

Here is the original recipe for the cookies that changed the world. It comes from the 1938 *Ruth Wakefield's Toll House Tried and True Recipes* and is made with chopped chocolate (you can substitute chocolate chips if you like). Notice that you dissolve the baking soda in a teaspoon of hot water, which is how it was done in the Toll House Inn in the 1930s.

PREP: 20 TO 25 MINUTES   BAKE: 7 TO 9 MINUTES

---

1. Place a rack in the center of the oven, and preheat the oven to 375°F. Set aside 2 ungreased baking sheets.

2. Place the soft butter and sugars in a large bowl and beat with an electric mixer on medium-high speed until creamy and light, 1 to 1½ minutes. Scrape down the sides of the bowl with a rubber spatula. Add the eggs, one at a time, and beat until just combined.

(continued on next page)

TOP TO BOTTOM: *Banana Drop Cookies and Ruth Wakefield's Chocolate Crunch Cookies*

3. Place the baking soda in a small measuring cup and stir in the teaspoon of hot water to dissolve the soda. Spoon this into the butter and sugar mixture along with the vanilla. Beat on low speed until just combined, 15 seconds. Whisk together the flour and salt in a medium-size bowl, and add to the batter, beating on low speed until just combined. Turn off the mixer, and fold in the nuts and chocolate with the spatula until well distributed.

4. Drop the dough by teaspoons onto the baking sheets, spacing the dough about 2" apart. Place 1 pan in the oven.

5. Bake the cookies until lightly golden brown, 7 to 9 minutes. Remove the pan from the oven and transfer the cookies to wire racks. Repeat with the remaining cookie dough. Store the cookies in an airtight container.

BAKING TIPS: *Ruth Wakefield's original recipe did not specify the type of butter to use—unsalted or salted. Connie Carter says unsalted butter makes a more moist cookie. Salted butter makes a crispy cookie: "It ties up the moisture." But Ruth Wakefield does call for 1 teaspoon salt, so that would lead you to believe the butter was unsalted. Her recipe didn't specify the brown sugar as "light" or "dark," so use the one that appeals to you most or what you have on hand. The chocolate is a generous addition to the recipe, so feel free to add less—12 ounces—and that is exactly what happened to the recipe over time. The amount of chopped chocolate—or chocolate chips—was reduced from 16 to 12 ounces. Ruth's recipe instructs you to chop the chocolate to the "size of a pea," or about the size of a chocolate chip.*

Chocolate Chip Cookie Bliss

I once talked to an oven repairman who said the best way to gauge if your oven is baking at the right temperature is to bake chocolate chip cookies. If you set the oven for 350°F, and the cookies bake in 10 minutes, then your oven works just fine.

"You get to eat the cookies, too," he said with a grin. "And you don't need to call me."

I've remembered that advice through the years, as I have tested chocolate chip cookie recipes just about any time I get the chance. I've made them with chips, chunks, and even disks of fine chocolate I've packed in my suitcases and carried home from stores in New York, Dallas, and Seattle. I've tried them with all dark brown sugar, with half butter and half shortening. I've added oats, dried cherries, and toasted pecans. They never disappoint.

At our house, chocolate chip cookies have been a panacea for what ails us—a broken heart, a flat tire, a tough exam, a lost cat. And they have celebrated happier times with us, too—a new house, a promotion, a birthday.

I am not one of those people who will overanalyze them. Oh no, you won't hear me criticizing a chocolate chip cookie even if it's cakey—too much flour or too many eggs. Or spreads on the pan—the flour needs to be higher in gluten. Or pale—it wasn't allowed to sit overnight in the fridge. Or too dark—the pan or the hot oven is the culprit here. No, I could care less if they are imperfect. Because even if they look hideous, they are always great. Any chocolate chip cookie is a delicious chocolate chip cookie as long as one thing happens . . .

You bake them yourself.

Not from premade dough. You make the dough, let it rest in the fridge, preferably overnight. Then you bake and serve them warm. Always warm. With cold milk.

That's it—that's the secret to Chocolate Chip Cookie bliss. And a happy home. And a reliable oven!

BANANA DROP COOKIES

2 large ripe bananas

10 tablespoons unsalted butter, at room temperature

½ cup light brown sugar, lightly packed

½ cup granulated sugar

1 teaspoon vanilla extract

2 large eggs

2¼ cups all-purpose flour

1 teaspoon baking powder

½ teaspoon baking soda

½ teaspoon salt

½ teaspoon ground cinnamon

MAKES: About 4 dozen (2½") cookies

BANANAS ARE INTERTWINED WITH the tropical cuisine of Hawaii, where they are grown in backyards and commercially. But in 1917, the Hawaii Agricultural Experiment Station had a bit of a problem on its hand because the banana crop was booming and America had just entered World War I. Ships that usually transported Hawaiian bananas to the US mainland were being used in the war effort. Station director J. M. Westgate pleaded that everyone in Hawaii—then a US territory and not a state until 1959—should eat a banana a day instead of a slice of bread, hoping this would boost banana consumption. And with a ripening, rotting surplus of Hawaiian bananas on hand, his wife got into the kitchen and started cooking up ideas. She developed recipes for banana pudding, bread, custard, dumplings, fritters, and this banana drop cookie recipe, which she shared with the Honolulu newspaper. Here is a slightly adapted version of that 1917 cookie. Bake these using ripe bananas, just as you would for banana bread.

PREP: 10 TO 15 MINUTES   BAKE: 8 TO 10 MINUTES

---

1. Place a rack in the center of the oven, and preheat the oven to 375°F. Set aside 2 ungreased baking sheets.

2. Peel and slice the bananas into a small bowl. Mash with a fork until smooth. Set aside. You should have a generous 1 cup.

3. Place the soft butter and sugars in a large mixing bowl and beat with an electric mixer until creamy, about 1 minute. Add the vanilla and eggs, and beat until incorporated, 30 seconds. Fold in the mashed bananas.

4. Whisk together the flour, baking powder, soda, salt, and cinnamon in a medium-size bowl. Add the flour mixture to the butter and sugar mixture and beat on low until combined, 30 to 45 seconds.

5. Spoon tablespoons of dough about 2" apart onto the prepared baking sheets.

6. Bake the cookies until golden brown around the edges but still a little soft in the center, about 8 minutes. Or bake them until crispy, a full 10 minutes. Let the cookies rest on the pans for 1 minute, then transfer them to wire racks to cool completely.

A Little Banana History

The ordinary banana didn't have an easy entry into America. The first British colonists on Roanoke Island, North Carolina, brought bananas with them from the Caribbean in the hopes they could grow them. But that didn't work in the temperate climate of this new land. So bananas were a luxury—imported into New York, Boston, Philadelphia, Charleston, and New Orleans. And they were costly. At 10 cents apiece wrapped in foil at the 1876 Philadelphia Centennial Exposition, bananas seemed new and different if you could afford them. When the invention of refrigerated steamships to transport bananas allowed shipping them at a constant temperature to slow their ripening, then prices fell and bananas became affordable. Which is how they became a fixture at the American breakfast table and how they were mashed and folded into banana bread, cookies, and cakes.

THE NEIMAN MARCUS $250 COOKIE

1 cup (2 sticks) unsalted butter, at room temperature

1 cup dark brown sugar, lightly packed

1 cup granulated sugar

2 large eggs

1 teaspoon vanilla extract

2½ cups old-fashioned oats (see Baking Tips)

2 cups all-purpose flour (see Baking Tips)

1 teaspoon baking soda

1 teaspoon baking powder

¾ teaspoon salt

2 cups (12 ounces) semisweet chocolate chips

4 ounces semisweet or milk chocolate, grated (see Baking Tips)

1½ cups chopped pecans or walnuts

MAKES: 7 to 8 dozen (2") cookies

BEFORE THE INTERNET, THIS recipe made its rounds via chain letters and word of mouth. It is the Neiman Marcus $250 Cookie recipe, and if you think Neiman Marcus would actually charge a customer that much for a cookie recipe, well, I've got some swampland I'd like to sell you . . . Truthfully, it is just a chocolate chip and oatmeal cookie recipe that was hugely popular in 1988 and into the 1990s. With a little grated semisweet or milk chocolate and pecans added, this cookie recipe has stayed at the front of recipe boxes across the country.

It is a great cookie, no doubt, and it is similar to the Quaker oatmeal cookies, but again, the allure has been the name. In the 1980s, anything over-the-top, rich, and decadent got everyone's attention.

Food writer, novelist, and university professor Alice Randall found this recipe in the files of a well-known caterer of Mobile, Alabama. Randall and her Vanderbilt University class were tracing the roots of soul food through recipe collections. She says this recipe speaks to how anything called "Neiman Marcus" has had a mystique embraced by the African American community. Home seamstresses have copycatted Neiman Marcus clothing, she says, and this recipe illustrates how they can do the same thing in the kitchen.

PREP: 20 TO 25 MINUTES   BAKE: 8 TO 10 MINUTES

---

1. Place a rack in the top third of the oven, and preheat the oven to 375°F. Set aside 2 ungreased baking sheets.

2. Place the soft butter and sugars in a large mixing bowl and beat with an electric mixer on medium speed until creamy, 1 to 2 minutes. Turn off the mixer, scrape down the sides of the bowl with a rubber spatula, and add the eggs and vanilla. Beat on low speed until combined and smooth, 1 minute.

3. In a food processor fitted with a steel blade, pulse the oats until finely ground, 10 to 15 seconds. Transfer the oatmeal to a medium-size bowl and add the flour, baking soda, baking powder, and salt. Whisk to combine the dry ingredients, and dump the oatmeal and flour mixture into the bowl with the batter. Beat on low speed until just combined, 30 seconds. Scrape down the sides of the bowl.

(continued on next page)

4. Fold in the chocolate chips, grated chocolate, and nuts. Drop the batter by heaping 1" tablespoonfuls, 2" apart on the baking sheets. Place in the oven.

5. Bake the cookies until they just begin to crisp around the edges but are still a little soft in the center, 8 to 10 minutes. Let rest on the pan for 1 minute, then transfer with a metal spatula to a wire rack to cool. Repeat with the remaining cookie dough. Store the cookies in an airtight container.

BAKING TIPS: *I used old-fashioned oats in this recipe. By pulsing them in a food processor, you break down the oats into a flourlike texture. If you have quick-cooking oats on hand, that is okay, just skip the step of pulsing in the food processor. As for flour, use bleached or unbleached. The unbleached will create a cookie with more shape and bite to it. The original recipe called for Hershey's milk chocolate, but our tastes today gravitate to a less sweet chocolate, so this addition of grated chocolate is your chance to customize this recipe. Use a bittersweet or semisweet for a stronger chocolate punch. Use milk chocolate if you like a sweet creaminess. Grate the chocolate with a cheese grater or cut the chocolate into shavings with a heavy, sharp knife.*

FOR A MODERN TOUCH: Use grated bittersweet chocolate and sprinkle the cookies with a little sea salt before baking. The salt really brings out the flavor of the dark chocolate.

Get the Scoop

Even if you don't eat ice cream, you need an ice cream scoop for baking cookies. It perfectly portions out cookie dough, which means you bake evenly shaped and sized cookies. Believe me, dropping cookie dough onto baking pans wasn't always this easy. I was taught to use 2 spoons. One spoon scoops down and shovels out a lump of dough, and the second spoon pushes the dough onto the pan. Credit Mrs. Field's, David's, or any of the famous cookie bakers, caterers, or pastry chefs who needed to keep their cookies the same size for this marvelous invention. The home kitchen thanks you. Choose ice cream scoops of all sizes for cookie baking. My favorites are about 1" across for small- to medium-size cookies and a larger scoop, about 2" across, to yield big 3" cookies.

FORGOTTEN CHOCOLATE COOKIES

2¾ cups confectioners' sugar

Generous ½ cup unsweetened cocoa powder

1 tablespoon cornstarch

Pinch salt

3 large egg whites

½ teaspoon vanilla extract

2 cups finely chopped pecans (see Baking Tips)

MAKES: 2 to 3 dozen (2 ½" to 3") cookies

HOW COULD A COOKIE this good ever be forgotten? The intense chocolate flavor, the irresistible chewiness, the crunch of the exterior, and the way the pecans toast effortlessly as the cookies bake? It can't. The name comes from the old method of making meringue cookies where the cookies first bake, then you turn off the oven and let the cookies remain in the oven, where they get nice and crispy and seem "forgotten."

It is a method of baking chocolate cookies that was popular in Jewish bakeries such as Gottlieb's Bakery in Savannah, Georgia. Their famous Chocolate Chewies were a meringue cookie with 2 tablespoons flour added, and the cookies were frozen for 1 hour after baking to make them even chewier. Gottlieb's opened in 1884 when Russian Jewish immigrant Isadore Gottlieb started his baking dynasty here. For generations those cookies, his cinnamon rolls, and his challah bread have been an important part of growing up in Savannah.

You can bake "forgotten" cookies in a myriad of ways, with a tablespoon of cornstarch like they do at the Central Market grocery stores in Texas or with the 2 tablespoons flour at Gottlieb's. They're incredibly adaptable and are not, under any circumstances, to be forgotten.

PREP: 10 MINUTES   BAKE: 12 TO 15 MINUTES

---

1. Place a rack in the center of the oven, and preheat the oven to 350°F. Line 2 baking sheets with parchment paper or a silicone baking mat.

2. Place the confectioners' sugar, cocoa, cornstarch, and salt in the bowl of an electric mixer and beat on low speed just to combine the dry ingredients. Add the egg whites and beat on low speed to incorporate the whites, then increase the speed to high and beat for 1 minute, or until very well combined. Stir in the vanilla and pecans.

3. Scoop or drop heaping tablespoonfuls of dough onto the baking pans. Place one pan in the oven.

(continued on next page)

4. Bake the cookies until shiny and firm on the outside but still a little soft inside, 12 to 15 minutes. (Gauge the baking time by the size of the cookie. Smaller cookies bake in about 12 minutes, and larger ones need more time.) Remove the cookie sheet from the oven and let the cookies rest for 2 minutes on the pan. With a metal spatula, transfer the cookies to a wire rack to cool. Serve, or store in a airtight container at room temperature for a week or in the freezer for 3 months.

BAKING TIPS: *For some reason, the cookies bake up glossiest when the dough is scooped immediately onto baking sheets and not left to linger in the bowl. Haven't figured out why that happens! I use pecans because they are always in my freezer. Use walnuts if that is what you have on hand.*

GOURMET'S CHOCOLATE MOCHA COOKIES

4 ounces unsweetened chocolate, chopped

3 cups (18 ounces) semisweet chocolate chips, divided use (see Baking Tips)

$\frac{1}{2}$ cup (1 stick) unsalted butter, cut into tablespoons

$1\frac{1}{2}$ cups granulated sugar

4 large eggs

$\frac{1}{2}$ cup all-purpose flour

$1\frac{1}{2}$ tablespoons espresso powder (see Baking Tips)

$\frac{1}{2}$ teaspoon baking powder

$\frac{1}{2}$ teaspoon salt

2 teaspoons vanilla extract

MAKES: About 5 dozen (2") cookies

WHEN *GOURMET* MAGAZINE SHARED this recipe in *The* Gourmet *Cookie Book* in 1990, little did they know the recipe would be duplicated countless times and morph into all sorts of chewy, gooey chocolate cookies across the country. If a cookie recipe spoke to a particular decade in America, this recipe encapsulated the 1990s—rich, decadent, unapologetic. *Gourmet* ceased operation in October 2009, a gray day in the food journalism world, because those who grew up reading about food in the previous decades knew *Gourmet* as the pinnacle of good taste.

Many caterers and pastry chefs have adopted this cookie as their own, as its deep, dark chocolate flavor accented with espresso powder is welcome anywhere. Nashville caterer Emily Frith makes these cookies in smaller, bite-size tastes, portioning out the cookies uniformly using a scoop. Make it your own by adding your favorite chocolate, omitting the espresso powder, adding a bit of almond extract, brushing with Kahlúa after baking . . . you get the picture. But for now, let's bake the one that started it all.

PREP: 20 TO 25 MINUTES   CHILL: 1 HOUR   BAKE: 7 TO 9 MINUTES
---

1. Place the chopped chocolate, 1 $\frac{1}{2}$ cups of the chocolate chips, and the butter in a medium-size heavy-bottomed saucepan over very low heat, Stir continuously until the chocolate just begins to melt, 2 to 3 minutes. Turn off the heat, and stir until the chocolate has completely melted.

2. Transfer the chocolate mixture to a large mixing bowl and, with a wooden spoon, stir in the sugar. Break the eggs, one at a time, into the mixture, stirring until smooth after each addition. Set aside.

3. Whisk together the flour, espresso powder, baking powder, and salt in a small mixing bowl. Turn the flour mixture into the chocolate mixture and stir until just combined. Stir in the vanilla, and fold in the remaining $1\frac{1}{2}$ cups chocolate chips.

4. Cover the bowl with plastic wrap, and place the bowl in the refrigerator to chill for 1 hour.

(continued on next page)

5. When ready to bake, preheat the oven to 350°F. Place a rack in the center of the oven. Drop the batter by heaping tablespoons onto ungreased baking sheets, spacing the batter 2" apart. (You can also line the baking sheet with parchment paper or a silicone baking mat for easy cleanup.)

6. Bake the cookies until they rise and are glossy on top, 7 to 9 minutes. Do not overbake. (They need to be a little soft and gooey to the bite.) Let the cookies rest 1 minute on the baking sheet, then transfer with a metal spatula to a wire rack to cool completely. These cookies freeze very well stored in gallon zipper-lock plastic bags for up to 3 months. And they are particularly delicious cold and chewy straight from the freezer!

BAKING TIPS: *Use whatever semisweet chocolate chips you like. The 60 percent cacao chips are less sweet and more chocolatey than Nestlé, but use whatever chocolate chips you desire. As for espresso powder, you can find it on the coffee aisle in many supermarkets.*

CHOCOLATE MUDSLIDES

7 ounces unsweetened chocolate, chopped

6 ounces bittersweet chocolate, chopped

1/2 cup (1 stick) unsalted butter

7 large eggs

2 1/4 cups granulated sugar

1 teaspoon vanilla extract

3/4 cup plus 2 tablespoons cake flour

1 tablespoon baking powder

1 teaspoon espresso powder

1/8 teaspoon salt

1 1/2 cups bittersweet or semisweet chocolate chips

1 1/3 cups chopped walnuts

MAKES: 30 (3") cookies

MUDSLIDES SOUND LIKE MOTHER Nature unleashing havoc... unless you are in the kitchen and baking chocolate cookies. Then you think of a different mudslide, a gooey and intensely chocolate cookie by the same name. Back in the early 1990s, talk of edible mudslides began. At a baking contest in Petaluma, California, pastry chef Robert Jörin, now a Culinary Institute of America at Greystone instructor, won for his Chocolate Mudslide Cookies. The name was catchy and described chocolate desserts, from cakes to cookies to pies.

A decade later, renowned pastry chef Jacques Torres was on television making Chocolate Mudslide Cookies. And this time the "mudslide" not only meant gooey chocolate but also an overload, an avalanche of more than 2 pounds of chocolate sliding into this cookie dough. And that cookie, or at least the name, has survived.

Today you can find mudslide cookies in bakeries like Talula's Daily in Philadelphia, where the cookie is deep and dark and rich and studded with walnuts. Here is a recipe should you want to try your hand at it, an adaptation of both Jacques Torres's recipe and one baked at the Culinary Institute of America in Hyde Park, New York.

What makes these cookies different is not just the sheer volume of chocolate in the recipe but that they intentionally contain more baking powder than you might usually add to a cookie dough. In fact, you might think the tablespoon of baking powder is a mistake. But it isn't. Chemically, the baking powder adds so much leavening that the cookies expand and fall slightly, which makes them more dense and fudgy. You don't want to overbake these cookies. Turn on the oven light and look for them to get opaque with a slight crust on top. But they should still be soft to the touch when you remove the pan from the oven. Let them cool completely on a wire rack before storing. These are good keepers, up to 5 days at room temperature or up to 6 months in the freezer. Pair them with a cup of coffee or tea or a glass of cold milk. And to really experience the mudslide, warm them slightly in the microwave before eating.

PREP: 18 TO 22 MINUTES   BAKE: 8 TO 10 MINUTES

(continued on next page)

1. Place the chocolates and butter in a large heavy-bottomed saucepan over low heat. Stir until the chocolate and butter have nearly melted and are smooth, 3 minutes. Turn off the heat and continue to stir until smooth. Set aside.

2. Place a rack in the center of the oven, and preheat the oven to 350°F. Line a baking sheet with parchment paper.

3. Place the eggs and sugar in a large bowl and beat with an electric mixer on medium-high speed until the eggs and sugar are light in color and texture, about 5 minutes. Pour in the vanilla, then pour in a third of the melted chocolate, and mix on low speed until just combined. Add another third of the chocolate and mix to combine, then add the final third of chocolate and mix briefly, 10 seconds.

4. Whisk together the flour, baking powder, espresso powder, and salt in a large bowl. Carefully turn the flour mixture on top of the chocolate batter, and mix on low speed until just combined, 10 seconds. Fold in the chocolate chips and walnuts.

5. With a $1/4$-cup ice cream scoop, drop 6 scoops of dough onto the prepared baking sheet. Place the pan in the oven.

6. Bake the cookies until opaque and firm on top but still soft when pressed, 8 to 10 minutes. Remove the pan from the oven, and let the cookies rest on the pan for 2 minutes. Using a metal spatula, transfer the cookies to a wire rack to cool completely. Repeat baking the rest of the cookies. Store the cookies in an airtight container up to 5 days at room temperature or up to 6 months in the freezer.

SARA'S RASPBERRY THUMBPRINT COOKIES

$\frac{1}{2}$ cup (1 stick) lightly salted butter, at room temperature

$\frac{1}{2}$ cup granulated sugar

$\frac{1}{4}$ cup light brown sugar, lightly packed

1 large egg

1 teaspoon vanilla extract

$1\frac{1}{4}$ cups all-purpose flour (see Baking Tips)

$1\frac{1}{2}$ to 2 cups chopped pecans (see Baking Tips)

$\frac{1}{3}$ cup raspberry jam

MAKES: 18 to 24 ($1\frac{1}{2}$") cookies

PRESS YOUR THUMB INTO a soft ball of cookie dough and you'll experience a simple joy of baking. It's no surprise that thumbprint cookies are found in recipe collections across the country. The earliest mentions of them are in newspapers and cookbooks in the late 1940s, where they were often called Norwegian Thumbprints.

And if thumbprints experienced a resurgence, it might have been in the 1980s. That's about the time Sara Franco of Atlanta started baking them. She had tried her friend Margaret Weiller's recipe and was hooked. She loved the chopped toasted pecans clinging to the sides of the cookie and the filling of bright red raspberry jam. "I have been baking these cookies for about 35 years . . . I can do it blindfolded," Franco says confidently.

And for good reason. People love them. They want to buy them from her—"I say write a check to charity, and I'll bake them for you."

Franco has perfected an already-perfect recipe. The original recipe suggested that the cookies bake for 10 minutes, then be pulled out of the oven and filled with jam. But she found that unnecessary, so she fills them before baking. And she just started using a cookie scoop to portion the dough out evenly onto the baking pan. Perfection in the smallest of details—that's what makes this an outstanding recipe. And it's why in Franco's world, she is known for these cookies and her challah bread. "Baking is my quiet time, and in the end I have something to show for it."

PREP: 25 TO 30 MINUTES   BAKE: 15 TO 18 MINUTES

---

1. Place the soft butter and sugars in a large mixing bowl and beat with an electric mixer on medium speed until the mixture is creamy, about 1 minute. Turn off the machine.

2. Separate the egg, placing the egg white in a small bowl and setting it aside. Place the egg yolk in the mixing bowl with the butter and sugar. Add the vanilla. Beat on low speed until the mixture is just combined and creamy, 30 seconds. Add 1 cup of the flour, beating on low speed. Scrape down the sides of the

(continued on next page)

TOP TO BOTTOM: *Schrafft's Butterscotch Cookies and Sara's Raspberry Thumbprint Cookies*

bowl with a rubber spatula. Add up to $1/4$ cup of the remaining flour, adding what is needed to pull the mixture into a ball, beating on low speed as you add the flour. Depending on the size of the egg yolk, you may or may not need all the flour.

3. Place a rack in the center of the oven, and preheat the oven to 350°F. Set aside 2 ungreased baking sheets.

4. Drop the dough into 18 to 24 balls on 2 ungreased baking sheets. Roll each ball in the palm of your hands gently, then dip on all sides in egg white and roll in the pecans. Place back on the baking sheet, and repeat with the remaining balls of dough. Using your thumb, press into the center of each ball to create a well. Spoon $1/2$ teaspoonful of jam into each well. Place one pan in the oven.

5. Bake the cookies until they are lightly golden brown, 15 to 18 minutes, depending on the size of the cookie. Repeat with the second pan. Store the cookies in an airtight container.

BAKING TIPS: *Use your favorite all-purpose flour in this recipe, bleached or unbleached. The unknown element is that the dough needs to pull together, and this depends on the size of the egg yolk and the generosity of your teaspoon of vanilla, as these are the only liquid components of the recipe. So don't add all the flour at once, and if you do, just correct it with a little more vanilla or a teaspoon of water. As for pecans, you can chop the pecans finely or coarsely or buy already chopped pecans. And while Franco prefers raspberry jam with seeds, you can use seedless if you choose. Or select another flavor jam if that is what's in the fridge.*

WILD PERSIMMON COOKIES

½ cup (1 stick) unsalted butter, at room temperature

½ cup light brown sugar, firmly packed

½ cup granulated sugar

1 large egg

1 cup wild persimmon pulp (see Prepping Wild Persimmons)

1 teaspoon vanilla extract

2 cups all-purpose flour

1 teaspoon baking powder

1 teaspoon salt

1 cup chopped pecans

1 cup raisins

MAKES: 5 to 6 dozen (2½") cookies

VALERIE FREY GREW UP in Athens, Georgia, with a yard full of persimmon trees. When the coral-colored round fruit dropped off the tree and onto the ground, her mom would race to gather the persimmons before critters snatched them. Deer, opossums, raccoons, and skunks all love sweet, ripe persimmons. And now Valerie does the same thing each fall, except she has to be a bit more creative because there are no wild persimmon trees in her yard. The last time she searched for persimmons, she posted on Facebook asking where to find them and someone directed her to a tree along a public sidewalk. There were so many persimmons on the ground, she quickly bagged the ripe fruit, took them home, and stashed them in her freezer.

Persimmons are a unique and indigenous American fruit that grows from Florida north to Connecticut, west to Kansas, and south to Texas. They are full of tannin and inedible when unripe and green. Once they ripen, however, their fruit turns orange and has the consistency of jam. You need to remove the skins and caps by rubbing the soft persimmons through a sieve. Then measure the pulp and turn it into cakes, pudding, and cookies as you would mashed bananas or pumpkin.

Frey's mother, Sharon Frey, saw this following cookie recipe in a 1971 *Southern Living* magazine and adapted it as her own. It contains raisins, nuts, and some vanilla, but no spices, and yet the most intoxicating aroma comes from your oven when you bake these moist, fruitcakelike cookies. The original recipe called for margarine or shortening and white sugar, but I opted for butter and a bit of brown sugar to complement the flavor of the persimmons. Can't find autumn wild persimmons? Use the Hachiya persimmons that come into market, or substitute pumpkin.

PREP: 20 TO 25 MINUTES   BAKE: 12 TO 15 MINUTES

---

1. Place a rack in the top third of the oven, and preheat the oven to 350°F. Set aside 2 ungreased baking sheets.

2. Place the soft butter and sugars in a large mixing bowl and beat with an electric mixer on medium-low speed until the mixture is creamy and light, 1 minute. Add the egg, persimmon pulp, and vanilla, and beat on medium-low speed until incorporated and smooth, 30 seconds. Stop the mixer.

(continued on next page)

3. Whisk together the flour, baking powder, and salt in a medium-size bowl. Add the pecans and raisins, and toss to combine. Turn the flour mixture into the bowl with the batter. Fold in with a rubber spatula until just combined.

4. Spoon tablespoons of dough about 2" apart onto the prepared baking sheet and place in the oven.

5. Bake the cookies until the edges turn lightly browned, 12 to 15 minutes. You can refrigerate the dough between batches. Cookies baked from chilled dough are more round than those baked from dough that has not been refrigerated. Let the cookies rest for 1 minute on the baking sheet, then transfer to a wire rack to cool completely. Repeat with the remaining cookies. These cookies keep up to a week at room temperature.

PREPPING WILD PERSIMMONS: Rinse and pat dry wild persimmons. Remove the caps. Place the persimmons in a sieve set over a large bowl. Press down on the persimmons to push the pulp through the holes of the sieve and into the bowl. You will need to scrape the pulp off the underside of the sieve. It takes 6 cups persimmons to yield about 1 cup pulp. Discard the seeds and skins.

VANISHING OATMEAL RAISIN COOKIES

14 tablespoons (1 stick plus 6 tablespoons) unsalted butter, at room temperature

³/₄ cup light brown sugar, firmly packed

¹/₂ cup granulated sugar

2 large eggs

1 teaspoon vanilla extract

1¹/₂ cups all-purpose flour

1 teaspoon baking soda

1 teaspoon ground cinnamon

¹/₂ teaspoon salt

3 cups old-fashioned or quick oats

1 cup raisins

MAKES: 4 dozen (2¹/₂") cookies

LONG BEFORE THE FIRST oatmeal cookie recipes were shared in the 1880s, cooks were folding oats into baked goods to stretch it, enhance it, and to make it seem healthier. Some early oatmeal cookie recipes called for butter and others for lard. Some used molasses and others used white sugar. By 1902, oatmeal cookies made with almond extract were said to taste like macaroons. And the oatmeal cookie secured its place in American baking during World War I rationing because these cookies not only tasted good, but they were patriotic. In 1918 the *Lincoln Star & Evening Journal* in Nebraska said that oatmeal raisin cookies were good for the country, a true "wheat-saving" recipe. And oats were also used to stretch ground beef in meat loaf and other cost-cutting recipes.

In more recent times, oats have been lauded as a health food, good for your heart. And the simple, no-nonsense oatmeal cookie, a cookie that needs no grocery list, no fanfare, is still as relevant today as it was more than a century ago.

The following recipe has been printed on the back of the round Quaker Oats box since 1939. It wasn't the first recipe to appear—that was an oat cake in 1908. The earlier version of this recipe contained a teaspoon of water in which you dissolved the baking soda. The word *Vanishing* was added in the 1990s to describe how these cookies seem to disappear before your very eyes.

PREP: 15 TO 20 MINUTES   BAKE: 8 TO 10 MINUTES

1. Place a rack in the center of the oven, and preheat the oven to 350°F. Set aside 2 ungreased baking sheets.

2. Place the soft butter and sugars in a large mixing bowl and beat with an electric mixer on medium speed until creamy, 1 to 1¹/₂ minutes. Add the eggs and vanilla, and beat long enough to blend the eggs, about 30 seconds.

3. Whisk together the flour, baking soda, cinnamon, and salt in a medium-size bowl. Add the flour mixture to the butter and sugar

(continued on page 52)

FOLLOWING PAGE, CLOCKWISE FROM TOP LEFT: *Brown Palace Macaroons, Dallas Junior League Cowboy Cookies, Coconut Macadamia Macaroons, Mexican Wedding Cookies, 1908 Rocks, Vanishing Oatmeal Raisin Cookies, Mexican Wedding Cookies, and Wild Persimmon Cookies*

mixture, and blend on low speed to just combine, 20 seconds. Add the oats and raisins, and blend on low until just combined, 20 seconds.

4. Drop the dough by rounded tablespoons onto the baking sheets, spacing them about 2" apart. Place a pan in the oven.

5. Bake the cookies until lightly golden brown, 8 to 10 minutes. Let the cookies cool on the pan for 1 minute, then remove to a wire rack to cool completely, 30 minutes. Repeat with the remaining cookie dough. Store the cookies in an airtight container.

CHANGE IT UP: Even a classic recipe benefits from some last-minute creativity. So don't feel like you have to follow this recipe to the letter. Use chocolate chips or dried cranberries instead of the raisins, for example. Omit the cinnamon. Use the old-fashioned oats or the quick-cooking oats, whatever you hand on hand. And if you don't have the time to portion out cookies, turn this dough onto an ungreased 13" × 9" baking sheet and bake at 350°F until golden brown, about 30 minutes.

DALLAS JUNIOR LEAGUE COWBOY COOKIES

1 cup (2 sticks)
unsalted butter, at
room temperature

1½ cups dark brown
sugar, lightly packed

½ cup granulated
sugar

2 large eggs

1½ teaspoons vanilla
extract

2 cups all-purpose
flour

1 teaspoon baking
soda

½ teaspoon salt

½ teaspoon ground
cinnamon, if desired

2 cups old-fashioned
oats

2 cups semisweet or
bittersweet chocolate
chips

1 cup unsweetened
dried coconut (see
Baking Tips)

1 cup finely chopped
pecans

MAKES: About 40 (3")
cookies

IN THE 1950S, COWBOYS and cowgirls were the stuff dreams were made of . . . thanks to television and the movies. Roy Rogers and Dale Evans on the screen opened up a whole new western world for children and all sorts of marketing opportunities for companies. The idea of a Cowboy Cookie likely originated in a test kitchen. You can find a recipe for them in a 1948 Quaker Oats cookbook. It was an oatmeal cookie with chocolate chips and peanuts added.

As one newspaper columnist admitted in 1952, "My grandson wouldn't try them when told they were Oatmeal Cookies, but when told they were Cowboy Cookies, that was different and he found them delicious."

A lot of people have liked the idea of Cowboy Cookies and many of them are Texans. Just as Roy Rogers was the King of the Cowboys, Texas is the king—or queen—of the Cowboy Cookies. That might have to do with former First Lady Laura Bush sharing her Cowboy Cookie recipe with *Family Circle* magazine during the 2000 presidential election. But in Texas, this cookie of oats, chocolate chips, coconut, pecans, and often cinnamon has been around a lot longer than that. In fact, it was featured in the 1976 *Dallas Junior League Cookbook* and shared by Mrs. David C. Smith. That recipe doesn't contain cinnamon, a more modern addition, so feel free to add ½ teaspoon. Just as those classic cowboy movies still have an appeal, so do these Cowboy Cookies!

PREP: 20 TO 25 MINUTES   BAKE: 10 TO 14 MINUTES

---

1. Place a rack in the upper third of the oven, and preheat the oven to 350°F. Set aside 2 ungreased baking pans.

2. Place the soft butter and sugars in a large bowl and beat with an electric mixer on medium-low speed until creamy, about 2 minutes. Add the eggs and vanilla, and beat until well combined and slightly thickened, 1 minute.

3. Whisk together the flour, baking soda, salt, and cinnamon, if desired, in a medium-size bowl. Pour the flour mixture over the butter and sugar mixture. Add the oats. Blend on low speed until just combined, about 30 seconds. Turn off the mixer, and scrape

(continued on next page)

down the sides of the bowl with rubber spatula. Add the chocolate chips, coconut, and pecans, and continue to beat on low until just combined, 30 to 45 seconds.

4. Using an ice cream scoop $1^3/_4$" to 2" wide, scoop 6 balls of dough onto each prepared baking sheet. Place a pan in the oven.

5. Bake the cookies until they have browned around the edges but are still a little soft in the center, 10 to 14 minutes. Remove the pan from the oven, and let the cookies rest on the pan for 1 minute. Remove with a metal spatula to a wire rack to cool completely. Repeat with the remaining batter. Store the cookies in an airtight container.

BAKING TIPS: *For a more modern Texas Cowboy Cookie flavor, add $1/_2$ teaspoon ground cinnamon to the flour mixture. Unsweetened dried coconut can be found at natural food stores, and if you cannot find it, use unsweetened flaked coconut. For a more pronounced flavor, sprinkle the cookies with a little finely ground sea salt before baking*

SCHOOL LUNCH PEANUT BUTTER COOKIES

½ cup creamy peanut butter

½ cup vegetable shortening

½ cup light or dark brown sugar, lightly packed (see Baking Tip)

½ cup granulated sugar, plus about 2 tablespoons for pressing into the top of cookies

½ teaspoon vanilla extract

1 large egg

1½ cups sifted all-purpose flour

1 teaspoon baking soda

½ teaspoon salt

MAKES: About 4 dozen (2") cookies

MAKING SOMETHING AS SIMPLY delicious as the peanut butter cookie didn't happen overnight. While peanut butter was invented in the 1890s, and George Washington Carver spent the 1920s extolling the benefits of both peanuts and peanut butter, it took hard times—the war years and the Depression—for peanut butter to gain the spotlight as a source of protein and B vitamins. What was childhood without a peanut butter and jelly sandwich? And what was school lunch without peanut butter cookies?

As farmers faced financial ruin due to price collapses on their commodities in the 1930s, as parents were out of work and their children hungry, the US government stepped in to help through the federally supported lunch program. Not only did the government purchase surplus crops from farmers and feed children a hot meal, but they also employed thousands of women to cook in the lunchrooms.

And to bake recipes such as peanut butter cookies. These cookies were perfect for the lunch program because they used lower-cost vegetable shortening instead of butter. They could be baked in bulk. And they could be stored at room temperature. They became a staple at public school lunchrooms as well as private. When the Chicago Tribune profiled the cafeteria manager of the Catholic Marquette Park School in 1961, they found a favorite peanut butter cookie recipe being baked for 1,300 girls by Sister Mary Trinita. Here is that 1961 recipe. And while today peanut allergies prevent many cafeterias from baking peanut butter cookies, you can bake a taste of the past with this recipe.

PREP: 10 TO 15 MINUTES   BAKE: 10 TO 12 MINUTES

1. Place a rack in the center of the oven, and preheat the oven to 375°F. Set aside 2 ungreased baking sheets.

2. Place the peanut butter, shortening, brown sugar, and ½ cup of the granulated sugar in a large mixing bowl and beat with an electric mixer on medium-low speed until creamy, about 1 minute. Add the vanilla and egg, and beat on medium-low until the mixture is smooth, about 45 seconds. Turn off the mixer and scrape down the sides of the bowl with a rubber spatula.

(continued on next page)

3. Whisk together the sifted flour, soda, and salt in a medium-size bowl and turn this into the peanut butter mixture. Beat with the mixer on low speed until the dry ingredients are just incorporated, 45 seconds to 1 minute.

4. Drop the dough in 1" pieces spaced about 3" apart on the pans. Press the top of each ball twice with a fork dipped in the remaining granulated sugar, creating a crosshatch pattern. Place one pan at a time in the oven.

5. Bake the cookies until lightly browned, 10 to 12 minutes. Let the cookies rest on the pan for 1 minute, then transfer the cookies to a wire rack to cool.

BAKING TIP: *Use whatever brown sugar you have on hand. Dark brown sugar creates a dark and flavorful cookie. But most people prefer light.*

Macaroons and Macarons

Down South in New Orleans, Creole macaroons were being made with the grated zest of two oranges, as shown in the 1901 *Picayune Creole Cookbook*. Coconut made its grand entrance into macaroons about that time, and in more recent years we've seen chocolate, cornflake, even macadamia macaroons.

And yet a discussion on macaroons isn't complete without considering Charleston and the effect that the refugees of the French Revolution and the Haitian Revolution had on pastry in this city. According to Charleston historian Nic Butler, a French-refugee confectioner calling himself "Monsieur Macaron" in advertisements made "macarons" there in the 1790s.

Today there has been a new interest in the Parisian style of French "macarons." A cousin of the more rustic macaroon, this macaron is made with almond flour and the batter is more liquid in texture. It puffs up while baking and has a characteristic smooth appearance, and it is sandwiched with chocolate ganache or a buttercream filling.

MACAROONS

THE SIMPLE YET EXQUISITE macaroon, containing just ground almonds, sugar, and egg whites, is a cookie with a past. Its roots are in present-day southern Iraq, according to Jewish foodways expert Joan Nathan. It found its way to other countries via Jewish refugees. Once rustic, now more refined, macaroons contain no wheat flour or leavening, and Jews around the world bake them during Passover.

The British called them "macaroons." In early America, if macaroons weren't imported from France and Italy along with flour, prunes, and liqueurs, then they were made at home. One of the first mentions of macaroon baking was among the Quakers. Jane Paxson Parry set up her household in the late 1700s in what is now called the Parry Mansion in New Hope, Pennsylvania. Parry wrote down her receipts (recipes) in a journal, and her Quaker macaroon recipe couldn't be closer to what is used today:

Take a half lb. of almonds, ³⁄₄ of sugar, the whites of 3 eggs, bake on paper 12 minutes.

Elizabeth Ellicott Lea wrote in her *A Quaker Woman's Cookbook* in 1821 that macaroons should contain ground blanched almonds, rose water, egg whites, flour, and sugar, and be "shaped on white paper with a spoon, and bake them on tin plates in a slow oven." That same method would appear in *The Virginia House-wife* in 1824 and also *The Carolina Housewife* in 1847. And when American artist Grandma Moses wrote a macaroon recipe in her 1870s journal, now in the Bennington Museum in Bennington, Vermont, you get a sense that macaroons were very much a part of 19th-century life in the Northeast. Her recipe contained a little nutmeg, a nice touch.

I share two recipes for macaroons on the following pages.

BROWN PALACE MACAROONS

3 large egg whites

8 ounces almond paste

1 cup confectioners' sugar

½ cup granulated sugar

MAKES: 5 dozen (1" to 1½") cookies

THIS RECIPE IS FROM the Brown Palace Hotel in Denver, known for serving macaroons at high tea. They begin with almond paste. The longer you bake them, the crispier they will be, and the less time you bake them, the chewier they will become.

PREP: 15 TO 20 MINUTES   BAKE: 12 TO 15 MINUTES

---

1. Place a rack in the center of the oven, and preheat the oven to 325°F. Line 2 baking sheets with parchment paper.

2. Place the egg whites in a large mixing bowl, and beat with an electric mixer on high power until soft peaks form, about 2 minutes.

3. Crumble the almond paste into pieces in a large mixing bowl or the bowl of a food processor fitted with a steel blade. Add the sugars and beat with an electric mixer or pulse the food processor until combined. Add a third of the beaten egg whites and beat or pulse until no lumps remain. Add the rest of the beaten egg whites, beating on low or pulsing gently.

4. Spoon nickel-size dollops of dough onto the prepared baking sheets. Or use a pastry bag and pipe out ¾" rounds. Place a pan in the oven.

5. Bake the macaroons until the edges are golden brown over the top, 12 to 15 minutes. Transfer to a wire rack to cool. Repeat with the remaining dough. Store the cookies in an airtight container.

COCONUT MACADAMIA MACAROONS

2 cups (4 ounces) unsweetened flaked coconut

$^3/_4$ cup ($3^1/_2$ ounces) macadamia nuts

2 large egg whites

$^1/_4$ teaspoon cream of tartar

Pinch of salt

$^3/_4$ cup granulated sugar

MAKES: 3 to 4 dozen ($1^1/_2$ to 2") cookies

THIS RECIPE WAS ORIGINALLY called Mary Jo's Coconut Macaroons and is from Lindsey Shere's book, *Chez Panisse Desserts*. Shere's trick to create egg whites with lots of volume is to gently warm the whites before beating.

PREP: 20 TO 25 MINUTES   BAKE: 10 TO 14 MINUTES

---

1. Place a rack in the center of the oven, and preheat the oven to 325°F.

2. Toast the coconut on a baking sheet in the oven until golden brown, about 10 minutes. Turn the coconut periodically to keep it from burning on one side. Then, on a separate baking sheet, toast the macadamia nuts until the color changes slightly, about 12 minutes. Let the nuts cool and chop them finely. Set the coconut and macadamia nuts aside.

3. Warm the egg whites in a small saucepan over low heat for 5 to 10 seconds. Pour the egg whites into the bowl of a stand mixer, add the cream of tartar and salt, and beat with the electric mixer on high speed until stiff peak forms, about 3 minutes. Add the sugar and beat on high speed until stiff peaks appear again, 3 minutes. Remove the bowl from the mixer. Fold in the coconut and macadamia nuts with a wooden spoon or rubber spatula.

4. Line a cookie sheet with parchment paper. Using a 1" cookie scoop, form 1" balls of dough and place 1" apart on the baking sheet. Place the pan in the oven.

5. Bake the macaroons until lightly browned, about 10 to 14 minutes. Remove the pan from the oven and let the cookies cool on a wire rack until ready to serve, about 5 minutes. Store the cookies in an airtight container.

AUNT IDA'S WINE DROPS

1 cup granulated sugar

½ cup vegetable shortening

1 cup molasses

1 cup buttermilk

1 teaspoon baking soda

4 cups all-purpose flour

2 teaspoons ground cinnamon

1 teaspoon ground cloves

½ teaspoon ground nutmeg

½ teaspoon salt

½ cup raisins

½ cup currants

MAKES: About 8 dozen (1½" to 2") cookies

FOUND HANDWRITTEN IN THE back of an old cookbook archived by the Virginia Tech library is this spice cookie recipe. It contains no wine, but it would have been a cookie enjoyed with wine, such as sherry or Madeira. If you look closely, this mystery recipe will give you clues about when it was baked. It calls for shortening—1911 and later—and "thick milk," which was a phrase used in Pennsylvania, the Hudson River Valley, and on various farms where you might have had access to clabbered milk. Today, we just use buttermilk in tandem with baking soda.

And the recipe adds that you can place an orange or lemon in the jar with your cookies and "you will them a delicious flavor." Who was Aunt Ida? An aunt who was known well enough for her cookies that her recipe was written in beautiful cursive on the back page of a book, and now shared here.

PREP: 20 TO 25 MINUTES   BAKE: 8 TO 10 MINUTES

---

1. Place a rack in the center of the oven, and preheat the oven to 375°F.

2. Place the sugar, shortening, and molasses in a large bowl and beat with an electric mixer on medium speed until combined, 15 seconds.

3. Pour the buttermilk into a liquid measuring cup and whisk in the soda until dissolved. Pour the buttermilk mixture into the molasses mixture and beat on medium speed until combined, about 15 seconds. Scrape down the sides of the bowl with a rubber spatula.

4. In a medium-size bowl, whisk together the flour, cinnamon, cloves, nutmeg, and salt. Add the raisins and currants and stir until they are coated with the dry ingredients. With a wooden spoon or rubber spatula, fold this into the sugar mixture until combined, about 30 seconds.

5. Drop 1½" balls of dough about 1" apart onto ungreased baking sheets. Place a pan in the oven.

6. Bake the cookies until browned around the edges and just firm in the center, 8 to 10 minutes. Let the cookies rest 1 minute on the pan, then transfer to a wire rack to cool completely. Store the cookies in a loosely covered container.

2

COOKIES
SHAPED, ROLLED
& REMEMBERED

Sometimes you don't want to simply drop cookie dough on a pan. Sometimes you want to roll it out on a lightly floured board and cut it into delicate rounds with a jelly glass. Or you want to shape it into balls and, after baking, dredge these fragile, buttery cookie balls in confectioners' sugar. And maybe enclose a date inside. Or spread on apricot preserves and cinnamon sugar before rolling triangles of dough into little crescents.

This chapter includes those cookies and speaks to times when a little extra care goes into the preparation. You aren't on the clock, you have some time, and the cookies might be for a special gift or birthday or religious holiday. That's when cookies are shaped, rolled, and remembered.

Throughout our country's history, cooks just like you have taken dough into their hands and modeled it into something memorable. The first sugar cookies eaten in America were called jumbles—often spelled jumbals—and were an old English recipe that was modified over and over until we arrived at the cutout sugar cookies we love today. Those first jumbles were rolled into ropes and shaped into rings on the baking pan. The Danish peppernuts are a version of this method, rolling the spiced dough into a rope, but then the rope is cut into tiny pieces—nuts.

Our earliest version of a rolled cookie was the classic gingersnap, an eggless cookie dough that was rolled into one sheet, baked, and then cut while hot into pieces. Similar were the spongy Creole Stage Planks, sliced into big fat rectangles before baking, and the more modern Crisp Gingerbread Stars, rolled and cut into star shapes.

All the cookies in this chapter are perfect for gift-giving. Uncle Milt's Christmas Cookies are loaded with goodies. Homemade Fig Newtons are full of complex fig and orange flavors. The Mexican Wedding Cookies have a touch of cinnamon, as do the old Apisas, Sagamore Hill Sand Tarts, and St. Augustine Crispes. Mrs. Wright's Cocoons is a Jackson, Mississippi, buttery sugar cookie recipe that has made the rounds in various shapes, from cocoon to crescent to balls. Holiday cookies are often marked by a distinct ingredient that sets them apart from everyday cookies. When that ingredient is anise, as in the New Mexico Bizcochitos and the Ursuline Anise Cookies of New Orleans, the cookies have a profound and sacred flavor. When the spice is nutmeg (as in the New Hope Jumbles) or coriander (as in Amelia Simmons's Coriander Cookies), you taste one vivid spice and understand how it made the cookies memorable.

AMERICAN GINGERSNAPS

½ cup light brown sugar, packed firmly

½ cup molasses

½ cup (1 stick) unsalted butter

2 cups unbleached flour, plus 3 to 4 tablespoons for rolling the dough

1 teaspoon baking soda

2 teaspoons ground ginger

1 teaspoon ground cinnamon

½ teaspoon ground allspice

½ teaspoon ground coriander

½ teaspoon salt

MAKES: About 5 dozen (2" to 2½") cookies

THE SPICY GINGERSNAP TRULY snaps when you break it into pieces. And real gingersnaps, the old-timers say, contain no eggs, plenty of butter, and molasses that has cooked down on top of the stove.

The first mention of gingersnaps took place around 1805, according to John Mariani in *The Dictionary of American Food & Drink*, although cooks were baking gingerbread long before then. What we call gingerbread cake and gingerbread cookies today were parts of the collection of "gingerbread" recipes baked in Colonial America. The oldest examples were hard gingerbread pieces pressed with a decorative pattern using a stamp. These early ginger cookies originated in Europe and came with the German, Dutch, and English settlers to America. Gingersnaps were named from the German or Middle Dutch word *snappen*, meaning "to seize quickly."

In the United States, gingersnaps were associated with Muster Day or Militia Day, a military training and social event the entire town attended. Food historian Betty Fussell says that after the Revolutionary War, America realized the importance of a town militia for protection, and on Muster Day after the new recruits were signed up and the drills took place, there was plenty of rum to drink, gingersnaps to eat, and games and festivities to enjoy.

The following method for making gingersnaps might seem odd. You thinly roll the dough and drape it onto a pan before baking. Then, while still warm, the cookies are cut into strips and diamonds with a pastry wheel or pizza cutter. Nothing is wasted—there are no scraps from cutting out rounds of dough to bake. It's resourceful and fast—an old technique that works with busy lives today.

PREP: 20 TO 25 MINUTES   CHILL: 2 HOURS   BAKE: 11 TO 13 MINUTES

1. Place the brown sugar, molasses, and butter in a large saucepan and heat, stirring constantly, over medium-low heat until the butter melts, 5 to 6 minutes. Remove the pan from the heat and stir well to combine.

(continued on next page)

LEFT TO RIGHT: *Ursuline Anise Cookies and American Gingersnaps*

2. Whisk together the flour, baking soda, ginger, cinnamon, allspice, coriander, and salt in a large mixing bowl. Spoon the flour mixture into the brown sugar mixture in the saucepan. Stir with a wooden spoon until well blended. Transfer the dough to a glass bowl, cover with plastic wrap, and place in the refrigerator to chill for at least 2 hours. (You can chill overnight, but you will need to allow $1\frac{1}{2}$ hours for the dough to warm back up to room temperature.)

3. Place a rack in the top third of the oven, and preheat the oven to 350°F. Set aside a $17\frac{1}{2}$" × 12" baking sheet.

4. Remove the dough from the refrigerator. Sprinkle the rolling pin and work surface with flour. Place about a third of the dough on the work surface and roll the dough $\frac{1}{8}$" to $\frac{1}{16}$" thick. Loosen the dough from the surface using a thin metal spatula. Carefully wrap the dough around a rolling pin and lift it onto the baking sheet. Unroll the dough so that it is centered on the pan. Place the pan in the oven.

5. Bake the dough until it is browned around the edges, 11 to 13 minutes. Remove the pan from the oven, and allow the dough to rest on the pan for 2 minutes. Using a pizza cutter or sharp knife, cut the dough into strips or diamonds. Let the gingersnaps cool on the pan for 10 minutes. Break apart the snaps and place them on a wire rack to cool completely. Repeat the process, rolling another third of the dough onto the cooled pan, bake, score, and cool. Repeat with the final third. Store the cooled cookies in an airtight metal container for up to 2 weeks.

Gingersnaps Survive the Hard Times
Gingersnaps were a revered cookie in hard times, especially the war years, because they contained no eggs, could use vegetable shortening or lard in place of the rationed butter, and could be made quickly. With a long shelf life—up to 2 weeks—the cookies shipped well to family members serving overseas.

URSULINE ANISE COOKIES

Vegetable shortening for prepping the pans

2 teaspoons anise seeds

½ cup (1 stick) unsalted butter, at room temperature

¾ cup granulated sugar

2 large eggs

2 cups all-purpose flour

½ teaspoon baking powder

¼ teaspoon salt

OPTIONAL ICING

1 cup confectioners' sugar

2 tablespoons milk

MAKES: About 4 dozen (1½" to 2") cookies

NEW ORLEANS'S FOOD HISTORY has benefited from the variety of cultures present in the city. One of these groups was the French Catholic nuns—12 of them, in fact—who came to New Orleans in 1727 to educate girls and women. They were part of a larger religious order called the Sisters of the Order of Saint Ursula, founded in Italy. Their original convent was located at the corner of Chartres Street and Ursulines Avenue, and their school became the Ursuline Academy, still in operation today and the oldest Catholic school in the United States.

It has been a tradition of those of the Catholic faith to bake anise cookies when St. Joseph's Day is celebrated on March 19. Anise, with a faint licorice flavor, has long been a celebratory flavoring of Europe, and originally it was prized for being a digestive. Sicilian immigrants brought the tradition of staging a St. Joseph's Day altar stacked with anise cookies to New Orleans. And this is the recipe that people still bake today for that altar and religious holiday. It is adapted from *Recipes and Reminiscences of New Orleans* by the Parents Club of Ursuline Academy, and also from *Cooking Up a Storm* by Judy Walker and Marcelle Bienvenu.

PREP: 25 TO 30 MINUTES   BAKE: 9 TO 11 MINUTES

1. Place a rack in the center of the oven, and preheat the oven to 350°F. Lightly grease 2 baking sheets.
2. Crush the anise seeds coarsely with a mortar and pestle (or between sheets of waxed paper with a rolling pin). Place in a large mixing bowl with the soft butter and beat with an electric mixer at medium speed until soft, about 1 minute. Gradually blend in the granulated sugar until creamy, about 1 minute. Beat the eggs into the mixture, one at a time, until well blended. Set aside.
3. Sift the flour with the baking powder and salt in a medium-size bowl. Using the mixer on low speed, gradually mix the flour mixture into the butter and sugar mixture until just blended, 30 seconds.

(continued on next page)

4. Shape the dough into 1" balls and place them 2" apart on the prepared baking sheets. Place a pan in the oven.

5. Bake the cookies until lightly browned around the bottom, about 9 to 11 minutes. Transfer the cookies to wire racks to cool, then store in airtight containers.

6. If desired, for an icing, whisk together the confectioners' sugar and milk in a small bowl. You can tint it red or green at Christmastime. Drizzle the icing over the cooled cookies, and let the icing set before serving.

ANOTHER DECORATING IDEA: Before baking, roll the balls of dough in a mixture of 3 tablespoons granulated sugar and $^3/_4$ teaspoon ground cinnamon.

Baking in New Orleans with an Italian Flavor

We know the French influence on the food of New Orleans, but the Italians, and the Sicilians in particular, were important to New Orleans foodways, says Poppy Tooker, local historian and radio host. According to Loyola University in New Orleans, in 1850 more Italians lived in New Orleans than any other US city.

Molasses

Molasses, America's revolutionary sweetener, is a critical ingredient in gingersnaps and other ginger cookies. This recipe calls for first boiling the molasses with butter and brown sugar, allowing moisture in the molasses to escape. No doubt molasses plays a major role in the taste and texture of gingersnaps. But which molasses to use?

Choose unsulfured, light molasses, which is the sweetest and the first boiling of molasses. It is made from the juice of sun-ripened sugarcane. "Second-boil" molasses is darker, and sulfured molasses is made from unripe, green sugarcane with the addition of sulfuric dioxide as a preservative. The heaviest molasses is called blackstrap—or as the old-timers put it, "the mother liquor." It is the dark, rich, third boil and slightly bitter in flavor, but full of vitamins and minerals.

MRS. LEFFERT'S NEW YEAR'S CAKES

8½ cups all-purpose flour

1 pound light brown sugar, firmly packed

1 teaspoon baking soda

1 teaspoon salt

10 ounces (2½ sticks) unsalted butter, at room temperature

1 large egg

1 cup milk, or more as needed

2 tablespoons caraway seeds

2 tablespoons orange zest (from 2 oranges)

MAKES: About 10 dozen (3") cookies

ON THE FIRST DAY of the New Year, 17th-century Dutch immigrants in the Hudson River Valley opened their homes to guests. It was their ritual. On the menu were punch and cookies, the latter flavored with caraway and orange. According to Dutch food historian Peter G. Rose, cookies are "distinctly Dutch." And New Year's Day was a special time for the Dutch to bake cookies and share them with others.

Maria Lott Leffert was a member of one of Brooklyn's leading Dutch founding families. She recorded her recipes in her 1820 dairy, and this recipe was first discovered by Peter Rose and placed in her book *Matters of Taste: Dutch Recipes with an American Connection*. Rose says Mrs. Leffert's original recipe called for 28 pounds flour, 10 pounds sugar, 5 pounds butter, caraway seeds, and orange zest. That would have fed a lot of visitors!

PREP: 20 TO 25 MINUTES   REST: 30 MINUTES   BAKE: 8 TO 10 MINUTES

---

1. Place the flour, brown sugar, baking soda, and salt in a large mixing bowl and stir to combine well. Add the soft butter and, with two knives, cut the butter into the dry ingredients until it looks like coarse meal.

2. Stir together the egg and milk in a small bowl, and whisk until the yolk is broken. Stir this into the flour mixture. Add the caraway seeds and orange zest. Stir until the dough is stiff. Add more milk if needed to pull it together. Cover the bowl with a kitchen towel, and let it rest for 30 minutes.

3. Place a rack in the center of the oven, and preheat the oven to 325°F.

4. Flour a work surface, and divide the dough into quarters. Roll out one quarter of the dough until it is quite thin, ¼" to ⅛" thick. Cut into 2½" diamond-shaped cookies. Place on an ungreased baking sheet, spacing them 1" apart, and place the pan in the oven.

5. Bake the cookies until golden brown around the edges and crisp, 8 to 10 minutes. Transfer the cookies to a wire rack to cool completely. Repeat with the remaining dough. Store covered for up to 1 week.

CREOLE STAGE PLANKS

3½ cups unbleached all-purpose flour, divided use, plus ¼ cup for rolling the dough

1 tablespoon ground ginger

1 teaspoon ground cinnamon

½ teaspoon ground cloves

½ teaspoon baking soda

¼ teaspoon salt

½ cup (1 stick) unsalted butter, at room temperature

¼ cup granulated sugar

¾ cup molasses

½ cup buttermilk

MAKES: 16 (6" × 2") cookies

A LARGE, STIFF GINGER cookie made with lard called Creole Stage Planks was on the menu of the New Orleans Press Club banquet in 1898. Oddly, it was better known at the time as *estomac mulatre*, meaning "mulatto's stomach," and was baked and sold by the Creoles of New Orleans. Dark with molasses and redolent of ginger, this cookie was a stomach settler for sailors. It was common for ginger cookies to be sold on docks in New Orleans as well as port cities along the East Coast.

These large, dense rectangles were so named because they resembled the planks on which you stepped to get from the dock to the ship. Made with plenty of flour, but without butter or eggs, they were and still are good keepers, able to stay fresh in a covered container for up to 2 weeks on sea or on land. Here is a recipe adapted from *The Picayune Creole Cook Book,* published in 1901.

PREP: 20 TO 25 MINUTES   BAKE: 10 TO 15 MINUTES

1. Place a rack in the center of the oven, and preheat the oven to 375°F. Line a baking sheet with parchment paper.

2. Whisk together 3 cups of the flour, the ginger, cinnamon, cloves, baking soda, and salt in a medium-size bowl.

3. Place the butter, sugar, and molasses in a large bowl and beat with an electric mixer on medium speed until combined, about 1 minute. With the mixer on low speed, alternate adding a third of the dry ingredients and half of the buttermilk to the sugar mixture. Once incorporated, scrape down the sides of the bowl with a rubber spatula. The dough should be sticky but still firm enough to roll out. Add another ½ cup flour if needed.

4. On a lightly floured surface, roll out the dough to a 16" × 12" rectangle, or until the dough is ¼" to ⅓" thick. With a pizza cutter, cut the dough horizontally across the median. Make 8 more cuts to create 16 rectangles. Transfer the planks to the prepared baking sheet and place in the oven.

5. Bake the planks until just firm at the center, 10 to 15 minutes. Remove the pan from the oven, and transfer the planks to wire racks to cool. Wait about 5 minutes before serving. Store lightly covered for up to 2 weeks.

BEATRICE'S PEPPERNUTS

1 cup (2 sticks) unsalted butter, at room temperature

1 cup light brown sugar, lightly packed

1 large egg

2½ cups all-purpose flour, plus extra for rolling the dough

1 teaspoon baking powder

½ teaspoon baking soda

1 teaspoon ground cardamom

½ teaspoon ground cinnamon

½ teaspoon ground cloves

½ teaspoon ground allspice

½ teaspoon ground nutmeg

1 cup ground toasted almonds (see Baking Tips)

MAKES: About 18 dozen (¾") cookies

BEATRICE OJAKANGAS IS A Finnish American cookbook author who knows much about Scandinavian baking. Raised on a farm in northern Minnesota, her large family preferred the simple taste of a vanilla butter cookie baked plain or rolled in spices and nuts. Yet other families with Scandinavian roots who settled in the upper Midwest weren't so simple. The Norwegians cooked their *krumkake* wafer cookies on irons on top of the stove. Swedes "have these little pans and little cookie cutters," tools handed down from generation to generation. Each recipe "reflected the economics of the past, and traditions are always based on economics of the past," according to Ojakangas. When people immigrated to America, they brought these traditions with them. It was a connection to their past, to their homeland, she says, and they made a point of baking these special cookies during the holidays to remind them of home. "You do what is familiar," says Ojakangas. To the Danes, familiarity meant peppernuts, the spicy cookie dough that is rolled into ropes and cut into nut-size pieces before baking. But "pepper" doesn't mean black pepper—although many peppernuts recipes do contain black pepper. It means anything flavored, she says, such as allspice, nutmeg, cloves, cinnamon, and cardamom, all present in this recipe.

Although Ojakangas isn't Danish, this recipe is one of her holiday favorites because you bake them once and they keep well throughout the holidays. Serve with coffee, tea, or wine. They embody the winter holidays—aromatic, fun, and reminiscent of the homeland.

PREP: 30 TO 35 MINUTES   BAKE: 8 TO 10 MINUTES

---

1. Place the soft butter and brown sugar in a large mixing bowl and beat with an electric mixer on medium-low speed until light and fluffy, 1 to 2 minutes. Add the egg and mix until incorporated, 30 seconds.

2. Using a fork, whisk together the flour, baking powder, baking soda, cardamom, cinnamon, cloves, allspice, and nutmeg in a medium-size bowl. Using the mixer on low speed, gradually add the flour mixture to the butter mixture. Scrape down the sides of

(continued on next page)

the bowl with a rubber spatula. Increase the mixer speed to medium, and mix just until combined, 1 to 2 minutes. Fold in the ground almonds with a wooden spoon or spatula. Cover the bowl with plastic wrap and place in the refrigerator until the dough is firm, at least 1 hour.

3. When ready to bake, place a rack in the center of the oven, and preheat the oven to 375°F.

4. Flour a clean working surface. Take a small section of the dough and roll between your hands on the floured surface until the dough forms a rope about $1/2$" in diameter. Cut the rope into $3/4$" pieces with a knife, separate those pieces, and place the squares on an ungreased baking sheet. Place the pan in the oven.

5. Bake the cookies until lightly golden, 8 to 10 minutes. Remove the pan from the oven and let the cookies cool on the pan for about 5 minutes. Store tightly covered for up to 2 weeks.

BAKING TIPS: *Toast 2 cups whole almonds in a 350°F oven for 6 to 7 minutes, or until toasted and fragrant. Cool to the touch. Grind in a food processor fitted with a steel blade, using 9 to 10 pulses. This dough may be stored covered in plastic wrap in the fridge for a few days to let the flavor enhance and the texture improve.*

COUNTERCLOCKWISE FROM TOP RIGHT: *Beatrice's Peppernuts, Creole Stage Planks, and Mrs. Leffert's New Year's Cakes*

AMELIA SIMMONS'S CORIANDER COOKIES

½ cup granulated sugar

¼ cup water

2 cups unbleached all-purpose flour

1 teaspoon coriander seeds, crushed

½ teaspoon baking powder

¼ teaspoon salt

½ cup (1 stick) unsalted butter, at room temperature, cut into tablespoons

---

MAKES: About 3 dozen (1½") cookies

ONE OF THE FIRST cookie recipes printed in an American cookbook, this recipe was just called "Cookies." It was a mixture of butter, flour, sugar, and a little pearlash leavening popular with the Dutch in what is now the Hudson River Valley of New York. And it contained crushed coriander seeds, a typical ingredient in cookies and cakes in early America. Spices of all types were routine in baking, and the port cities of Philadelphia, Boston, New York, and Charleston had access to cinnamon and nutmeg and other spices. But coriander seeds were a little different, says Patty Erd of the Spice House. They grew freely in early America, and it's possible that the spice-trading Dutch settlers brought the seeds with them from their homeland.

In these early days of American baking, a simple add-in, be it coriander or nutmeg or caraway seeds, was folded into a basic cookie or cake batter. That flavor shone and was significant to a holiday or an occasion. And before there was granulated sugar, before you could cream butter and sugar together with an electric mixer, you needed to dissolve sugar by boiling it in water in a pot over the fire. Cookie recipes back then, versus now, had a lot more flour in the dough. This original recipe calls for "two and a half pounds." That equals somewhere around 10 cups. As early cooks didn't have the benefit of refrigeration and air-conditioning to keep the dough cool, they had to add a lot of flour to the dough to make it workable. As a result, their cookies were hard and dry in comparison to the crispy, softer cookies we enjoy today. The following is a slightly modernized version of Amelia Simmons's recipe.

PREP: 25 TO 30 MINUTES   BAKE: 10 TO 12 MINUTES

---

1. Place a rack in the center of the oven, and preheat the oven to 350°F.
2. Place the sugar and water in a small saucepan over low heat and stir constantly until the sugar dissolves, 4 to 5 minutes. Turn off the heat and let the sugar syrup cool.
3. Meanwhile, place the flour in a large mixing bowl and whisk in the crushed coriander seeds, baking powder, and salt to distribute well. Pour in the cooled sugar syrup. Add the soft butter. Mix with a wooden spoon until the cookie dough comes

together into a ball. (You can facilitate this process using a food processor.)

4. With floured hands, divide the dough into thirds. Place two-thirds of the dough in a cool place. Working with one third, roll it with your hands to about a $\frac{1}{2}$"-thick rope. Cut the rope into 3" sections, and twist each section into a loop and place on an ungreased baking sheet. Place the pan in the oven.

5. Bake the cookies until lightly golden brown around the edges, 10 to 12 minutes. Transfer the cookies to a wire rack to cool, and repeat with the remaining dough. Store the cookies in a metal or plastic container for up to 1 week.

Decoding Old Recipes

Old recipes are a joy to read, but they pose a challenge if you want them to work in today's kitchen. Here is how Amelia Simmons described the process of shaping her cookies in 1796:

"Make roles half an inch thick and cut to the shape you please..."

Hmm. Do you roll out the dough to a $\frac{1}{2}$" thickness and cut into rounds? Or do you roll it into a $\frac{1}{2}$"-thick log and cut into crosswise slices like slice-and-bake cookies? But these thin cookies might have burned in a wood-fired oven. Could she have meant to roll the log into a "role" and cut into various lengths and twist these into pretzel shapes and rings? I chose two methods. First, I rolled the dough to a $\frac{1}{2}$" thickness on a floured surface and cut it into rounds. They baked well at 350°F for 10 to 12 minutes. And then I chose the method of twisting ropes of dough into shapes, which is the recipe above. They are decorative and able to withstand the heat of the early-American oven. I believe this is the method Amelia Simmons intended.

CRISP GINGERBREAD STARS

1 cup (2 sticks) unsalted butter, at room temperature

1½ cups granulated sugar

1 large egg

4 teaspoons grated orange zest

2 tablespoons dark corn syrup, molasses, or sorghum

3¼ cups all-purpose flour

2 teaspoons baking soda

2 teaspoons ground cinnamon

1 teaspoon ground ginger

½ teaspoon ground cloves

½ teaspoon salt

ICING

2 cups confectioners' sugar

2 tablespoons orange juice or water, or as needed

MAKES: 5 dozen (2½" to 3") cookies

THEY SAY EVERYONE HAS a story, and the same can be said for cookies. This Crisp Gingerbread Stars recipe came out of a food writers' luncheon I attended in the late 1980s. I cannot remember the venue or the rest of the meal, but I fell in love with the cookies, fragrant with orange and deep and dark with cinnamon and ginger. They were crisp and buttery, yet light. And at my house during the Christmas holidays, they are the cookies that go onto trays to give to friends.

The secret of making great cutout cookies is not only the recipe but the tools. You need a heavy rolling pin. A maple French rolling pin bought at E. Dehillerin while in cooking school in Paris decades ago is my favorite. I lugged it back with me in a carry-on bag, something you wouldn't be able to do today. It is long and tough and can roll anything out as thin as paper. The trick to crispy, thin, rolled cookies is to bash the dough first before rolling. Then roll from the center out to the desired thickness. Keep the counter lightly floured, and flip the dough often to prevent it from sticking.

Years ago I picked up a set of tin cookie cutters in graduated sizes of stars. I like to cut stars of all sizes not only because they look like one big star family on the platter but also because people like cookies of different sizes. You have the "I'll eat only one bite" sort of people, and they choose the small stars. (And then go back for a second!) Then you have those folks who say bigger is better and want the biggest cookie on the plate. I relate to both.

To decorate these stars, I whisk together confectioners' sugar and enough orange juice to make a smooth and slightly thickened icing. Pour this into a plastic squeeze bottle. Once the cookies are cool, drizzle the icing over the cookies in zigzags, or however you like! Let the icing dry before storing.

PREP: 45 MINUTES   CHILL: 2 HOURS TO OVERNIGHT   BAKE: 8 TO 10 MINUTES

---

1. Place the soft butter and granulated sugar in a large bowl and beat with an electric mixer on medium speed until creamy and soft, 1 to 2 minutes. Add the egg and beat until light and fluffy, 1 minute. Fold in the orange zest and corn syrup, molasses, or sorghum until combined.

(continued on next page)

2. Sift the flour, baking soda, cinnamon, ginger, cloves, and salt into a medium-size bowl. Fold the flour mixture into the butter and sugar mixture with a rubber spatula until combined. Chill the dough, covered, at least 2 hours, or overnight.

3. When ready to bake, place a rack in the center of the oven, and preheat the oven to 375°F. Lightly flour a work surface and remove the dough from the refrigerator. Scrape about half of the dough onto the work surface. Lightly flour a rolling pin, and firmly tap the dough with the rolling pin until it is about 1" thick. Roll out the dough to about $\frac{1}{4}$" thickness, lightly rolling from the center out to the edges and flipping the dough over every so often so that it does not stick to the work surface. Dust the dough and surface with flour as needed. Cut the dough with star cutters (or the cookie cutter of your choice), pressing firmly down on one stroke. With the help of a metal spatula, transfer the cutouts to ungreased cookie sheets, placing the cookies about 1" apart. Keep the remaining dough chilled, press the scraps into a loose ball, and roll the scraps and rest of the dough and cut into shapes. Place a pan in the oven.

4. Bake the cookies until they are well browned and crisp, 8 to 10 minutes. Remove the pan from the oven, and let the cookies cool on the pan 1 minute. Transfer them to a wire rack to cool completely.

5. For the icing, whisk together the confectioners' sugar and orange juice or water in a small bowl until smooth. Using a knife, spread the cookies with icing, and let it set before eating. Or pour the icing into a plastic squeeze bottle and pipe out squiggles, lines, or designs to decorate. These cookies keep up to 1 week in a tightly covered metal container.

VIRGINIA TAVERN BISCUITS

2 cups unbleached flour, plus a little flour for rolling the dough

1/2 cup plus 2 tablespoons granulated sugar

1/4 teaspoon ground nutmeg

1/2 cup (1 stick) unsalted butter, cut into tablespoons, at room temperature

3 tablespoons milk

2 tablespoons brandy or rum

MAKES: About 3 dozen (2") cookies

SWEET, SIMPLE COOKIES BAKED with brandy or rum were called tavern biscuits in Virginia and the rest of the Colonies. Whether they were actually baked in a tavern or were called "tavern" because of the addition of liquor isn't certain. One of the first mentions of a tavern biscuit in an American cookbook was in *The Virginia House-wife* by Mary Randolph, published in 1824. Tavern biscuits were long baked in England.

Taverns were essential facilities in the Colonies, located on busy roads, serving good hearty meals and plenty of alcohol, and often offering lodging for the weary. They were where people gathered to dine, drink, share the news of the day, and establish the early militia.

Here is a simple recipe for tavern biscuits adapted from *The Virginia House-wife*. Another tavern biscuit is the Joe Froggers recipe (page 6) from Massachusetts.

PREP: 10 TO 15 MINUTES   BAKE: 15 TO 18 MINUTES

---

1. Place a rack in the center of the oven, and preheat the oven to 375°F.

2. Stir together the flour, sugar, and nutmeg in a large mixing bowl. Distribute the soft butter around the bowl. Add the milk and brandy or rum. Stir until the dough just begins to pull together. With clean hands, knead the dough until it comes together in one mass, about 2 minutes.

3. Dust a work surface with a little flour. Roll the dough out to 1/4" thickness and cut into desired shapes with floured cookie cutters or with a knife. With the help of a metal spatula, transfer the shapes on an ungreased baking sheet, setting the cookies about 1" apart. Place the pan in the oven.

4. Bake until the cookies are just golden brown but still a little soft, 15 to 18 minutes. Remove the pan from the oven, and transfer the cookies to a wire rack to cool completely. Repeat with the remaining dough. The cookies keep in an airtight container for 2 weeks.

MAMMAW HYTKEN'S MATZO COOKIES

Vegetable shortening for prepping the pans

1 cup matzo meal

1 cup matzo farfel (see Baking Tip)

³/₄ cup granulated sugar

1 teaspoon ground cinnamon

¹/₄ teaspoon salt

2 large eggs, at room temperature

²/₃ cup vegetable oil

1 cup (4 ounces) chopped pecans, if desired

³/₄ to 1 cup semisweet chocolate chips, if desired

MAKES: About 30 (2") cookies

BAKING TIP: *Matzo farfel is matzo broken into pieces. If you cannot find it, substitute 4 sheets large matzo crackers, coarsely crushed to pea-size.*

JENNIE HYTKEN EMIGRATED FROM Latvia to rural Mississippi in the early 1900s. She married and raised her family in Belzoni, Mississippi, and according to her granddaughter Julie Kramer of Nashville, Tennessee, there were few Jewish immigrants in this small southern town. So to shop for ingredients in Jewish recipes, Mammaw Hytken had to travel to Memphis. And she eventually moved to Memphis.

Known for her good cooking, Mammaw Hytken stuffed matzo balls with ground seasoned beef brisket and baked these cookies for as long as Kramer can remember. Most Jews eat matzo just at Passover, but her grandmother made these cookies year-round. "I don't know where the idea of matzo cookies came from, but I feel like she probably invented it. She was an excellent and innovative cook."

Here is the family recipe.

PREP: 15 TO 20 MINUTES   BAKE: 11 TO 13 MINUTES

---

1. Place a rack in the center of the oven, and preheat the oven to 350°F. Generously grease 2 baking sheets with shortening, and set them aside.

2. Toss together the matzo meal, matzo farfel, sugar, cinnamon, and salt in a large bowl.

3. Place the eggs in a medium-size bowl and whisk to break the yolks. Add the oil and whisk to combine well. Pour this egg and oil mixture over the matzo mixture. Add the pecans and chocolate chips, if desired. Stir with a wooden spoon until the batter is well combined. The batter will be thick.

4. Dollop the batter onto the prepared baking sheets, placing the dough 1¹/₂" to 2" apart. Place a pan in the oven.

5. Bake the cookies until slightly golden brown around the edges, 11 to 13 minutes. Allow the cookies to rest on the pan for 2 to 3 minutes, then transfer them with a metal spatula to a wire rack to cool completely. Repeat with the remaining dough. Store the cookies covered for up to 1 week.

CLOCKWISE TOP TO BOTTOM: *Virginia Tavern Biscuits, New Mexico Bizcochitos, and Mammaw Hytken's Matzo Cookies*

NEW MEXICO BIZCOCHITOS

DOUGH

1 cup (8 ounces) lard, at room temperature

¾ cup granulated sugar

1 large egg

1 teaspoon anise seeds, crushed (see Baking Tip)

1½ cups whole wheat flour

1½ cups all-purpose flour, plus more for rolling the dough

1½ teaspoons baking powder

½ teaspoon salt

¼ cup brandy

TOPPING

½ cup granulated sugar

1 teaspoon ground cinnamon

MAKES: About 6 dozen (2") cookies

THE STATE COOKIE OF New Mexico, bizcochitos are an anise-flavored confection traditionally baked at Christmas and religious holidays. They are related to the Spanish *mantecados*, a shortbread made with lard. The first reference to them in America was in a Taos, New Mexico, newspaper 5 years before New Mexico was granted statehood in 1912.

A crisp and simple cookie with a multitude of baking variations, bizcochitos may call for lard or butter; whole wheat flour or white. But the key flavor here is anise, a medicinal herb and tiny aromatic seed beneficial to digestion.

Even the spelling was debated when the New Mexico legislature introduced a bill in 1989 to make bizcochitos the state cookie. It was introduced as "biscochito," but Spanish-language scholars insisted the right spelling was with a *z* rather than an *s*.

So what you have is a decidedly regional cookie with strong flavor and heritage, first baked in *horno*, or clay ovens. And the smell of bizcochitos baking tells you it's a special time. According to the *Santa Fe New Mexican* magazine, "the sweet smell of bizcochitos baking means it's holiday time in New Mexico. . . . Everyone has an opinion on who creates the finest bizcochitos, our state cookie. In most cases, probably it is your grandmother." They can or cannot use cinnamon, and the Mexican canela cinnamon, which is warmer and softer in flavor, is preferred.

This recipe is good enough to satisfy a grandmother. It is adapted from one shared by Jane Butel, New Mexico foodways expert, in her 1965 cookbook called *Favorite Mexican Foods*.

PREP: 30 TO 35 MINUTES   BAKE: 12 TO 14 MINUTES

---

1. Place a rack in the center of the oven, and preheat the oven to 350°F.

2. For the dough, place the lard and sugar in a large bowl and beat with an electric mixer on medium speed until fluffy and light, 1 minute. Scrape down the sides of the bowl with a rubber spatula. Add the egg and anise seeds. Beat on medium speed until just combined, 30 seconds.

3. Place the flours in a large bowl. Stir in the baking powder and salt to combine. Alternately add the brandy and the flour mixture to the lard mixture, beating on low speed after each addition until just combined.

4. Divide the dough into thirds. On a lightly floured surface, place 1 ball of dough. Roll it out to $\frac{1}{8}$" thickness and, with a 2"-diameter decorative cutter, cut into rounds, diamonds, or stars. Transfer the cookies to an ungreased baking sheet, arranging them 1" apart.

5. For the topping, place the sugar in a small bowl, and stir in the cinnamon to combine. Sprinkle the cinnamon-sugar mixture generously over the cookies on the baking sheet. Place the pan in the oven.

6. Bake the cookies until barely golden brown, 12 to 14 minutes. Remove the pan from the oven and transfer the cookies to a wire rack to cool completely. Repeat with the remaining dough, using the scraps from all 3 rolls to make a fourth roll of dough. These cookies actually improve with age and are better the next day. Store covered for up to 1 week.

BAKING TIP: *Place the anise seeds in a small bowl and crush using the end of a rolling pin. Or crush them with a mortar and pestle.*

NEW HOPE JUMBLES

1 cup (2 sticks) lightly salted butter, at room temperature

1¾ cups granulated sugar

1 large egg

2½ cups unbleached all-purpose flour

¼ teaspoon ground nutmeg

MAKES: About 90 (2¼") cookies

JUMBLES ARE RING-SHAPED COOKIES native to medieval Europe and the forerunner to our sugar cookies. There's a good chance your family recipe box holds a jumble recipe.

Jumbles were especially dear to the Quakers. In *A Quaker Lady's Cookbook*, a cookbook that shares recipes from four generations of the Parry family of New Hope, Pennsylvania, all generations of women recorded their jumble recipes. The earlier recipes of this family who lived in the Parry Mansion from 1787 to 1900 contained currants, spices, wine or brandy, and less sugar. Later versions contained baking powder, which is how the firm, crispy jumble morphed into the softer and cakier American sugar cookie we know.

Jumbles have been loved throughout America. *The Carolina Housewife*, written in 1847, contains three jumble recipes, all flavored with rose water and spices, but one rolled and cut into small pieces; one not specifying how the cookie is prepared for baking; and a third rolled, cut into strips, twisted into the characteristic ring shape, and then baked. Food writer Annabella Hill of Georgia describes jumbles made with rose water and nutmeg in her 1872 *Mrs. Hill's New Cook Book*. In *The Settlement Cookbook* of 1903, published in Milwaukee, Wisconsin, jumbles were cut into the shape of a doughnut to mirror their earlier ring shape. Here is Elizabeth Van Etten Parry's 1850s Quaker recipe, which is lightly flavored with nutmeg.

PREP: 20 TO 25 MINUTES   BAKE: 8 TO 12 MINUTES

1. Place a rack in the center of the oven, and preheat the oven to 375°F.

2. Place the soft butter and sugar in a large bowl and beat with an electric mixer on medium-low speed until light and fluffy, 2 minutes. Add the egg and beat until combined, 1 minute more.

3. Sift together the flour and nutmeg into a medium-size bowl. Add a third of the flour mixture to the butter and sugar mixture and mix with the mixer on low speed until just incorporated. Scrape down the sides of the bowl with a rubber spatula. Repeat with the remaining flour until all the ingredients are well combined.

(continued on next page)

4. On a floured surface, roll out a fourth of the dough to about $\frac{1}{3}$" thick. Cut with a ring-shaped cookie cutter and transfer cookies to an ungreased baking sheet, keeping them at least 1" apart. Place the pan in the oven.

5. Bake the cookies until the edges are light brown, 8 to 12 minutes. Cool on wire racks before serving. Store covered for up to 1 week.

Weather, Farming & Jumbles

Jumbles were one of the most popular cookie recipes in early farmer's almanacs. That's not surprising when you consider why people read the almanacs—to know what was coming around the bend and how to deal with it. By 1820 Americans relied on the good advice—and recipes— found in farmer's almanacs. With a world that was unpredictable— economic depression, the War of 1812, and an unusually cold summer of 1816—there was comfort in knowing what weather patterns would affect crops and livestock. And in upturns and downturns, nothing soothed more than home baking, especially the simple, economical jumble cookie recipes in the almanacs.

THE 1922 GIRL SCOUT COOKIES

½ cup (1 stick) lightly salted butter, at room temperature

½ cup granulated sugar

1 large egg, at room temperature

½ teaspoon vanilla extract

1 cup all-purpose flour, plus extra for rolling the dough

½ teaspoon baking powder

MAKES: 5 to 6 dozen (3") cookies

GIRL SCOUT COOKIES ARE one of the great fund-raising success stories in America. But before these cookies were commercially baked and sold, they were baked at home to raise monies to send girls to camp. Florence Neil, a Girl Scout director in Chicago, created the recipe for the Scouts to follow, and it was printed in the July 1922 issue of *American Girl* magazine, published by the Girl Scouts of the USA. That cookie was round, not the trefoil shape of today.

The cookies were packaged in waxed paper and tied into a bundle with a string. The expense of baking those cookies cost each Scout and her mother 26 to 36 cents per six- or seven-dozen cookies, and the cookies sold for 25 to 30 cents a dozen, producing a nice profit. But there was a caveat—the girls had to use self-control and not nibble the cookies. As Florence Neil advised: "Don't eat too many before selling, or the Girl Scouts won't make enough money to pay for camp this summer."

Here is my adaptation of the original recipe. I halved the recipe and omitted the milk because it made the dough sticky and difficult to roll. These are very nice cookies, and it must have been hard for the Scouts to bake them and not be able to eat a few!

PREP: 10 TO 15 MINUTES   CHILL: 3 HOURS TO OVERNIGHT   BAKE: 8 TO 10 MINUTES

---

1. Place the soft butter and sugar in a large bowl and beat with an electric mixer on medium speed until creamy, 2 minutes. Add the egg and vanilla, and beat just to combine, 1 to 2 minutes. Scrape down the bowl with a rubber spatula.

2. Whisk together the flour and baking powder in a small bowl. Using the mixer on low speed, add the flour mixture to the butter and sugar mixture in 3 batches, mixing until blended. Scrape down the bowl. Turn the dough into an airtight container and place in the refrigerator for at least 3 hours, up to overnight.

3. Place a rack in the center of the oven, and preheat the oven to 375°F.

(continued on next page)

4. Remove the dough from the refrigerator and divide it into quarters. Generously flour a work surface and roll one portion of dough at a time into a 7"-diameter circle that is about $\frac{1}{8}$" thick. Flour a $2\frac{1}{2}$"-round cookie cutter and cut the dough into circles. Transfer the rounds onto ungreased baking sheets. Place a pan in the oven.

5. Bake the cookies until lightly browned, 8 to 10 minutes. Remove the cookies to wire racks to cool completely. Repeat with the remaining dough. Store the cookies covered for up to 1 week.

KATHLEEN'S SUGAR COOKIES

1 cup (2 sticks) unsalted butter, at room temperature

1 cup granulated sugar

2 large eggs

2 teaspoons vanilla extract

3 cups all-purpose flour

1 large egg white, lightly beaten with a fork

Colored sugars of your choice

MAKES: About 5 dozen (2" to 2½") cookies

WHEN MY CHILDREN WERE little, we would bake and decorate sugar cookies any chance we got. The drill went something like this: I draped the kitchen floor with an old sheet. With a little advance planning, I had made the dough the night before, and now I pulled it from the fridge to warm a bit. Then we gathered up all the sugar sprinkles on a tray and pulled our favorite cookie cutters from the kitchen cabinet, and I whisked an egg white for the "paint" needed to adhere the sprinkles to the cookies.

Halloween, Christmas, Valentine's Day, and Easter were more festive because of these decorated cookies. They were named after my older daughter because she took ownership of the recipe and loved to instruct her younger siblings on cookie art. It was a wonderful, messy sugar fest with often more sprinkles on the floor than on the cookies, but after it was over and done, I took the sheet outside and shook it in the wind. And we sat down and savored those cookies.

PREP: 10 TO 15 MINUTES FOR THE DOUGH, PLUS 1 HOUR FOR DECORATING
CHILL: 1 HOUR TO OVERNIGHT   BAKE: 10 TO 12 MINUTES

1. Place the soft butter and granulated sugar in a large bowl and beat with an electric mixer on medium speed until light and fluffy, 1 to 2 minutes. Add the eggs and vanilla and beat well. Beat in the flour on low speed just until combined, 1 to 1½ minutes. Cover the bowl and refrigerate the dough for at least 1 hour, but preferably overnight.

2. When ready to bake, place a rack in the center of the oven, and preheat the oven to 350°F. Line a baking sheet with parchment paper or leave ungreased.

3. Working with a little of the dough at a time, roll it out on a floured surface to about ⅛" thickness. Keep the remaining dough refrigerated. Cut with cookie cutters and transfer the cookies carefully to the baking sheet, spacing them about 1" apart. If you like, and if there is enough room in your refrigerator, chill the cookies on the baking sheets for about 5 minutes before baking. This helps the cookies retain their shape.

(continued on next page)

4. To decorate the cookies with colored sugars, brush the cookies with a little egg white before sprinkling on the sugar. Place a pan in the oven.

5. Bake the cookies until golden brown, 10 to 12 minutes. Let the cookies cool on the pan for about 1 minute. Then, using a spatula, transfer the cookies to wire racks to cool. Repeat with the remaining cookie dough. Store the cookies covered for up to 1 week.

APISAS

1 cup (2 sticks) lightly salted butter, at room temperature

1 cup plus 2 tablespoons granulated sugar

3¾ cups unbleached flour, sifted, plus about ⅓ cup for rolling

1 teaspoon ground cinnamon, if desired

⅓ cup rose water

¼ cup ice water

MAKES: About 95 (2") cookies

A SIMPLE SCALLOPED-EDGED SUGAR cookie baked by the Quakers in the 18th century is known by a collection of names. Is the name for this rose water–flavored cookie apisas or apeas or apees, or the initials "A. P."? Historian and cookbook author Joanne Lamb Hayes says whatever you want to call the cookie, the origin is most likely Pennsylvania Dutch. She heard the story that somewhere in rural Pennsylvania a woman named Ann Page etched her initials into each cookie before baking them. Ruth Hutchison writes in *The Pennsylvania Dutch Cook Book* in 1948 that the name might have come from the French *pain d'épices*, or spice bread. Some versions contain cinnamon and others do not, and it's possible that sand tarts (page 111) and apisas are one and the same. Or did "A. P." mean *anis plätzchen*—what were known as German anise cookies? Yet another explanation is that the cookies were so named because they looked like "a piece," meaning a gold coin.

You get the idea. This cookie discussion could go on forever.

What distinguishes this recipe from other sugar cookies is the rose water. An ingredient in old English recipes, rose water is found today in Middle Eastern markets, and it's made by steaming the petals of roses. Open the bottle and take a whiff before adding to the recipe: You will find it smells a lot like perfume. For an added touch, sprinkle the unbaked cookies with a mixture of ⅓ cup sugar and 1 teaspoon ground cinnamon just before baking.

PREP: 25 TO 30 MINUTES BAKE: 11 TO 13 MINUTES

---

1. Place a rack in the center of the oven, and preheat the oven to 350°F.
2. Place the soft butter and sugar in a large bowl and beat with an electric mixer on medium-high speed until light and fluffy, about 2 minutes. Scrape down the sides of the bowl with a rubber spatula.

(continued on page 100)

FOLLOWING PAGE: ① *Amelia Simmons's Coriander Cookies,* ② *Apisas,* ③ *Mrs. Wright's Cocoons,* ④ *Mexican Wedding Cookies,* and ⑤ *Apricot and Raisin Rugelach*

3. Whisk together the 3¾ cups of flour and the cinnamon in a medium-size bowl. Add about a third of the flour mixture to the butter and sugar mixture. Using the mixer on low speed, mix just to combine, about 15 seconds. Add the rose water and beat just to combine, 15 seconds. Beat in another third of the flour mixture on low speed, just to combine. Add the cold water, then the remaining flour. Beat just to combine, then scrape down the sides of the bowl.

4. Generously flour the working surface and rolling pin. Gently form one-third of the dough into a ball. Roll to the thickness of a silver dollar, about ⅝" (like a thickish pie crust). Dip a cookie cutter into flour and cut the dough into shapes. Place the cookies ½" to ¾" apart on an ungreased baking sheet. Place the pan in the oven.

5. Bake the cookies until they barely change color, 11 to 13 minutes. Allow the cookies to cool on the pan for about 5 minutes, then transfer to a wire rack. Repeat with the remaining two-thirds of dough, saving the scraps. Make a final roll with the scraps from the 3 batches. Discard any remaining scraps. Store the cookies covered for up to 1 week.

MEXICAN WEDDING COOKIES

1 cup (2 sticks) unsalted butter, at room temperature

1½ cups confectioners' sugar, divided use

1 teaspoon vanilla extract

¼ teaspoon salt

1¾ cups all-purpose flour

1 teaspoon ground cinnamon

1 cup ground toasted pecans, walnuts, or almonds

MAKES: About 30 to 36 (1" to 1½") cookies

IN SAN ANTONIO, TEXAS, everyone—from home cooks to Mexican bakeries—bakes Mexican wedding cookies. According to Karen Haram, a longtime San Antonio food writer, sometimes they are crescent-shaped, but most often they are round balls, baked and then dredged twice in powdered sugar. "Always twice, once after baking and then again before serving," Haram adds. "They need to be well coated."

So well coated that the sugar falls off the cookie and onto your clothes, and the only way to eat a Mexican wedding cookie without showering yourself in powdered sugar is to hold it at arm's length—in front of you, savoring each and every bite.

The key ingredient is *canela*, or Mexican cinnamon, "which gives them a lovely warm flavor," says Haram. Often called "true" cinnamon—compared to the cinnamon most often found on the American grocery shelf, which is powdered cassia bark—canela is milder and warmer. You can find it at Mexican groceries or at spice shops.

Which brings us to the cookie name. While they were so named because they showed up at wedding receptions, they are most often served at parties of all sorts, bridal showers, baby showers, and Christmas. Other variations call for a tablespoon of bourbon or rum, and older versions call for anise seeds or anise oil. Regardless, they are similar to crescent cookies and Mrs. Wright's Cocoons, except they taste of cinnamon, which is bright and festive. This recipe is adapted from *Sweet on Texas* by Denise Gee. I made them slightly smaller, but you can bake 24 larger ones, which will need about 20 minutes to bake.

PREP: 10 TO 15 MINUTES   CHILL: 1 HOUR OR LONGER   BAKE: ABOUT 15 MINUTES

1. With a hand mixer on medium-high speed, cream the soft butter in a medium-size bowl until fluffy, about 1 minute. Add ½ cup of the confectioners' sugar and mix until just combined, about 15 seconds. Then add the vanilla and salt and mix until just combined, 15 seconds.

2. In a separate medium-size bowl, sift together the flour and cinnamon. Add the ground nuts, and combine with a fork.

(continued on next page)

Gradually incorporate the flour mixture into the butter and sugar mixture, using a wooden spoon or rubber spatula, just until combined. Cover and refrigerate the dough for at least 1 hour.

3. When ready to bake, place a rack in the center of the oven, and preheat the oven to 350°F.

4. Use a cookie scoop to portion the dough and roll it into 1" balls. Place the balls at least 1" apart on an ungreased baking sheet. Place the pan in the oven.

5. Bake the cookies until the bottom edges turn golden, about 15 minutes. The cookies will not change color very much. Remove the pan from the oven and cool the cookies on wire racks for about 5 minutes.

6. In a small bowl, sift the remaining 1 cup confectioners' sugar and roll the warm cookies in the sugar to achieve a first coating. After the cookies are completely cool, after about 25 minutes, roll them in the sugar for a second coating. Store the cookies up to 1 week in metal containers between layers of waxed paper.

MRS. WRIGHT'S COCOONS

14 tablespoons
(1¾ sticks) lightly
salted butter, at room
temperature

4 tablespoons
confectioners' sugar,
plus ½ cup for
dredging the cookies

1 teaspoon water

2 teaspoons vanilla
extract

2 cups all-purpose
flour, sifted

1 cup finely chopped
pecans

MAKES: 3 dozen
(2" to 2½") cookies

ACCLAIMED SHORT STORY WRITER and novelist Eudora Welty contributed a foreword to *The Jackson Cookbook* in 1971. What a coup that must have been for the Symphony League cookbook committee to get Welty's contribution to their book. Two years later, she would win the Pulitzer Prize for her novel *The Optimist's Daughter*. Welty not only knew how to stretch out a story, but she understood Jackson, Mississippi. Welty was born and raised in Jackson and had covered the news of its society as a young reporter for the Memphis *Commercial Appeal*. She knew Jackson entertained at home. She knew how important entertaining was in Jackson, and she understood Jackson party food—it was pretty, a bit of trouble for the hostess to make, and "thunderously rich." Mrs. Wright's Cocoons, one of her favorite recipes included in *The Jackson Cookbook*, met the three criteria.

In this cookie recipe, the dough is shaped into cocoons—not crescents, not balls, but cocoons. Which makes them a little challenging. They are pretty to look at, all dusted with powdered sugar. And they are rich. Mrs. Wright was Mrs. William R. Wright, and because her name is attached to the recipe, Welty said, Mrs. Wright was connected to it. "To make a friend's fine recipe is to celebrate her once more."

PREP: 20 TO 25 MINUTES   CHILL: 20 MINUTES OR LONGER   BAKE: 15 TO 20 MINUTES

1. Place the soft butter and the 4 tablespoons of confectioners' sugar in a medium-size mixing bowl and beat with an electric mixer on medium speed until creamy, about 30 seconds. Add the water and vanilla and mix on medium speed until combined, about 30 seconds. Scrape down the sides of the bowl with a rubber spatula.

2. With the mixer running, gradually incorporate the flour into the butter and sugar mixture, beating on low speed until thick and creamy, about 1 minute. Scrape down the sides of the bowl, and fold in the chopped pecans, until just combined. Cover the bowl with plastic wrap and refrigerate for at least 20 minutes.

3. Place a rack in the center of the oven, and preheat the oven to 325°F.

(continued on next page)

4. Remove the dough from the refrigerator. Take spoonfuls of the dough and roll them into cocoons about 2" in length and 1" in width at the centermost point. Place on an ungreased baking sheet, and place the pan in the oven.

5. Bake the cookies until the bottom edges are golden brown and they are firm to the touch, 15 to 20 minutes. Transfer the cookies to a wire rack to cool for at least 5 minutes. Place the remaining $\frac{1}{2}$ cup confectioners' sugar in a shallow bowl, then dredge each cookie in the sugar. Serve, or store the cookies up to 1 week in metal containers between layers of waxed paper.

DEE'S CHEESE DATE COOKIES

½ cup (1 stick) unsalted butter, at room temperature

2 cups (8 ounces) freshly shredded sharp Cheddar cheese

1½ cups all-purpose flour

¼ teaspoon salt

1 pound pitted dates, well chopped (see Baking Tips)

¾ cup finely chopped pecans

½ cup confectioners' sugar for dusting

MAKES: About 6 dozen (2") cookies

MY GRANDMOTHER, ELIZA CARR, was a strong and loving woman we called Dee. She was widowed when my mother was 12 and raised five daughters on her own. Dee didn't have a lot of time for baking, but when she did bake, it was memorable. These Cheese Date Cookies were the recipe she baked each Thanksgiving. I can recall as a child everyone gathering around her cookie tray and ogling. The cookies exercised every one of our tastebuds. The dates made them sweet and sticky, the pecans crunchy, and the Cheddar cheese salty and oddly complementary. It was an otherworldly sort of flavor to a child. You didn't expect cookies to be salty and sweet. And yet, that's why the flavor stayed with you. And that's why this recipe has endured the years.

A recent family reunion gave me a good reason to revisit this recipe and bake it for my family. My cousins and I guess this recipe was first baked by Dee in the early 1900s. Dates were a common grocery ingredient then, and it's quite possible she found this recipe in a ladies' magazine. It seems this recipe is a spin-off of a cheese biscuit or wafer, popular across the United States and specifically in the South. Savory cheese cookie dough wrapped around chopped dates and pecans, then baked until golden and rolled in confectioners' sugar: Did they know they were creating possibly the best cookie in the world?

PREP: 25 TO 30 MINUTES   CHILL: OVERNIGHT   BAKE: 15 TO 20 MINUTES

1. Place the butter, cheese, flour, and salt in a large mixing bowl and blend with an electric mixer on medium speed until the mixture looks like coarse crumbs, about 1 minute. Continue blending or working with your hands until the mixture comes together into a ball. Flatten it out, wrap in plastic wrap, and place in the refrigerator overnight.

2. The next day, make the filling: Combine the chopped dates and pecans in a small bowl. Set aside.

3. Preheat the oven to 350°F. Remove the dough from the refrigerator, and cut it into two halves. Work with one half at a time. Return the other to the fridge to stay cold.

(continued on next page)

4. Lightly flour a work surface, and roll the dough out to ¼" thickness. With a knife, cut it into rough 1½" squares. Place a teaspoon of filling onto each square. Roll the filling into the dough like a small jelly roll. Press the dough to seal any cracks, and place about 18 cookies at a time on an ungreased baking sheet. Place the pan in the oven.

5. Bake the cookies until golden brown and firm, 15 to 20 minutes. Remove the pan from the oven, transfer the cookies to a wire rack, and, when cool enough to handle, dredge in the confectioners' sugar. Let cool before serving. Repeat with the remaining dough and filling. Store for up to 1 week in a covered metal container between sheets of waxed paper.

BAKING TIPS: *Look for a pound-size container of pitted whole dates. You will need to finely chop the dates and combine them with the finely chopped pecans. This can be done a day ahead and set aside, covered, at room temperature.*

ST. AUGUSTINE CRISPES

DOUGH

½ cup (1 stick) unsalted butter, at room temperature

6 ounces cream cheese, at room temperature

2 cups all-purpose flour

½ teaspoon salt

FILLING

1 large egg

½ cup granulated sugar

1 teaspoon ground cinnamon

MAKES: About 44 (2") cookies

FOR A COOKIE TO be rolled and remembered, it has to be a recipe that can survive the years and be relevant no matter the generation. In our history, this cookie has been quick to make, cheap, and uses ingredients at hand.

A good example is the old Minorcan Crispes—pronounced "cro-sprays"—which is a cinnamon-scented pastrylike cookie. Although you won't find them served at St. Augustine restaurants today, they are a part of the story of the Minorcan people who came from the island of Minorca in the Mediterranean to farm indigo in Florida. One of the early customs of the Minorcans, of Catholic heritage, was to stroll the streets and carol on the night before Easter. They sang religious songs and folk carols, requesting sweets for their singing. A cookie associated with this ritual was the crispe, essentially pie pastry dough cut into rounds, topped with an egg, sugar, and cinnamon mixture, and baked until golden.

PREP: 20 TO 25 MINUTES   CHILL: 2 HOURS OR LONGER
BAKE: 17 TO 22 MINUTES

---

1. For the pastry dough, place the soft butter and cream cheese in a large mixing bowl and beat with an electric mixer on medium speed until creamy, 30 seconds. Add the flour and salt, and beat on low speed until the mixture looks like coarse crumbs, 1 minute. With your hands, work the crumbs into a ball. Press down slightly on the ball, wrap in waxed paper or plastic wrap, and chill at least 2 hours.

2. Remove the dough from the refrigerator and divide it into 2 pieces. On a lightly floured surface, roll one half of the dough to ¼" thickness. Cut into about 22 (2") rounds with a cookie cutter or water glass, and transfer them to 2 baking sheets. Turn up the edges of each round and crimp them with your fingertips as you would a pastry crust. Prick the bottom of each round a few times with a fork. Place the pans in the fridge while you make the filling.

3. Place a rack in the center of the oven, and preheat the oven to 350°F. For the filling, crack the egg into a small bowl and whisk

(continued on next page)

to break up the yolk. Add the sugar and cinnamon, and whisk until smooth.

4. Remove the pans from the refrigerator. Place a pan in the oven, and bake until the dough is just set, 2 to 3 minutes. Remove the pan from the oven. Spoon a teaspoon of filling onto each pastry circle, trying to not let it run off. Return the pan to the oven, and bake the cookies until golden brown on top, 15 to 19 minutes. Remove the pan from the oven, and transfer the cookies to a wire rack to cool. Repeat with the remaining pan of pastry circles.

5. Serve warm or at room temperature. These keep lightly covered at room temperature for 2 to 3 days.

A Little Florida Food History

About 200 years before the beginnings of the American Revolution, before our 13 colonies were formed and our founding fathers had given thought to a democratic style of government, the area that is now known as Florida was settled. The Spanish first came to the St. Augustine area in 1565 and named the historic coastal town after the Catholic Saint Augustine. They brought with them citrus trees, rice, and sugarcane, as well as cattle, pigs, peaches, and date palms. These crops and livestock would flourish in southeastern coastal America and define the foodways of this region, according to Charles Tingley at the St. Augustine Historical Society research library.

Britain then bought Florida from the Spain in 1763, and a 3,000-strong colony of Minorcans, people from the island of Minorca, as well as Italy and Greece, arrived at nearby New Smyrna 5 years later to farm indigo. When that opportunity went bust, there were only 600 Minorcans surviving 9 years later. Those Minorcans migrated to the more bustling St. Augustine area, where they farmed citrus and where their descendants live today. Over the years, Florida would return to Spanish rule, and then cede to the United States in 1821 and become the 27th state in the Union 24 years later. To put this into perspective, at the end of the Civil War, St. Augustine was already 300 years old.

SAGAMORE HILL SAND TARTS

DOUGH

1 cup (2 sticks) lightly salted butter, at room temperature

2 cups granulated sugar

3 large eggs, divided use

2 teaspoons vanilla extract

4 cups sifted all-purpose flour

TOPPING

⅓ cup granulated sugar

¼ teaspoon ground cinnamon

MAKES: About 6 dozen (3") cookies

SAND TARTS ARE AN old cousin of the snickerdoodle. Originally a German recipe, the dough used to be rolled so thinly that some cooks got downright competitive about it. The dough was then cut into squares or circles, and according to an 1858 recipe from Ohio, you would "strew them over with pounded almonds and cinnamon." Those ground almonds and/or cinnamon on top gave the cookies their sandy appearance and, thus, their name.

This recipe was a favorite of Edith Roosevelt, wife of America's 26th president, Theodore Roosevelt. Serving two terms, Roosevelt and his family were in the White House from 1901 to 1909. But when they weren't in Washington, DC, they were at Sagamore Hill, on Oyster Bay, Long Island.

This cookie was said to be a fixture on the Christmas cookie tray at Sagamore Hill. It was served with coffee to friends and family who came by to visit during the holidays. Edith Roosevelt liked sand tarts so much that she wrote this recipe inside the cover of her favorite cookbook, *Housekeepers' and Mothers' Manual* by Elizabeth Winston Rosser, published in 1895.

Some recipes today call for a little almond extract. Others instruct to sprinkle ground almonds on top of the cookies along with sugar and cinnamon. Or some omit the cinnamon and use just ground almonds. Purists place 3 almond halves on top before baking. But it's up to you.

**PREP: 10 TO 15 MINUTES   CHILL: 2 HOURS (SEE BAKING TIP)
BAKE: 8 TO 10 MINUTES**

---

1. Place the soft butter in a large mixing bowl and beat with an electric mixer on medium speed until it has the consistency of mayonnaise, 1 minute. Add the 2 cups sugar gradually, and beat on medium until light and fluffy, 1 to 2 minutes. Scrape down the sides of the bowl with a rubber spatula. Add 2 of the eggs, one at a time, beating well after each addition. Separate the third egg. Reserve the egg white. Add the yolk to the bowl with the butter and sugar mixture. Add the vanilla. Beat on medium speed until incorporated, 30 seconds.

(continued on next page)

2. Scrape down the sides of the bowl and add the flour. Stir the flour into the mixture until well incorporated. Cover the bowl with plastic wrap, and place the bowl in the refrigerator until chilled and easy to handle, at least 2 hours.

3. Meanwhile, for the topping, place the $\frac{1}{3}$ cup sugar and the cinnamon in a small bowl and stir to combine. Set aside.

4. Place a rack in the center of the oven, and preheat the oven to 350°F.

5. On a lightly floured surface, roll the dough $\frac{1}{4}$" to $\frac{1}{8}$" thick. Cut into $2\frac{1}{2}$" rounds. Transfer the rounds to a baking sheet and brush with the reserved egg white. Sprinkle with the cinnamon-sugar mixture. Place the pan in the oven.

6. Bake the cookies until lightly browned around the edges, 8 to 10 minutes. Remove the pan from the oven, and transfer the cookies to a wire rack to cool completely. Repeat with the remaining dough. Store covered for up to 1 week.

BAKING TIP: *Allowing the dough to rest in the fridge, even for 2 hours, makes the dough much easier to roll out thinly.*

HOMEMADE FIG NEWTONS

DOUGH

½ cup (1 stick) unsalted butter, at room temperature

½ cup vegetable shortening

1½ cups granulated sugar

3 large eggs

1 tablespoon vanilla extract

5 cups all-purpose flour

3½ teaspoons baking powder

½ teaspoon salt

½ cup whole milk

FILLING

2 pounds dried figs, stems removed and coarsely chopped

8 ounces (about 1½ cups) raisins

1 large orange

1 heaping teaspoon lemon zest

1 large apple, peeled and chopped

¾ to 1 cup finely chopped pecans, toasted, from 1 heaping cup pecan halves

¼ cup granulated sugar

1 teaspoon ground cinnamon

6 tablespoons brandy, water, or apple juice

FIGS HAVE MADE THEIR way into the regional cakes and cookies of America. And while they have taken to the warm coastal US climates, the tradition of baking with them comes from other countries. The Italians, specifically the Sicilians, bake fig cookies at Christmas, and their descendants living in America have continued this cookie tradition.

The most popular fig cookie in America, however, is the commercial cookie called the Newton, or what until 2012 was known as the Fig Newton. Made by Nabisco, this soft cakelike cookie with fig filling was created in 1891 and named after Newton, Massachusetts, where the F.A. Kennedy Steam Bakery that made them was located.

Martha Bowden's cookie memories are more of New England ginger cookies than the fig- and citrus-scented flavors of this recipe that resembles the Newton. But she is an avid cookie baker and a curious cook. Looking at a recipe for fig cookies, she could taste the complex flavors just by reading the recipe. So she took on the challenge of baking fig cookies and has adopted the Italian fig cookie as her own. They are her Homemade Fig Newtons.

PREP: 55 TO 60 MINUTES   CHILL: 3 HOURS   BAKE: 11 TO 14 MINUTES

---

1. For the dough, place the soft butter and shortening in a large bowl and beat with an electric mixer on medium speed until creamy, 1 minute. Add the 1½ cups sugar and beat until combined, 1 minute more. Add the eggs, one at a time, beating to combine. Blend in the vanilla.

2. Whisk together the flour, baking powder, and salt in a medium-size bowl. Add a third of the flour mixture to the butter and sugar mixture, beating on low to combine. Add half of the milk, then beat until combined. Add another third of the flour mixture, followed by the rest of the milk, then the last third of the flour, beating until smooth, and scraping down the bowl with a rubber spatula as needed. Divide the dough into 4 equal portions.

3. To shape the dough portions into perfect rectangles, line a 9½" × 5" loaf pan with plastic wrap. Press one portion of dough at a time into the bottom of the loaf pan, pressing the dough evenly to the edges. Using the plastic wrap, lift the rectangle out of the

(continued on next page)

BAKING TIPS: *If it
seems too difficult to
flip the long piece of
dough, cut a slit
halfway across the
dough so you are
flipping two shorter
pieces. If desired, after
cooling cut the strips
into 3 to 4 bite-sized
cookies.*

pan, and wrap the dough completely in the wrap. Place in the refrigerator to chill at least 3 hours, or overnight. Line the loaf pan again with plastic and repeat with the remaining dough.

4. Meanwhile, for the filling, place a fourth of the chopped figs in a large food processor fitted with a steel blade and pulse until finely chopped, about 30 seconds. Transfer to a bowl and repeat the process with the remaining figs. Place the raisins in the processor bowl and pulse until well chopped, 15 to 20 seconds. Transfer the raisins into the bowl with the figs.

5. Zest orange and add zest to the fig mixture. Slice the orange in half and squeeze the juice to yield $1/2$ cup. Remove seeds. Stir orange juice into the fig mixture. Add the lemon zest. Place the apple pieces in the same food processor bowl, and pulse until finely chopped. Turn the apples into the bowl with the fig mixture. Add the toasted pecans, sugar, cinnamon, and brandy. Stir the fig mixture until well blended. Set the mixture aside.

6. Place a rack in the center of the oven, and preheat the oven to 375°F.

7. Generously flour a work surface and rolling pin. Remove 1 rectangle of dough from the refrigerator and remove the plastic wrap. Roll this rectangle into a large rectangle, 16" × 8". Score the rectangle vertically down the center with a dull knife. Divide the fig filling into fourths. Place one-fourth of the filling just to the left of the center line of the rectangle, leaving about $1/2$" border. Brush this border with cold water. Using floured spatulas, flip the empty side of the rectangle over the filling and press the dough edges together to seal them.

8. With a sharp knife, cut the rectangle into strips about 1" wide. Carefully transfer the strips to an ungreased baking sheet, placing each cookie 1" to 2" apart. Place the pan in the oven.

9. Bake the cookies until barely browned on top, well browned on the underside, and just firm to the tough, 11 to 14 minutes. Immediately transfer the cookies to a wire rack to cool to room temperature. Repeat the process with the remaining dough and filling.

APRICOT AND RAISIN RUGELACH

DOUGH

1 cup (2 sticks) unsalted butter, at room temperature

8 ounces cream cheese, at room temperature

$\frac{1}{2}$ teaspoon salt

2 cups unbleached all-purpose flour, plus extra for rolling the dough

FILLING

1 to 2 teaspoons ground cinnamon

$\frac{1}{2}$ cup granulated sugar

1 cup raisins, finely chopped

1 cup (4 ounces) walnuts, finely chopped

1 cup apricot preserves

EGG WASH

1 large egg white

1 teaspoon water

MAKES: 3 dozen (2") pastries

THE IMMIGRANTS WHO HAVE migrated to America throughout our history have shared their cultures and recipes. Rugelach is a recipe of Austrian-Hungarian roots that has been beautifully adapted and modernized by the Jewish in America.

It originally was a yeast-leavened pastry and time consuming to make. But the addition of cream cheese made the pastry rich and easy to shape around fillings of nuts, raisins, spices, and preserves. Interestingly, cream cheese came about because of a lack of refrigeration in 19th-century America. If you wanted to bake with fresh cream, you had to be a dairy farmer or live near one. A New York cheesemaker named William Lawrence created cream cheese, similar to the French Neufchâtel. Cream cheese was spread onto Jewish bagels and went into cheesecake, and it is what makes rugelach dough easy to work with and flaky, too.

Rugelach can either be shaped in long slabs and cut into pieces, or rolled into crescent-shaped horns and filled with raisins, nuts, spices, and often jam or preserves before baking. The following recipe is an adaptation of two recipes: The filling comes from a cookbook called *Gourmet's Favorite Cookies*, and the method of shaping the rugelach comes from Maida Heatter, who calls these delicacies "walnut horns."

PREP: 60 TO 75 MINUTES   CHILL: OVERNIGHT   BAKE: 20 TO 25 MINUTES

---

1. For the dough, place the soft butter and cream cheese in a large bowl and beat with an electric mixer on low speed until smooth, 1 minute. Add the salt and the 2 cups flour, beating on low speed until the dough just comes together. Scrape down the sides of the bowl with a rubber spatula. Flour your hands and work the dough until all the ingredients are well combined. Roll the dough into a ball and divide it into three sections. Wrap each section in plastic wrap and press down on the dough slightly. Refrigerate the dough overnight.

2. When ready to bake, place a rack in the center of the oven, and preheat the oven to 350°F. Cover a baking sheet with aluminum foil and set aside.

(continued on next page)

3. On a well-floured surface, unwrap one of the balls of dough. Using a floured rolling pin, create a 12" circle with the dough. Do not worry about the edges. Transfer the dough to an ungreased baking sheet and place in the fridge to keep the dough from becoming too soft.

4. For the filling, whisk together the cinnamon and sugar in a small bowl. Combine the raisins and walnuts in a medium-size bowl.

5. Take the rolled dough out of the fridge and transfer back to the floured surface. Spread $\frac{1}{3}$ cup of the apricot preserves evenly over the dough. Then sprinkle one-third of the cinnamon-sugar mixture over the preserves, followed by one-third of the raisin and walnut mixture. Using a pizza cutter, cut the dough into 12 even wedges. Starting from the outside, tightly roll the wedge inward to the tip. Transfer the pastries to the prepared baking sheet with the tip down.

6. For the egg wash, combine the egg white and water in a small bowl. Lightly brush each pastry with the egg wash. Place the pan in the oven.

7. Bake the pastries until the sides are golden brown, 20 to 25 minutes. Using a metal spatula, transfer the pastries to a wire rack. Let the pastries for cool 5 minutes before serving. Repeat with the remaining dough and filling. Store the rugelach covered at room temperature for up to 3 days or freeze in a zipper-lock bag for up to 3 months.

UNCLE MILT'S CHRISTMAS COOKIES

8 ounces candied or dried pineapple, finely chopped

1 pound candied cherries, coarsely chopped

1 pound pitted dates, chopped

2$\frac{1}{3}$ cups all-purpose flour, divided use

1 cup chopped walnuts

1 cup chopped hazelnuts

1 cup chopped pecans

1 cup (2 sticks) unsalted butter, at room temperature

1$\frac{1}{2}$ cups light brown sugar, lightly packed

2 large eggs, at room temperature

1 teaspoon baking soda

1 teaspoon ground cinnamon

$\frac{1}{4}$ teaspoon salt

MAKES: 12 dozen (1$\frac{1}{2}$") or 9 dozen (2$\frac{1}{2}$") cookies

---

MILTON HOWARD CARTER MOVED west from Vermont, married a girl from Washington State, and spent a happy life in Oregon, according to his niece Connie Carter. She says Uncle Milt and his family were known for their joyous, warm, western hospitality—as in "nothing is too much trouble." Uncle Milt was also known for his fruitcake cookies, possibly the most perfect fruitcake cookie you will ever taste. They were always baked for Christmas.

And true to his living in the Pacific Northwest, these loaded cookies contained both hazelnuts and walnuts, as well as dates, pecans, cherries, and pineapple. Today they are the cookie to bake when dried fruits and nuts come into the supermarket for holiday shopping. They are the perfect cookie for gift-giving.

But should you not be able to find an ingredient—I couldn't find candied pineapple off-season and used dried pineapple instead—you can successfully substitute. Although Connie says Uncle Milt was particular about his recipe, didn't like to share it with just anyone, and didn't like substitutions, you can improvise. My deep apologies to Uncle Milt, who died in 1982, but this wonderful fruitcake cookie recipe is ripe for improvisation. It easily could be delicious with chopped dried peaches instead of the pineapple. You could omit the dates and use raisins. But be forewarned that this is a big recipe, yielding more than 100 cookies. Choose an afternoon to spend a couple hours chopping, scooping, baking, and packaging. It's worth it!

PREP: 40 TO 45 MINUTES   BAKE: 11 TO 13 MINUTES

---

1. In a large bowl, toss the pineapple, cherries, and dates with $\frac{1}{3}$ cup of the flour. Add the walnuts, hazelnuts, and pecans to the fruit mixture. Toss again, and set aside.

2. Place a rack in the center of the oven, and preheat the oven to 350°F. Line 2 baking sheets with parchment paper.

3. Place the soft butter and sugar in a large mixing bowl and beat with an electric mixer on medium speed until light and creamy, about 2 minutes. Add the eggs, one at a time, and beat after each

(continued on next page)

addition. Scrape down the sides of the bowl with a rubber spatula.

4. Stir together the remaining 2 cups flour with the baking soda, cinnamon, and salt in a medium-size bowl. Fold half of the flour mixture into the butter and sugar mixture and beat on low speed until just combined, about 1 minute. Add the other half of the dry ingredients and beat until combined, 1 minute. Fold in the fruit and nut mixture a little at a time. The dough will be stiff, and you may need to mix it with your hands to get all the ingredients incorporated. If you have disposable plastic gloves, use them.

5. Drop the dough onto the prepared pans using a small cookie scoop or roll the dough into balls and place them on the pans. Space the balls $1\frac{1}{2}$" to 2" apart. Place a pan in the oven.

6. Bake the cookies until browned around the edges but still a little soft in the center, 11 to 13 minutes. Remove the pan from the oven, and let the cookies cool on the pan 2 minutes. Transfer them with a metal spatula to a wire rack to cool completely. Repeat with the remaining dough. Store the cookies up to 1 week at room temperature.

Lavender Tea Cookies

Irma Rombauer's Refrig. Lace Cookies

Butterscotch Pecan Wafers

3

WAFERS, ICEBOX COOKIES & PLANNING AHEAD

Once upon a time, people made cookie dough ahead of time and stashed it in the refrigerator until they were ready to bake. They didn't keep store-bought cookies in their cupboard. They made the dough themselves and took pride in their recipes. And there must have been some satisfaction knowing they could bake up cookies hot and fresh at any moment.

That was the 1930s, the beginning of what we now call "slice and bake" cookies. The cookie dough you might see today in the supermarket refrigerator case is the offspring of real cookie dough made at a time when planning ahead was the norm.

Back in the day, though, these cookies were called icebox cookies, named after the early word for a refrigerator. The dough was chilled long enough to make it easy to slice, then baked, and you emerged from the kitchen a hero holding a plate piled with warm, fresh cookies.

If you look through old cookbooks of the 1940s and '50s you will see that these recipes stayed popular for decades. In *The Joy of Cooking*, author Irma Rombauer devotes a section to icebox cookies, and her stand-out recipe is a "lace" cookie containing grated orange zest and oats. Rombauer knew that women in the 1930s and '40s were working outside the home either in jobs or with the war effort. They were busy, and to be able to chill cookie dough in waxed paper or small milk cartons for baking later was thrifty and smart.

But icebox cookies, or wafers as they were often called, work today, too. Their simplicity of ingredients, their do-ahead ability, and their sheer nostalgia make them a perfect cookie for our busy times. You are not on the clock with these recipes. They work around your busy schedule!

It's because you chill the dough first that you're able to slice the log so thinly and bake waferlike cookies. The method works well with the Benne Icebox Wafer recipe, and it's much easier than dropping half teaspoonfuls of soft benne dough onto baking sheets. In the case of the Moravian black walnut cookie, it's easier to slice from a log than to roll out the dough and cut into rounds. Remember, though: When you are slicing cookie rounds from the chilled logs, use a sharp knife and return unsliced rolls to the fridge to stay chilled.

Today's flavors work beautifully with these old methods—the Lavender Tea Cookies are seemingly Victorian in their appearance and delicate flavor. And yet, adding your own home-grown lavender to a cookie recipe is a fresh adaptation. And while the Cornmeal Pistachio Cookies feel new, cornmeal has been used in Appalachian cookie baking since World War I, when wheat flour was scarce. Adding pistachios or the nut of your choice, however, is a modern riff.

The possibilities for icebox cookies are endless. Make, chill, slice, and bake.

No-Bake Cookies

Right out of the Depression, the 1930s, and then World War II came a need to bake quickly, economically, and efficiently. If that meant *not* baking a cookie, so be it! You used ingredients right in your kitchen, stirred everything together with a spoon and a bowl, and you didn't have to turn on the oven.

These no-bake cookies of the early 1950s were known as Chinese noodle cookies, spider cookies, or haystacks, made by stirring together melted chocolate chips, butterscotch chips, often peanut butter, and crunchy Chinese noodles or coconut. And they gave way to Preacher Cookies and Cow Pies of chocolate, peanut butter, and oats, stirred together over the stovetop, then dropped onto waxed paper and chilled. They were ready when you were to entertain the preacher or whoever might drop by. And they were the easy recipe taught in home economics class.

One of the easiest no-bake confections was chocolate bark, an assembly of melted chocolates and add-ins like nuts and dried fruit, left to set, then broken into pieces. It dates to the early 1950s and is still popular for gift-giving today.

CORNMEAL PISTACHIO COOKIES

Butter for prepping the pan

1 cup plus 2 tablespoons all-purpose flour

$1/3$ cup yellow cornmeal

$1/8$ teaspoon salt

$1/3$ cup ($1^{1}/_{2}$ ounces) finely chopped pistachios

$1/2$ cup (1 stick) unsalted butter, at room temperature

$1/2$ cup granulated sugar

1 large egg yolk

$1/4$ teaspoon vanilla extract

$1/4$ teaspoon almond extract

$1/2$ teaspoon lemon zest (from 1 small lemon)

MAKES: About 50 ($1^{1}/_{2}$" to 2") cookies

CORNMEAL MAY SEEM LIKE a modern addition to cookies, but really, it's an old addition that first appeared in the southern mountains, where corn could be more easily grown than wheat. Corn was an important part of the Appalachian diet. It was the thickener in the original chess pie, and during World War I when Americans conserved wheat for the war efforts, cornmeal was used in baking. The following recipe is one I have made for years, and I adapted it from a magazine recipe. The pistachios are the perfect complement to the cornmeal!

PREP: 15 TO 20 MINUTES   CHILL: 3 TO 24 HOURS   BAKE: 9 TO 11 MINUTES

1. Place the flour, cornmeal, salt, and pistachios in a large bowl and stir together with a fork.

2. Place the soft butter and sugar in a large bowl and beat with an electric mixer on medium-high speed until light and fluffy, 1 to 2 minutes. Scrape down the sides of the bowl with a rubber spatula. Add the egg yolk, vanilla, almond extract, and lemon zest and beat to combine well, about 30 seconds. Scrape down the sides of the bowl. Add the flour mixture in 2 batches, beating on low speed just until combined. Scrape down the sides of the bowl. The dough will appear loose and dry.

3. Tear off a piece of waxed paper about 15" long and place it on a flat surface. Dump the dough onto the paper. Wrap the paper around the dough to press it into a 13" log. Wrap plastic wrap around the waxed paper and store the dough in the fridge for 3 to 24 hours.

4. When ready to bake, place a rack in the center of the oven, and preheat the oven to 400°F. Lightly butter a baking sheet.

5. Remove the dough from the fridge and unwrap it. On a cutting surface, slice the dough into $1/4$" rounds. Place the rounds about 1" apart on the prepared baking sheet, and place the pan in the oven.

6. Bake the cookies until the edges are lightly browned, 9 to 11 minutes. Remove the pan from the oven, and with a metal spatula transfer the cookies to a rack to cool. Repeat with the remaining dough. Store the cooled cookies in a tightly covered container for up to 1 week.

BENNE ICEBOX WAFERS

½ cup benne seeds

½ cup (1 cup) lightly salted butter, at room temperature

1 cup light brown sugar, firmly packed

1 large egg

1 teaspoon vanilla extract

1 cup all-purpose flour

¼ teaspoon baking powder

MAKES: 5 to 6 dozen (2") cookies

MY FIRST TASTE OF a benne seed was in a souvenir cookie from Charleston, South Carolina. While Charleston and neighboring Mt. Pleasant love their benne wafers, this West African sesame plant, first domesticated in India, was prized in Europe and Asia long before it was sown in America. The seeds came to our country with the enslaved people, according to Charleston historian Nic Butler, either directly from Africa or via Jamaica. The word for "sesame" is *benne* in Senegal's Wolof language, according to Charleston cookbook author Nathalie Dupree.

Butler says early colonists were interested in growing the benne plants for their oil. In 1720s South Carolina, rice was an established and profitable crop in the fertile Low Country soil. So investors and planters looked for other crops to grow, and they were interested in benne to provide them with "salad oil" to wean them from their dependence on imported Mediterranean olive oil. Although producing benne oil didn't work out, the benne plants themselves continued to grow "for several more generations in the small patches of slave gardens on various low country plantations," Butler says. But after the Civil War, the benne story and the growing of it was mostly lost.

Tourism and the heritage seed and grain producer Anson Mills have helped fuel a benne comeback today. You can buy benne wafers easily in the Charleston area, and you can order benne seeds to make your own at home. The most traditional method of making benne wafers has been to drop the dough by tiny teaspoonfuls onto a baking pan. You can still do this, but it's tedious. So I created an icebox version of this cookie dough that can be stashed in the fridge to chill, then you simply cut slices off the log and bake. What you get is a light, crispy wafer cookie with crunchy benne seeds and an irresistible butterscotch flavor. It is the perfect complement to peach ice cream.

PREP: 15 TO 20 MINUTES   CHILL: 2 TO 3 HOURS TO OVERNIGHT, OR FREEZE 1 HOUR   BAKE: 10 TO 12 MINUTES

---

1. Place a rack in the center of the oven, and preheat the oven to 350°F. Spread the benne seeds in a small baking pan, and place

(continued on page 130)

FOLLOWING PAGE, LEFT TO RIGHT: *Cornmeal Pistachio Cookies, Benne Icebox Wafers, and Chocolate Icebox Wafers*

the pan in the oven. Let the seeds toast until they take on a little color, 4 to 5 minutes. Watch them so they do not burn. Remove the pan from the oven to let the seeds cool. Turn off the oven.

2. Place the soft butter and brown sugar in a large mixing bowl and beat with an electric mixer on medium speed until creamy and light, about 1 minute. Add the egg and vanilla and beat on low speed until combined, 30 seconds.

3. Stir together the flour and baking powder in a small bowl. Add to the butter and sugar mixture along with the benne seeds. Fold into the dough until well incorporated.

4. Tear off an 18"-long sheet of waxed or parchment paper. Turn the dough out onto the paper, and with floured hands, form into a $1\frac{1}{2}$"-diameter roll. Wrap the paper around the roll, and chill it in the refrigerator for 2 to 3 hours and up to overnight, or freeze for 1 hour.

5. Place a rack in the center of the oven, and preheat the oven to 350°F. Remove the dough from the refrigerator or freezer and slice it into $\frac{1}{4}$"-wide slices. Place these 1"to 2" apart on ungreased baking sheets or on pans lined with parchment paper. Place a pan in the oven.

6. Bake the cookies until golden brown around the edges, 10 to 12 minutes. Remove the pan from the oven, and immediately transfer the cookies to a wire rack to cool using a metal spatula. Repeat with the remaining dough. When cool, store the cookies in a tightly covered container for up to 1 week.

Finding Benne Seeds

If you live in the coastal South Carolina or Georgia area, then you can find benne seeds at the local market. Or you might have a benne plant in your backyard. But for the rest of us, we can either substitute sesame seeds for the smaller benne seeds or order at ansonmills.com or from Web sites that sell seeds to feed wild birds. Benne seeds are a favorite of quail and dove.

CHOCOLATE ICEBOX WAFERS

2 ounces unsweetened chocolate, chopped

½ cup (1 stick) unsalted butter, at room temperature

1⅓ cups granulated sugar

2 large eggs

½ teaspoon vanilla extract

1¼ cups unbleached all-purpose flour

¼ teaspoon salt

MAKES: 4 to 5 dozen (2") cookies

THE FIRST CHOCOLATE WAFER cookies were commercially baked, not homemade. In the 1870s you would have imported these chocolate "biscuits" from England. Even the most popular store-bought cookie in America—the Oreo, invented in 1912—was initially called a "biscuit."

But today we call this a cookie, and this is a chocolatey, chewy, and comforting cookie to bake on weekends. That's when you might have more time to ponder how the shorter stay in the oven results in a less-done and chewier cookie, whereas a few more minutes creates caramelization, browning, and crispness. It's really up to you! With chocolate cookies, I bake at a little lower temperature—350°F—and then I have a wafer that is crisp around the edges but still a little soft inside.

When testing chocolate wafer recipes, I found many recipes out of the 1930s were so full of baking powder and milk that they became cakelike in texture. I removed the baking powder and milk in this recipe so that this cookie tasted like a cookie! Actually, it's a cross between shortbread and a brownie and is delicious sandwiched with your favorite ice cream.

PREP: 15 TO 20 MINUTES   CHILL: 2 TO 3 HOURS TO OVERNIGHT
BAKE: 8 TO 10 MINUTES

1. Place the chopped chocolate in a small heavy-bottomed saucepan over low heat and stir until the chocolate has melted, 3 to 4 minutes. You can also melt the chocolate in a glass bowl in the microwave on high power for 1 to 1½ minutes, stirring at intervals. Set the chocolate aside to cool.

2. Place the soft butter and sugar in a large bowl and beat with an electric mixer on medium speed until smooth and creamy, about 1 minute. Add the eggs and vanilla, and beat just until combined, 30 seconds. Fold in the cooled melted chocolate.

3. Stir together the flour and salt in a small bowl. Dump the flour mixture in the bowl with the butter and chocolate mixture. Beat on low speed, scraping down the sides of the bowl once with a rubber spatula, until all the flour is incorporated, 1 to 2 minutes.

4. Tear off a sheet of waxed or parchment paper about 15" long.

(continued on next page)

Spoon the dough onto the paper to form a log. Wrap the paper up around the dough and chill for 2 to 3 hours, or freeze for 1 hour, until firm.

5. Remove the dough from the refrigerator and, with floured hands, roll the dough into a log about $1\frac{1}{2}$" in diameter. Place in the freezer while you preheat the oven. Place a rack in the center of the oven, and preheat the oven to 350°F.

6. Remove the dough from the freezer and slice the dough into $\frac{1}{4}$" rounds. Arrange them 1" to 2" apart on a baking pan. Place the pan in the oven.

7. Bake the cookies until crispy around the edges and not quite firm to the touch, 8 to 10 minutes. Transfer the cookies immediately to a wire rack to cool completely. Repeat with the remaining dough. Store the cookies in a tightly covered container for up to 1 week.

Give Old Recipes a Modern Touch

Our obsession with dark chocolate, the need for bold spice flavor, our fascination with pairing citrus with herbs—these are modern ways of flavoring baked goods. And they work with old cookie recipes, too. Simply read through old recipes, and don't be afraid of upping the vanilla a bit. Or adding grated dark chocolate. Or adding finely chopped orange zest. It's really up to you. Like cardamom? Add $\frac{1}{4}$ teaspoon to the chocolate wafer recipe. A fan of coriander? Add it to the tea cookies instead of lavender. Want some heat? Add a pinch of grated lime zest and chili powder to the cornmeal cookies. And true to today's faster schedules, let your icebox dough chill even more quickly in the freezer.

MORAVIAN BLACK WALNUT COOKIES

1 cup vegetable shortening (see Baking Tips)

$\frac{1}{2}$ cup light brown sugar, firmly packed

$\frac{1}{2}$ cup granulated sugar

1 large egg

2 cups all-purpose flour

$\frac{1}{2}$ teaspoon baking soda

$\frac{1}{2}$ teaspoon salt

1 cup finely chopped black walnuts (see Baking Tips)

MAKES: About 4 to 5 dozen (2") cookies

MOST MORAVIAN COOKIES ARE rolled and cut. In fact, they are rolled so thinly you can almost see through the dough—but this is a very labor-intensive and intricate task. So another method of making these cookies is to roll the dough into a log and refrigerate it before slicing and baking. And when you think of Moravian cookies, you probably think of the ginger-scented recipe, but there are other variations. This one comes from the Spach family, whose descendants were charter members of the Trinity Moravian Church in Winston-Salem, North Carolina. The Moravians were Protestant refugees who came to America from what is now the Czech Republic. They settled in Bethlehem, Pennsylvania, in 1740 and a decade later in North Carolina. Like other immigrants, their hope was to find prosperity and peace in this new land. This recipe and others are included in *The Old Salem Museum & Gardens Cookbook*. Old Salem is a historic living village where you can see and taste Moravian flavors today.

PREP: 15 TO 20 MINUTES   CHILL: 1 TO 2 HOURS, OR FREEZE 1 HOUR
BAKE: 9 TO 11 MINUTES

---

1. Place the shortening and sugars in a large bowl and beat with an electric mixer on medium speed until creamy and combined, about 1 minute. Add the egg and beat on low until just combined and smooth, 30 seconds.

2. Place the flour, baking soda, and salt in a small bowl and stir to combine well. Stir half of the flour mixture into the sugar and egg mixture. Add the walnuts, and stir to combine. Add the remaining flour mixture. You may need to knead the dough together with your hands until everything is combined. Divide the dough in half.

3. Tear off 2 sheets of waxed paper, each 12" to 15" long. Place half of the dough on each sheet of paper. With your floured hands, roll the dough into a $1\frac{1}{2}$"-diameter log. Wrap the logs in the waxed paper, and place them in the refrigerator to chill for 1 to 2 hours, or freeze for 1 hour, until easy to slice.

(continued on next page)

4. Just before baking, place a rack in the center of the oven, and preheat the oven to 375°F. Remove one dough log from the refrigerator and slice it into $\frac{1}{4}$" rounds. Arrange the rounds 1" to 2" apart on a baking pan, and place the pan in the oven.

5. Bake the cookies until lightly browned around the edges, 9 to 11 minutes. Let the cookies rest for 1 minute on the pan, then transfer them with a metal spatula to a wire rack to cool completely. Repeat with the remaining dough. Store the cookies in a tightly covered container for up to 1 week.

BAKING TIPS: *Vegetable shortening is a common ingredient in Moravian sugar cookie recipes because the dough doesn't have to be chilled as long before slicing as it would if you used butter in the recipe. You can substitute finely chopped pecans in this recipe. For best flavor, toast the pecans first at 350°F for 3 to 4 minutes.*

Storing Icebox Cookies & Wafers

Unbaked dough keeps in the fridge for up to 3 days and in the freezer for up to 3 months. Once you bake these cookies, be sure to store them in airtight containers so they stay crispy up to 1 week. If you want to store them longer, freeze them in zipper-lock plastic bags. Cookies left uncovered will still be delicious, but they will lose their crispness.

LEFT TO RIGHT: *Moravian Black Walnut Cookies, 1886 Vanilla Wafers, and Butterscotch Pecan Wafers*

1886 VANILLA WAFERS

10 tablespoons
unsalted butter, at
room temperature

1 cup granulated sugar

1 large egg

1 tablespoon vanilla
extract

2 cups unbleached
all-purpose flour

1 teaspoon cream of
tartar

$\frac{1}{2}$ teaspoon baking
soda

$\frac{1}{4}$ teaspoon salt

4 tablespoons milk

MAKES: 4 to 5 dozen
(2") cookies

LONG BEFORE VANILLA WAFERS lined the sides of a pan full of banana pudding, cooks made their own vanilla wafers at home. You will find a recipe in the 1851 Pennsylvania Dutch cookbook called the *Die Geschickte Hausfrau* (*The Handy Housewife*) by Gustav Peters, and you will find this recipe in *The Woman Suffrage Cook Book*, an early charity cookbook published in 1886.

Not long before these recipes were published, Boston pharmacist Joseph Burnett had bottled the first vanilla extract for a customer who had sampled vanilla desserts while traveling in Paris.

In this recipe from *The Women's Suffrage Cook Book* by Hattie A. Burr, the cookie shows its age because it calls for baking soda and cream of tartar, early leaveners before there was baking powder. As a result, the cookies are crisp and light, characteristic of wafers. And they would be a delicious homemade stand-in for banana pudding any day.

**PREP: 15 TO 20 MINUTES   CHILL: 2 TO 3 HOURS TO OVERNIGHT, OR FREEZE
1 HOUR   BAKE: 8 TO 10 MINUTES**

---

1. Place the soft butter and sugar in a large mixing bowl and beat with an electric mixer on medium speed until creamy, about 1 minute. Add the egg and vanilla and beat until well combined, 30 seconds.

2. Whisk together the flour, cream of tartar, baking soda, and salt in a medium-size bowl. Alternately add the flour mixture to the butter and sugar mixture with the milk, beginning and ending with the flour mixture. Beat on low speed until just combined.

3. Tear off an 18" sheet of waxed paper or parchment paper. Spoon the batter into a log on the paper and roll the paper up around it to secure. Place the log of dough in the refrigerator for at least 2 to 3 hours and up to overnight, or freeze for 1 hour.

4. When ready to bake, place a rack in the center of the oven, and preheat the oven to 375°F.

5. Unwrap the dough and slice into $\frac{1}{4}$" rounds. Place them 1" to 2" apart on an ungreased baking sheet, and place the pan in the oven.

6. Bake the cookies until lightly browned, 8 to 10 minutes. Transfer the cookies to a rack to cool. Repeat with remaining dough. Store in a covered container for up to 10 days.

BUTTERSCOTCH PECAN WAFERS

½ cup (1 stick) unsalted butter, at room temperature

¾ cup light brown sugar, firmly packed

1 large egg

½ teaspoon vanilla extract

1¼ cups unbleached all-purpose flour

¼ teaspoon salt

⅓ cup finely chopped pecans or almonds

MAKES: 4 to 5 dozen (2") cookies

YOU CAN EASILY CREATE butterscotch flavor by combining brown sugar, butter, and vanilla. This trio bakes into the most aromatic and nostalgic flavor and just might take you back to a time when your mother or aunt baked cookies like this for you. The recipe was based on a recipe my own Aunt Elizabeth baked, one she kept in logs in the freezer, ready to slice and bake for surprise guests. It also was influenced by a midwestern recipe from Glenn Andrews, author of *Food from the Heartland.* As Andrews recalls, her mother baked the cookies when someone pleaded enough! Homemade slice-and-bake dough, Andrews adds, tastes so much better.

PREP: 15 TO 20 MINUTES   CHILL: 2 TO 3 HOURS TO OVERNIGHT, OR FREEZE 1 HOUR   BAKE: 8 TO 10 MINUTES

1. Place the soft butter and brown sugar in a large bowl and beat with an electric mixer on medium speed until smooth and creamy, about 1 minute. Add the egg and vanilla and beat just until combined.

2. Stir together the flour and salt in a small bowl. Dump the flour mixture along with the pecans in the bowl with the butter and sugar mixture. Beat on low speed, scraping down the sides of the bowl once, until all the flour is incorporated, 1 to 2 minutes.

3. Tear off a sheet of waxed or parchment paper about 15" long. Spoon the dough onto the paper to form a log. Wrap the paper up around the dough and chill for 2 to 3 hours and up to overnight, or freeze for 1 hour until firm.

4. Remove the dough from the refrigerator, and with floured hands, roll the dough into a log about 1½" in diameter. Place in the freezer while you preheat the oven. Place a rack in the center of the oven, and preheat the oven to 375°F.

5. Remove the dough from the freezer, and slice into ¼" rounds. Arrange them 1" to 2" apart on an ungreased baking sheet. Place the pan in the oven.

6. Bake the cookies until golden brown and crispy around the edges, 8 to 10 minutes. Transfer the cookies immediately to a wire rack to cool completely. Repeat with the remaining dough. Store the cookies in a tightly covered container for up to 1 week.

IRMA ROMBAUER'S REFRIGERATOR LACE COOKIES

½ cup granulated sugar

½ cup light brown sugar, lightly packed

½ cup (1 stick) unsalted butter, at room temperature

1 large egg

1 tablespoon whole milk

½ teaspoon vanilla extract

1½ teaspoons lemon zest (from 1 medium lemon)

1½ cups old-fashioned oats

1 cup all-purpose flour, sifted

½ teaspoon salt

½ teaspoon baking soda

MAKES: 4 dozen (2" to 2½") cookies

A FINE ARTS STUDENT at Washington University, Irma Rombauer had a flair for decorating cakes and baking cookies before she wrote *The Joy of Cooking*. So no surprise that there are umpteen cookie recipes inside *Joy*, many of them icebox. It was the 1930s, a time of planning and baking ahead. And Rombauer tells us these plain and simple chocolate, spice, oatmeal, and butterscotch cookies "are all so good that is hard to decide upon the best." I love her lace cookies, made with oats and so named because after baking, the oats create a lacy, almost see-through effect.

Rombauer's rules for making icebox cookies were simple: Combine the ingredients as directed. Shape the dough into long rolls about 2" in diameter. If the dough is too soft to roll, chill it until you can handle it and roll into a log, instead of adding more flour. That's because extra flour makes your cookies dry. Her cookies are a true overnight icebox cookie, which not only makes for easy slicing but gives the dough a time to rest, which improves its texture. And Rombauer baked in a hot oven—400°F—so keep an eye on them!

PREP: 15 TO 20 MINUTES   CHILL: 12 TO 24 HOURS   BAKE: 8 TO 10 MINUTES

1. Place the sugars and soft butter in a large bowl and beat with an electric mixer on medium speed until the mixture is well blended, 1 minute. Beat in the egg, milk, vanilla, and lemon zest until combined, 30 to 45 seconds. Scrape down the sides of the bowl with a rubber spatula. Beat in the oats on low speed, just till combined.

2. With a fork, stir together the flour, salt, and baking soda in a medium-size bowl. Add to the oats mixture in 2 batches, beating on low speed just until the flour is blended, 30 seconds. Scrape down the sides of the bowl.

3. Place a 16" to 17" piece of waxed paper on the countertop. Drop spoonfuls of dough lengthwise on the paper, making a line about 12" long. Fold the paper lengthwise over the dough and make a log, rolling to 1¾" to 2" in diameter and 13" to 14" long. Place the log in the fridge for 12 to 24 hours.

(continued on next page)

4. When ready to bake, place a rack in the center of the oven, and preheat the oven to 400°F.

5. Remove the dough from the fridge, and place on a cutting surface. Remove the waxed paper. Cut the dough into $\frac{1}{4}$" slices and place on an ungreased baking sheet $2\frac{1}{2}$" apart. Place the pan in the oven.

6. Bake the cookies until the edges are golden brown, 8 to 10 minutes. Remove from the oven and allow to cool on the pan no longer than 1 minute. Transfer the cookies to a wire rack with a metal spatula and cool completely. Repeat with the remaining dough. Store the cookies in a tightly covered container for up to 1 week.

The Joy of Cooking

Devastated by her husband's suicide, with no income except $6,000 in savings, and dealing with the uncertainty of the Great Depression, Irma Rombauer did the unexpected. The 54-year-old St. Louis, Missouri, native and homemaker gathered favorite recipes and in 1931 invested half her savings to print 3,000 copies of a cookbook titled The Joy of Cooking: A Compilation of Reliable Recipes with a Casual Culinary Chat. *It was written the same year the Empire State Building was built, and it was revised seven more times. The second edition in 1936 was organized as more of a conversation, with ingredients listed as they were called for in prose. The third edition in 1943 included much-needed wartime rationing ideas, and it alone went on to sell 600,000 copies. In total,* The Joy of Cooking *has sold more than 18 million copies and has been America's perennial wedding gift. In 2012 the Library of Congress included Joy in a list of 88 books that shaped America.*

Cookie Swaps for Busy Cooks Through History

You might think that the cookie swap—where you bake cookies and bring them to a party and trade with other people who also bring cookies—is a modern phenomenon. It's perfectly logical that people today would want a fabulous spread of holiday cookies *without* spending a lot of time in the kitchen baking them.

But swaps, or "exchanges" as they were first called, have been taking place in America for nearly 100 years. They were annual holiday events, from California to New Jersey, offering friendship, festivity, and most of all cookies!

In the 1920s, when the first references were made to "cookie exchanges" in local newspapers, they were held at churches throughout the Midwest. A 1934 Indiana newspaper explained the rules—you baked and shared one cookie with each participant. But by the 1950s, the stakes were clearly higher. You brought a batch of your best cookies and, according to the Brownsville, Texas, newspaper food columnist in 1952, took home as many cookies as you had brought less the number you had eaten. So you didn't want to go hungry to the cookie swap!

Bridge clubs, church groups, newcomer organizations, Girl Scout leaders, neighbors—they all held cookie swaps in the weeks before Christmas. Some had rules that were discussed a month in advance. Often, you were encouraged to bake a "new" recipe, although many cooks resorted to a family favorite. Most of the time, you had to bring copies of your recipe for the other participants. And if you were hosting, you had to give some thought as to how people might take that bevy of cookies home. One hostess painted cookie jars for each of her guests.

By 1960, syndicated food columnist Clementine Paddleford declared "cookie swaps are sweeping the nation." The appeal, she said, was the dazzling array of cookies you could come home with and gift to others. And as a result, you had more time "to enjoy the last mad holiday rush."

More than a half century later, many of us can relate to that statement. Cookie swaps allow us to savor more cookies than we'd ever end up baking by ourselves. And they're a great way to taste other people's cookies or to exercise our creative skills in the kitchen with a new recipe.

Planning on baking cookies from *American Cookie* for a cookie swap? Here are my top-10 suggestions and why:

1. Irma Rombauer's Refrigerator Lace Cookies: an American classic
2. Sara's Raspberry Thumbprint Cookies: simply a real treat
3. Coconut Macadamia Macaroons: for their chewy, crunchy, almond-y texture
4. Beatrice's Peppernuts: the recipe makes a ton
5. Kathleen's Sugar Cookies: fun to decorate with others using colored sprinkles
6. Apricot and Raisin Rugelach: exotic and delicious
7. Cornmeal Pistachio Cookies: wonderful wafers for sharing
8. Mexican Wedding Cookies: everybody loves them—enough said!
9. Chocolate Pinwheel Cookies: a dazzling addition to the holiday spread
10. Kate's Pecan Tassies: sheer bliss in one bite

LAVENDER TEA COOKIES

½ cup (1 stick) unsalted butter

1 cup granulated sugar

2 large eggs

½ teaspoon vanilla extract

1 teaspoon dried food-grade lavender flowers, finely chopped (see Baking Tip)

1½ cups unbleached all-purpose flour

1 teaspoon baking powder

¼ teaspoon salt

MAKES: About 5 dozen (2") cookies

BAKING TIP: *To remove lavender blossoms from the stalk, simply run your fingers up and down the flower stalk. Collect these blossoms, then let them dry in a low oven—300 to 325°F— until dry, 8 to 10 minutes. Chop finely with a heavy kitchen knife. You need 1 teaspoon for this recipe, but you can certainly use more.*

AN OLD AND FRAGRANT herb, lavender has been grown and loved in Europe for centuries. It scented Roman baths. And it had a multitude of medicinal uses, from keeping away headaches to easing aches and pains to inducing sleep and even repelling insects in the home. But lavender in the kitchen was a slow entry, and you can find a few old recipes for pound cakes and cookies delicately scented with the chopped and dried lavender blossoms.

In this simple tea cookie recipe, lavender and vanilla work hand in hand to lift up the flavor and yet not overwhelm. You could use a little grated lemon zest instead of the vanilla. These cookies are different from other wafers in this chapter because they contain baking powder, which makes them soft and cakelike. If you don't have lavender growing in your garden, perhaps you can find some in a friend's garden. And if not, it is often sold in the produce section of Whole Foods Markets.

PREP: 10 TO 15 MINUTES   CHILL: 2 TO 3 HOURS, OR FREEZE 1 HOUR
BAKE: 8 TO 10 MINUTES

---

1. Place the soft butter and sugar in a large mixing bowl and beat with an electric mixer on medium speed until light and fluffy, 1 minute. Add the eggs, vanilla, and lavender and beat just to combine, 30 to 45 seconds.

2. Stir together the flour, baking powder and salt in a medium-size bowl. Add to the butter and sugar mixture, and stir to combine well.

3. Tear off an 18" sheet of waxed or parchment paper and turn the dough onto the sheet. With floured hands, form the dough into a 1½"-diameter log. Wrap in the paper and place in the refrigerator for 2 to 3 hours, or freeze for 1 hour, until chilled.

4. When ready to bake, place a rack in the center of the oven, and preheat the oven to 375°F. Remove the dough from the refrigerator or freezer, and slice into ¼" rounds. Place the rounds 1" to 2" apart on ungreased baking sheets or pans lined with parchment paper. Place a pan in the oven.

5. Bake the cookies until crispy around the edges, 8 to 10 minutes. Cool on the pan for 1 minute, then transfer the cookies to a wire rack to cool completely. Repeat with the remaining dough. Store the cookies in a tightly covered container for up to 1 week.

CHOCOLATE PINWHEEL COOKIES

½ cup (1 stick) unsalted butter, at room temperature

¾ cup granulated sugar

1 large egg

½ teaspoon vanilla extract

1¼ cups unbleached all-purpose flour

¼ teaspoon salt

1 ounce unsweetened chocolate

MAKES: 5 to 6 dozen (2") cookies

THE KITCHEN OF MY youth was filled with chocolate cake, pudding, and brownies, but sadly, it did not include pinwheel cookies. I had to read about these cookies that are most likely German in origin and popularized in the late 1920s. And I had to read how clever cooks divided their sugar cookie dough in half and added melted chocolate to one half, then laid the chocolate dough on top of the other and rolled them up before slicing into pinwheels. It is this visual spiral that intrigues me about this old recipe and surely has contributed to its popularity through the years. They are especially loved in the Midwest, where author Glenn Andrews recalled her mother making these cookies that, when baked, were so pretty they "seemed downright miraculous to me." That is the mystique of pinwheel cookies, and yet they're easier to make than you think.

Just follow the recipe below. Or use your favorite sugar cookie dough, divide in half, and add 1 ounce melted unsweetened chocolate to one half. For the best contrast of colors, lay the chocolate dough on top of the white so the white wraps around it. And be careful not to overbake so the white portion stays light. From there the possibilities are endless—you could substitute spices or grated orange zest or molasses for the chocolate.

PREP: 25 TO 30 MINUTES   CHILL: 2 TO 3 HOURS, OR FREEZE 1 HOUR
BAKE: 8 TO 10 MINUTES

---

1. Place the soft butter and sugar in a large bowl and beat with an electric mixer on medium speed until smooth and creamy, about 1 minute. Add the egg and vanilla and beat just until combined, 30 to 45 seconds.

2. Stir together the flour and salt in a small bowl. Dump the flour mixture in the bowl with the butter and sugar mixture. Beat on low speed, scraping down the sides of the bowl once with a rubber spatula, until all the flour is incorporated, 1 to 2 minutes. Set aside.

(continued on next page)

3. Chop the chocolate and place in a small glass bowl. Heat in the microwave oven on high power for 1 minute, stirring at intervals, until melted. Let cool.

4. Tear off 4 sheets of waxed or parchment paper, each about 15" long. Divide the dough in half. Place one half onto one sheet of waxed paper and press with your fingertips into a rectangle. Cover with another sheet of waxed paper and place in the refrigerator for 2 to 3 hours, or freeze for 1 hour. Pour the melted chocolate into the bowl with the second half of the dough. Beat with the electric mixer on medium speed to combine, 1 minute. Wrap the paper around the chocolate dough and chill 2 to 3 hours, or freeze for 1 hour, until firm.

5. Remove the plain dough from the refrigerator or freezer, and with floured hands, place the dough onto a floured work surface (or roll it between the sheets of the waxed paper). Roll to $1/4$" thickness. Carefully place the chocolate dough on top of the white, and roll the doughs up into a jelly roll, beginning with the longer side. Wrap the roll in the waxed paper, and place it in the freezer while you preheat the oven.

6. Place a rack in the center of the oven, and preheat the oven to 375°F. Remove the dough from the freezer, and slice the dough into $1/4$" rounds. Arrange them 1" to 2" apart on ungreased baking sheets. Place the pan in the oven.

7. Bake the cookies until they are just firm and begin to brown around the edges, 8 to 10 minutes. Remove the pan from the oven, and transfer the cookies immediately to a wire rack to cool completely. Repeat with the remaining dough. Store the cookies in a tightly covered container for up to 1 week.

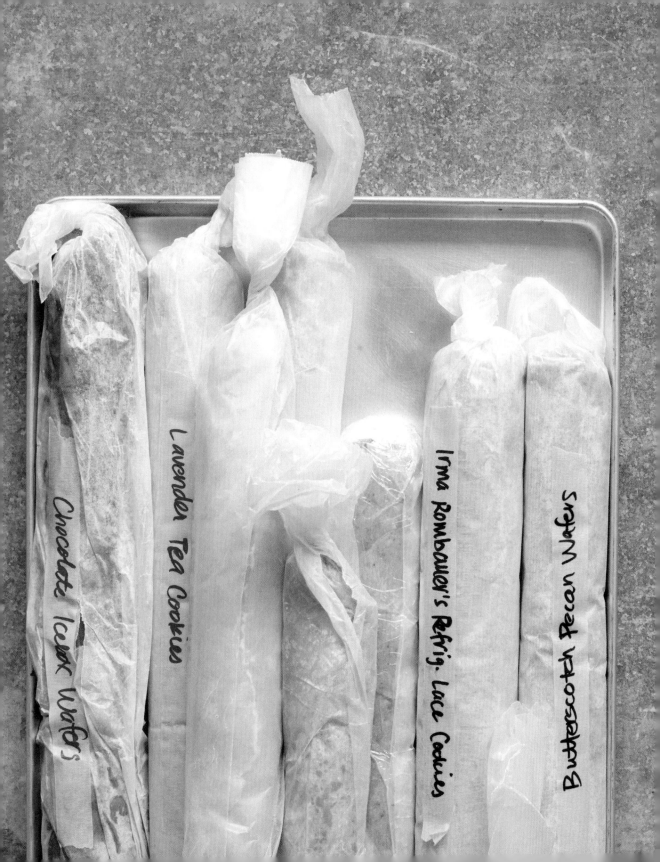

Chocolate Icebox Wafers

Lavender Tea Cookies

Irma Rombauer's Refrig. Lace Cookies

Butterscotch Pecan Wafers

4

BARS, BROWNIES & BAKING FOR OTHERS

The first snickerdoodle and hermit cookie recipes weren't cookies at all. They were bars. The dough was made, turned into a pan, baked, and cut into little squares often called "cakes." If you think back to a time when ovens were smaller, pans were smaller, and women were short on time, then you can understand the convenience of baking bar cookies.

But there were no 13" × 9" pans before the 1950s. The pan sizes were smaller. People baked bars of all types in 8" square pans—bars like hermits with raisins and spices or blondies made with brown sugar. Interestingly, brown sugar has been used in baking for centuries. I share an Alderney cakes recipe in this chapter, and it comes from 1840s Charleston, where brown sugar was imported by wealthy families.

And then there were bar cookies created just by plopping the batter into a pan, baking, and breaking up the pieces of the crispy cinnamon shortbread by hand. This is a family recipe that goes by myriad names. It has weathered time, temperature, and recipe files and is still delicious today.

Other recipes that have survived the years are Hello Dollies and lemon squares. The former are also known as seven-layer bars or magic bars and use every pantry baking staple you've got to layer the most chewy and delicious bar cookie on earth. And the latter is an old British recipe in which shortbread is baked and topped with lemon curd. But the 1960s versions that made the bridge party circuit across America called for a lemon filling that you poured on top of the half-baked crust, then returned to the oven to bake through. I tested my way through a lot of lemon bar recipes and share my favorite.

I also share bars made of maple syrup and oats, staples of the American rural kitchen. And I share brownies, the beloved fudgy chocolate bar that originated at the turn of the 20th century. The brownie was first showcased at the Chicago World's Fair in 1893 and was baked later in kitchens of Boston and Philadelphia cooking schools to use the newly packaged American baking chocolate. The brownie recipes in this chapter are cult favorites—Katharine Hepburn's brownies, plus an over-the-top decadent classic brownie from Maida Heatter and a more modern way to adapt the brownie to the gluten-free kitchen.

Ending the chapter is an insanely delicious chocolate, graham cracker, and coconut bar popular in the Pacific Northwest and Canada. It's named for the town Nanaimo on Vancouver Island where the bars were first baked.

Bars and brownies have been with us through the years, and they aren't going anywhere. That's because we can bake and take them with us—right in the pan. This makes them the perfect recipe to bake for others. Katharine Hepburn did that, as did Emily Dickinson with her rice cakes a century earlier. Hermits, so the story goes, were baked for sailors heading out to sea. Bars and brownies are the most adaptable of all the cookies, and people have known this for a long, long time. Enjoy!

EMILY DICKINSON'S RICE CAKES

Soft butter for prepping the pan

½ cup (1 stick) unsalted butter, at room temperature

2 large eggs

1 cup confectioners' sugar

2 teaspoons milk

¼ teaspoon baking soda

1 cup ground rice flour (see Baking Tip)

¼ teaspoon ground mace or nutmeg

MAKES: 16 (2") pieces

FANS OF THE 19TH-CENTURY American poet Emily Dickinson might know that she loved to bake. She often wrote poems on recipe cards and chocolate wrappers, and one of her favorite cakes to bake for others was this rice cake.

Dickinson lived with her family in Amherst, Massachusetts, in what is now called the Dickinson Homestead. She was said to be shy and reclusive, and yet her poetry has empowered and enlightened readers for more than 100 years.

In the *Boston School-Cooking Magazine* of 1906, Helen Knight Wyman, a cousin of Emily Dickinson, writes about her deceased famous relative as both poet and cook. She said rice cake was Dickinson's "company cake," and "carefully placed in a large tin pail and only used when outside persons came to tea." Wyman had access to the published letters of Dickinson and concluded that while the poet's mind was occupied with "all mysteries and knowledge," her hands "were often busy in most humble household ways."

These are nice shortbreadlike cakes. They are lightly flavored with mace or nutmeg, a bit like the Alderney cakes baked by *The Carolina Housewife*'s Sarah Rutledge. They're perfect for baking on a winter's day and serving with tea and Dickinson's poetry. This recipe is adapted from a small cookbook called *Emily Dickinson: Profile of the Poet as Cook*, published by the Emily Dickinson Museum.

PREP: 15 TO 20 MINUTES   BAKE: 18 TO 21 MINUTES

---

1. Place a rack in the center of the oven, and preheat the oven to 350°F. Lightly grease an 8" square pan with butter.

2. Place the soft butter in a medium-size bowl and beat with an electric mixer on medium speed until creamy, 30 seconds.

3. Crack the eggs into a separate medium-size bowl and whisk with a fork to break up the yolks. Add the confectioners' sugar, and whisk with the fork until well blended, 30 seconds. Turn the egg and sugar mixture into the butter, and beat with the mixer on

(continued on next page)

TOP TO BOTTOM: *Shirley's Cinnamon Shortbread and Emily Dickinson's Rice Cakes*

low speed until creamy and combined, 30 seconds to 1 minute. Scrape down the bowl with a rubber spatula.

4. Place the milk in a small bowl, and whisk in the baking soda to dissolve. Add the milk mixture to the batter along with the rice flour and ground mace or nutmeg. Blend on low speed to incorporate, 20 to 30 seconds. Turn the batter into the prepared pan, and place the pan in the oven.

5. Bake the cake until lightly golden on top, 18 to 21 minutes. Remove the pan from the oven, let it rest 10 minutes, then cut the cake into serving pieces. Store covered at room temperature for up to 4 days, in the fridge for up to a week, or in the freezer for up to 4 months.

BAKING TIP: *We used Bob's Red Mill white rice flour for this recipe.*

The Rice Flour Fascination

Emily Dickinson wasn't the only early-American baker fascinated by baking with rice flour. About 60 years before Dickinson was born, bakers in Charleston, South Carolina, were making cakes with local rice flour, as noted in A Colonial Plantation Cookbook: The Receipt Book of Harriott Pinckney Horry, 1770. *By the mid-1800s, rice flour baking had arrived in New England, and recipes for rice flour sponge cakes were found in* The New England Economical Housekeeper *by Esther Allen Howland (1845),* Miss Parloa's New Cook Book *(1880),* Jennie June's American Cookery Book *(1870), and* Domestic Cookery *by Elizabeth Lea (1869), the latter a Quaker cookbook that contained both sponge cake and pound cake recipes using rice flour. Why was rice flour so popular in the mid- to late 1800s? South Carolina food historian David Shields says it had to do with the texture of rice flour versus wheat flour at the time. "Rice flour had a finer texture," says Shields, and made the cake batter smooth and the baked cake itself light. You just had to be careful and not add too much rice flour or the cake went stale quickly, he says. Cooks also made rice flour waffles and a mid-19th-century thickening agent for sauces containing rice called "creme de ris."*

SHIRLEY'S CINNAMON SHORTBREAD

1 cup granulated sugar

1 tablespoon ground cinnamon

2 cups all-purpose flour

$^1/_2$ teaspoon salt

1 large egg, separated

1 cup (2 sticks) unsalted butter, at room temperature

1 teaspoon vanilla extract

$^2/_3$ cup finely chopped pecans or sliced almonds

MAKES: About 24 (3") pieces

SIMILAR TO THE OLD-FASHIONED gingersnaps where the dough is draped onto the pan and baked, this shortbreadlike cookie is just as simple and straightforward. It begins with ingredients you would have on hand if you did much baking—butter, sugar, flour, and an egg. And that's how the recipe got its start—it was quick to make with what was in the cupboard.

In German American kitchens, it might be called a "blitz kuchen," meaning a "lightning-fast cake." In old cookbooks of the 1940s and '50s, it was called cinnamon thins. But to Martha Bowden, who grew up in Tennessee in the 1960s, it was her mother Shirley Hutson's cinnamon shortbread she looked forward to most in her lunch box. Lucky girl!

PREP: 20 TO 25 MINUTES   BAKE: 20 TO 25 MINUTES

---

1. Place a rack in the center of the oven, and preheat the oven to 350°F. Mist an 18" × 12" pan with vegetable oil spray, and line the pan with parchment paper. Set aside.

2. Place the sugar and cinnamon in a small bowl and stir to combine.

3. Stir the flour and salt in a large mixing bowl to combine. Add the egg yolk, soft butter, vanilla, and half of the cinnamon-sugar mixture. Blend with an electric mixer on low speed until well combined, 1 minute. Turn the dough out onto the prepared pan. Press the dough to the edges of the pan, using a spatula.

4. In a small bowl, beat the egg white with a fork until it is frothy, 1 minute. Spread the egg white over the dough using a pastry brush or the back of a large spoon. Sprinkle the nuts over the egg white, and top with the remaining cinnamon-sugar mixture. Place the pan in the oven.

5. Bake the shortbread until golden brown, 20 to 25 minutes. Remove the pan to a rack to cool completely, 1 hour. Break the shortbread into 24 pieces with your hands. It keeps tightly covered at room temperature for up to 5 days.

BROWN SUGAR SAUCEPAN BLONDIES

Vegetable shortening or butter and flour for prepping the pan

12 tablespoons (1½ sticks) unsalted butter

1⅓ cups light brown sugar, firmly packed

⅓ cup granulated sugar

2 cups all-purpose flour

2 teaspoons baking powder

½ teaspoon salt

3 large eggs, beaten

1 teaspoon vanilla extract

1 cup chopped pecans, if desired

MAKES: 32
(2¼" × 1½") blondies

BLONDIES—THE FAIR-HAIRED COUSIN OF Brownies—likely originated during World War II due to the need to bake without rationed ingredients like chocolate and white sugar. It seems odd, I know, because packed as this treat is with butter, brown sugar, and eggs, it just doesn't seem like a recipe in which you are doing without something you love.

The first recipe for blondies shared in America came from one of the most prolific newspaper food columnists—Mrs. Alexander George of the Associated Press. Mrs. George was a home economics teacher turned columnist and known from 1929 through War World II for guiding home cooks through rationing, planning Victory meals, and leading them to nutrient-dense foods. And so it was with economy in mind that Mrs. George shared the recipe for blondies—"Light Colored Brownies"—in 1943 as a way to cut back on chocolate. She made those first blondies with vegetable shortening, dark brown sugar, and a handful of chocolate "pieces." Later versions of blondies contain some white sugar as well as butterscotch chips, chocolate, pecans, you name it!

The following version is a much simpler and less sweet recipe. It's a saucepan method of making blondies that might take you back to World War II America. You don't need a mixing bowl—you mix in the pan—and you don't need to cream the butter and sugar together, add eggs, then flour, etc. I'm sure Mrs. George would be glad to know her economical recipe had staying power.

PREP: 15 TO 20 MINUTES   BAKE: 20 TO 25 MINUTES

---

1. Place a rack in the center of the oven, and preheat the oven to 350°F. Lightly grease and flour a 13" × 9" baking pan and set it aside.

2. Place the butter in a large saucepan over medium heat and stir until melted. Add the brown sugar and stir with a wooden spoon until the sugar dissolves and the mixture thickens, about 3 minutes. Turn off the heat. Add the granulated sugar and stir until well combined, 1 minute. Let cool slightly.

3. Whisk together the flour, baking powder and salt in a medium-size bowl. Add a third of the flour mixture to the saucepan and

stir to combine and bring down the temperature of the butter and sugar mixture, 30 seconds. Add half of the beaten eggs and the vanilla. Stir to combine, 30 seconds. Add another third of flour mixture, stir to combine, then add the rest of the eggs, then the last of the flour, and stir until smooth. Turn the batter into the prepared pan and sprinkle the top with pecans, if desired. Place the pan in the oven.

4. Bake the blondies until nut brown around the edges and just firm in the center, 20 to 25 minutes. You do not want to overbake.

5. Remove the pan from the oven, and place it on a wire rack to cool. Score the blondies into pieces with a sharp knife. When completely cool, slice into pieces and serve. These blondies keep covered at room temperature for up to 4 days and in the freezer for up to 4 months.

The Best Way to Slice Bar Cookies

If you've even baked one recipe of brownies, you know that the center pieces are flat and the ones around the sides are taller and chewier. Some people like the ooey-gooey center pieces, while others prefer their crispy side servings. Pastry shops will cut off those outside edges to make their squares and bars perfectly flat and uniform in size. And they always remove their bar cakes from the pan before slicing, not only to make slicing and removing from the pan easier but to save their precious bakeware from knife nicks. How to do this at home? Spray or butter your 13" × 9" pan, then line it lengthwise with enough parchment or waxed paper so you will be able to lift out the entire pan of unsliced bars in one piece once baked. You may have to run a knife around the edges first to separate the bar from the pan, and you might need to run a spatula underneath to get the process going. But once you do, you can move the bars to a cutting board and slice them into perfect pieces. You've saved time, saved your pan, and the bars look much more professional.

FOLLOWING PAGE, CLOCKWISE FROM UPPER LEFT: *Katharine Hepburn Brownies, Brown Sugar Saucepan Blondies, Flourless Chocolate Brownies, and Hello Dollies*

KATHARINE HEPBURN BROWNIES

Butter and flour for prepping the pan

2 ounces unsweetened chocolate, chopped

$\frac{1}{2}$ cup (1 stick) unsalted butter

1 cup granulated sugar

2 large eggs, lightly beaten

$\frac{1}{2}$ teaspoon vanilla extract

$\frac{1}{4}$ cup all-purpose flour

$\frac{1}{4}$ teaspoon salt

1 cup chopped walnuts (see Baking Tip)

MAKES: 16 (2") brownies

IT'S JUST A SAUCEPAN brownie, but then it's a wonderful brownie from a simply wonderful actress whom we all loved. Katharine Hepburn's brownie recipe was first shared in a big way in the *New York Times* in July 2003 by a former neighbor of Hepburn's, Heather Henderson. Many years earlier, when Henderson was in college and living in the same building as Hepburn, she awoke one morning to a phone call from the actress saying, "Is this the young woman who wants to quit Bryn Mawr?" Henderson wasn't happy in college, and her father was looking for ways to encourage her to stay in school. Knowing her neighbor Hepburn was a Bryn Mawr graduate, he dropped a note to Hepburn to please intervene. Henderson and Hepburn would meet for tea and Hepburn's homemade brownies. And yes, Henderson stayed at Bryn Mawr and graduated.

When Katharine Hepburn died 20 years later, Henderson felt the need to share this story and recipe with *New York Times* readers. Only the recipe she shared wasn't correct, said the late Frederick Winship, whose actress wife had been a close friend of Hepburn. So he shared the real recipe, containing unsweetened chocolate instead of cocoa powder. But both recipes were in agreement that only $\frac{1}{4}$ cup flour is needed. That was the secret of Hepburn's brownie recipe. In fact, Henderson said that Hepburn shared with her three rules of living: "Never quit. Be yourself. Don't put too much flour in your brownies."

It's obvious that other people have known of the Hepburn brownie before it was printed in the *Times*. It was on the menu for a March of Dimes fund-raising luncheon in California in 1977. But that's due to the fact that it was no secret, and the actress was happy to share with anyone who asked. Here is the Hepburn recipe. Be careful not to bake too long. This is the only difficult part of this recipe, and of baking brownies in general. Pull them from the oven when the toothpick inserted shows moist, fudgy crumbs.

PREP: 10 TO 15 MINUTES   BAKE: 35 TO 40 MINUTES

---

1. Place a rack in the center of the oven, and preheat the oven to 325°F. Rub an 8" square baking pan with butter and dust with flour. Shake out the excess flour and set the pan aside.

2. Place the chocolate and butter in a large heavy saucepan over low heat. Stir until the chocolate and butter melt, 4 to 5 minutes.

Remove the pan from the heat and stir in the sugar. Add the eggs and vanilla and stir to combine well. Add the flour, salt, and the walnuts. Stir just to combine. Turn the batter into the prepared pan, and place the pan in the oven.

3. Bake until a toothpick inserted in the center comes out with moist and fudgy crumbs, 35 to 40 minutes. Remove the pan to a wire rack to cool completely, about 1 hour. Cut into bars or squares, and store covered at room temperature for up to 5 days, or freeze for up to 2 months.

BAKING TIP: *To make these brownies even more delicious, toast the walnuts before chopping. Place the nuts in the oven while it preheats, then remove and chop.*

A Little Brownie History

One of the most beloved cakes in American history is the simple brownie. It wasn't developed to be heavy with chocolate like you find in bakeries today. It was designed to be a light bar cake to enjoy with a glass of milk. At the 1893 World's Columbian Exposition in Chicago, Palmer House Hotel chefs created a chocolate cake that could be cut into squares for ladies' box lunches. This chocolate and buttery cakelike confection sounded like today's brownie and was covered in apricot jam. A few years later, brownies were mentioned as a chocolate candy in a Sears, Roebuck and Co. catalog in 1897. Fannie Farmer had included them in her landmark *The Boston Cooking-School Cookbook* in 1896, but they were brown from molasses and chopped nuts and contained no chocolate. By the 1905 revision, Fannie Farmer would put chocolate in her recipe, but by then chocolatey brownies were popping up everywhere in cookbooks and chocolate company recipe brochures. And they were so loved and a part of American baking that during the war years people substituted cocoa for the bar chocolate and used corn syrup instead of granulated sugar, which was rationed. When Gallup polled people at the end of World War II on what rationed ingredient they missed the most during the war years, half said sugar. Today brownies come in myriad flavors and forms. Dropping the batter onto baking pans has created something new—the brookie—a cross between a brownie and a cookie.

MAPLE SIRUP BARS

CRUST

¹⁄₂ cup (1 stick) lightly salted butter, at room temperature

¹⁄₄ cup granulated sugar

1 cup all-purpose flour

FILLING

¹⁄₃ cup light brown sugar, lightly packed

¹⁄₃ cup maple syrup

1 tablespoon lightly salted butter, melted

1 large egg

¹⁄₂ teaspoon vanilla extract

¹⁄₃ cup finely chopped pecans

MAKES: 24 bars (1¹⁄₂" × 2¹⁄₄") bars

MAPLE SYRUP—OR "SIRUP," AS it used to be spelled in the Midwest—has been an important ingredient in rural American baking. It was the frontier's sweetener, and you were fortunate if you had sugar maples on your land. The Native Americans discovered the sweet sap that trickled out of the maple trees, and settlers in New England and the Midwest have benefited from maple trees' bounty.

Because it wasn't white sugar, which they called "slave sugar," abolitionists sought out maple syrup and sugar. In 1804, the *Old Farmer's Almanac* advised that maple syrup "possesses no mingled tears of misery; no desponding slave ever groaned over my cauldrons or fanned them with his sighs."

While maple syrup production is tops in Vermont, midwestern states like Illinois and Indiana have also produced it. In 1824 Issac Funk came to the rural area outside what is now Bloomington, Illinois, from Kentucky in search of fertile soil and timber. He found both, and he also found maple trees, which would become the livelihood of many generations of his family. Today Funks Grove is a working maple syrup farm located on historic Route 66. The family shared a maple recipe with Marian Clark and Michael Wallis, the authors of *The Route 66 Cookbook*, which is where I learned about Funks Grove. Here is an adaptation of that recipe, which is the lemon square to maple lovers.

PREP: 20 TO 25 MINUTES   BAKE: 37 TO 42 MINUTES

---

1. Place a rack in the center of the oven, and preheat the oven to 350°F. Set aside a 9" square pan.

2. For the crust, place the soft butter and ¹⁄₄ cup granulated sugar in a medium-size bowl and beat with an electric mixer on medium speed until creamy, 30 seconds. Add the flour and beat until just combined. Turn out the dough into the pan, and press it to the edges using your fingers that have been dipped in flour. Place the pan in the oven. Bake until the crust is lightly browned, about 15 minutes. Remove the pan from the oven and let the pan cool. Leave the oven on.

3. For the filling, place the brown sugar, maple syrup, and melted butter in a medium-size bowl and beat with the same mixer beaters on medium speed until combined, 15 seconds. Add the egg and vanilla and beat until just combined, 30 seconds. Pour the filling over the baked dough. Sprinkle the top with the pecans. Place the pan in the oven.

4. Bake the bars until golden brown on top, 22 to 27 minutes. Cool to room temperature, then cut into individual bars. Store covered at room temperature for up to 3 days or in the refrigerator for up to 1 week.

ALDERNEY CAKES

1 cup (2 sticks) lightly salted butter, at room temperature (see Baking Tip)

1 cup light brown sugar, firmly packed

1½ cups unbleached all-purpose flour

¼ teaspoon ground nutmeg

½ cup whole milk

½ teaspoon baking soda

MAKES: 4 dozen (1") squares

I'D GIVE ANYTHING TO be in the kitchen with Sarah Rutledge, author of *The Carolina Housewife*, published in 1847. That one encounter would tell me volumes about early-American baking. Rutledge spent her childhood in England, and she was a member of an old and prestigious Charleston family. Her father, Edward Rutledge, and uncle, Arthur Middleton, were both signers of the Declaration of Independence. Rutledge's family kitchen would not have wanted for ingredients with which to bake. They would have imported brown sugar, and they would have been able to find the prized Alderney butter.

Alderney cakes in *The Carolina Housewife* are a rich, rolled cookie. The key ingredient—and a lot of it—is this butter, so named after the Alderney cow, known as the "gentleman's cow" in England, and originating in Alderney, the northernmost of the Channel Islands. A Philadelphia newspaper columnist gushed about the butter in 1853: "Nothing could be finer or sweeter in taste." It was a little spicy, too, reports the Pennsylvania State Agricultural Society in 1877.

If Rutledge were here, she might confirm that the buttery cakes were an early homage to the prized butter. But she isn't, so we make educated guesses. And we can take a little license with her recipe, which she rolled out and cut into shapes with a "tumbler." I have turned the dough into one pan and baked as squares. They are akin to our blondies, but not as sweet as cakes and bars we are accustomed to today.

PREP: 15 TO 20 MINUTES   BAKE: 25 TO 30 MINUTES

---

1. Place a rack in the center of the oven, and preheat the oven to 350°F. Set aside a 13" × 9" baking pan.

2. Place the soft butter and brown sugar in a large bowl and beat with a wooden spoon until creamy and well combined, 1 minute. Stir together the flour and nutmeg in a medium-size bowl. Measure the milk into a glass measuring cup and dissolve the baking soda in it. Add the flour mixture and milk mixture alternately to the butter and sugar mixture, beginning and ending with the flour. When smooth, after about 1 minute of stirring, turn the batter into the reserved pan. Place the pan in the oven.

3. Bake the cake until golden brown around the edges, 25 to 30 minutes. Remove the pan from the oven and, with a sharp knife, score it to make 48 (1") squares. Let the pan cool on a wire rack for 20 minutes, then separate the squares and serve. Store the squares in a tightly covered container.

BAKING TIP: *To duplicate the flavor of the Alderney butter, I used a European-style lightly salted butter. It has a higher butterfat than regular butter and greatly contributes to the flavor in this recipe.*

Fresh Milk and Nutmeg
These cakes are soft and spongy from the addition of baking soda combined not with buttermilk but with "fresh milk"—another benefit of having an Alderney cow nearby. And they are flavored delicately with nutmeg, which makes them perfect for teatime.

FOLLOWING PAGE, LEFT TO RIGHT: *New England Hermits, Nanaimo Bars, Maple Sirup Bars, Alderney Cakes, and more Nanaimo Bars*

NEW ENGLAND HERMITS

Butter and flour for prepping the pan

2 cups all-purpose flour

1 teaspoon ground cinnamon

³/₄ teaspoon baking powder

³/₄ teaspoon baking soda

¹/₂ teaspoon salt

¹/₂ teaspoon ground nutmeg

¹/₄ teaspoon ground allspice

¹/₈ teaspoon ground cloves

1 cup raisins or currants

1 cup boiling water for soaking the raisins

¹/₂ cup (1 stick) unsalted butter, at room temperature

¹/₂ cup granulated sugar

2 large eggs

¹/₂ cup molasses

1 cup chopped walnuts or pecans

1 teaspoon confectioners' sugar for dusting

MAKES: About 24 (1¹/₂" × 3") bars

ONE OF THE SIMPLEST and most loved American cookies was the hermit. Packed with spice, dried fruit, and nuts, this near-fruitcake cookie was as commonplace in the 1880s cookie jar as chocolate chip cookies are today.

It was born across New England, from Maine south to Cape Cod, and described as a spice cookie that stored well. It didn't need refrigeration and actually improved in texture days after baking. It was the foodstuff of sailors, and purists say the true hermit was not a cookie at all—but a bar. Baked in one pan, the cake was sliced into bars or squares.

For a little history of the name, think how these brown molasses and spice cookies or bars looked after baking. A hermit was the name for a religious recluse, possibly a monk, who wore a brown robe. These edible hermits might have slightly resembled them. Today, hermits aren't baked as often as they used to be. They were once made with coffee and called "tramp cookies" during the Depression and mailed to World War II soldiers away from home. But maybe they'll make a comeback.

PREP: 20 TO 25 MINUTES   BAKE: 28 TO 33 MINUTES

---

1. Place a rack in the center of the oven, and preheat the oven to 350°F. Lightly butter and flour a 13" × 9" baking pan and set aside.

2. Whisk together the flour, cinnamon, baking powder, baking soda, salt, nutmeg, allspice, and cloves in a large bowl. Set aside.

3. Place the raisins or currants in a large glass measuring cup or small glass bowl and pour the boiling water over them. Let them stand for a few minutes while you prepare the batter.

4. Place the soft butter in a large bowl and beat with an electric mixer on low speed until creamy, 15 seconds. Add the granulated sugar and beat well to combine, 15 seconds. Add the eggs and molasses and beat until combined. The mixture will look curdled but will come back together once the dry ingredients are added. Fold in the flour mixture with a wooden spoon until smooth. Drain the raisins, and add them to the bowl. Add the nuts and stir to combine. Turn the batter into the prepared pan, smoothing the top. Place the pan in the oven.

5. Bake the hermits until the cake springs back when lightly pressed in the center, 28 to 33 minutes. Remove the pan from the oven and transfer to a wire rack to cool. Dust the top with confectioners' sugar while the cake is still warm. Cut into bars and serve. The bars keep covered for up to 4 days at room temperature or up to 3 months in the freezer.

A&P Spanish Bar Cake

A bakery cake that rates high on the nostalgia scale is the A&P Spanish Bar Cake. It was a spice cake, like the hermits, packed with raisins and assembled in layers with a buttercream frosting and sold at A&P stores. Grocery leader A&P—the Atlantic & Pacific Tea Company—began in New York City in 1859. By the 1930s, there were 16,000 A&P stores across America, which means a lot of people raised in the 1940s remember this cake. In the '50s and '60s, A&P began to lose market share to other retailers, but a few hundred stores remain in the Northeast today. Sadly, they do not bake the spice cake. But online you can find all sorts of copycat recipes. Some contain coffee, applesauce, even cocoa. Some are made with butter; others use vegetable shortening. Some recipes look exactly like a hermit bar recipe with buttercream frosting between the layers and on top. This is a cake left largely to memory.

HELLO DOLLIES

½ cup (1 stick) lightly salted butter

1½ cups graham cracker crumbs (from 8 whole crackers)

1 cup finely chopped pecans or walnuts

1 cup sweetened shredded coconut

1½ cups semisweet chocolate chips

½ cup butterscotch chips

1 can (14 ounces) sweetened condensed milk

MAKES: 24 (2") squares

WHEN I TASTE THESE seven-layer bars, my mouth gets so happy that all I can say is, "Hello Dollies!" And I would add, "it's so nice to have you back where you belong." But I'd better stop because the copyright police will arrest me for reeling off the words of the title song of the 1960s Broadway musical called *Hello, Dolly!* and starring Carol Channing. Which is possibly how that name got attached to this '60s bar cookie of graham cracker crumbs, coconut, nuts, chocolate, butterscotch, butter, and sweetened condensed milk. That's how it works with naming recipes. If it sounds good and everyone is talking about it, then the name sticks.

These bars were also called magic bars, seven-layer bars, or yum-yum bars, depending on where you lived in the country. And there were slight regional differences exhibited in Hello Dollies, such as pecans used in Texas and walnuts in Minnesota. With the assortment of food manufacturers represented in this recipe, it's possible this recipe was shared on the back of a package. And you found it in newspaper columns and community cookbooks in a postwar period when convenience was king and seemingly effortless recipes like this represented the new prosperity.

But that's getting terribly technical about a recipe created for pleasure. Here is that original recipe, adapted to suit the modern palate.

PREP: 5 TO 10 MINUTES   BAKE: 25 TO 30 MINUTES

---

1. Place a rack in the center of the oven, and preheat the oven to 350°F. Place the stick of butter in a 13" × 9" baking pan, and place the pan in the oven so the butter can melt, 5 to 7 minutes, depending on your oven.

2. Remove the pan from the oven, and tip the pan to let the melted butter coat the bottom evenly. Pack the graham cracker crumbs on top of the butter to create an even bottom crust. Scatter on the nuts, then the coconut. Add a layer of chocolate chips, then butterscotch chips. Finally, pour the condensed milk on top, tipping the pan as needed to let the milk run evenly throughout the pan. Place the pan in the oven.

3. Bake the squares until well browned around the edges, 25 to 30 minutes. Remove the pan from the oven, and let it cool for 20 minutes before cutting into squares. These store covered at room temperature up to 1 week or in the fridge for up to 2 weeks.

THE BEST LEMON SQUARES

CRUST

1 cup (2 sticks) unsalted butter, at room temperature

$1/2$ cup confectioners' sugar

$1/2$ teaspoon salt

2 cups all-purpose flour

FILLING

3 cups granulated sugar

$1/2$ cup plus 1 tablespoon all-purpose flour

2 large or 3 medium lemons

6 large eggs

TOPPING

2 teaspoons confectioners' sugar, for dusting

MAKES: 24 ($2^1/_4$") squares

PICK UP AN OLD Junior League cookbook and you might find telltale smudges on the lemon squares recipes. With their shortbreadlike crust and intense lemon curd–like filling, they were the favorite, iconic dessert of the 1960s, served after tomato aspic and shrimp salad at white-gloved luncheons across the country.

But lemon squares are much older than you might imagine. At the end of the 19th century, department store cooking schools offered classes in baking bread and desserts to better acquaint the cook with the new modern gas range. In the basement of the John Wanamaker store in Philadelphia in June of 1899, women were baking lemon squares, which were square lemon layer cakes. By the 1930s, lemon squares had become less of a cake and more of a bakery cookie popular in the Midwest. The first recipe for the confection resembling what we bake today appeared in the *Des Moines Register* in January 1940, and columnist Wilma Phillips Stewart writes how to roll the biscuit dough $1/2$" thick, cut it into squares, press a sugar cube into each square, and moisten with lemon juice and grated rind before baking. There is also a good chance that our lemon squares are native to England and came to us via Canada. Canadian food writers wrote in the 1940s how this recipe was a favorite. But it took Cecily Brownstone, the *Associated Press* food writer, to mention them in 1951, and for their popularity to explode. Lemon squares became dear to caterers and home cooks as the perfect do-ahead, pickup dessert for weddings, funerals, teas, and, yes, the ladies' lunch. The lemon square remains a perennial American favorite. What's not to like? A crisp, buttery crust and plenty of mouth-puckering fresh lemon flavor in the curdlike filling. Yum!

PREP: 30 TO 35 MINUTES   BAKE: 40 TO 46 MINUTES

---

1. Place a rack in the center of the oven, and preheat the oven to 350°F. Set aside an ungreased metal 13"× 9" baking pan.

2. For the crust, place the butter in the bowl of an electric mixer and beat on low speed until the butter is creamed, about 1 minute. Add the confectioners' sugar and salt, and blend until fluffy, 30 seconds. Turn off the mixer and scrape down the sides of the bowl with a rubber spatula. Add half of the flour to the

(continued on next page)

bowl, then blend on low until incorporated, 30 to 45 seconds. Add the remaining flour and blend until just combined, 15 to 20 seconds. Turn the dough into the pan and, with floured fingertips, press the dough evenly across the bottom of the pan. Prick the dough with a fork in 12 to 15 places (this lets steam escape when baking so the dough won't bubble). Place the pan in the oven and bake the crust until lightly golden, 12 to 14 minutes. Remove the pan from the oven.

3. While the crust is baking, make the filling. Whisk together the granulated sugar and flour in a medium-size bowl. Set aside. Rinse and pat dry the lemons. Grate enough zest to yield 1 tablespoon zest. Cut the lemons in half and juice them to yield $\frac{1}{2}$ cup plus 1 tablespoon fresh lemon juice. Add the lemon juice, zest, and eggs to the sugar and flour mixture and beat with an electric mixer on low speed until just combined, but not frothy, about 1 minute. Pour the filling over the warm baked crust and return it to the oven.

4. Bake the lemon squares until the center is set and they are lightly golden, 28 to 32 minutes. Remove the pan from the oven, and place it on a rack to cool to room temperature, about 1 hour. Cut into squares. For the topping, dust the squares with confectioners' sugar and serve. Lemon squares keep covered up to 4 days at room temperature, a week in the fridge, and up to 2 months in the freezer.

Berry Good Lemon Squares

You can create blueberry, blackberry, or raspberry lemon squares by adding 1 cup fresh fruit to the recipe. First, rinse the fruit and drain it very well on paper towels. If the blackberries are large, cut them in half. After you have poured the lemon filling onto the crust, and the squares have baked 20 minutes, open the oven and carefully scatter the fruit evenly on top. Press down gently onto the fruit with your fingers to anchor it in the filling. Close the oven door and continue baking another 8 to 12 minutes.

ZUCCHINI SPICE BARS

Vegetable oil spray and waxed paper for prepping the pan

3 cups all-purpose flour

1 tablespoon ground cinnamon

1 teaspoon ground nutmeg

1 teaspoon baking soda

$\frac{1}{2}$ teaspoon salt

$\frac{1}{2}$ teaspoon baking powder

$\frac{1}{4}$ teaspoon ground ginger or cloves

2 large eggs

2 cups granulated sugar

1 cup vegetable oil

1 teaspoon vanilla extract

2 packed cups grated zucchini (1 pound)

CREAMY BROWN SUGAR GLAZE

4 ounces cream cheese, at room temperature

4 tablespoons lightly salted butter, at room temperature

$\frac{1}{2}$ cup light brown sugar, firmly packed

$\frac{1}{2}$ teaspoon vanilla extract

MAKES: About 4 dozen (3" × 1$\frac{1}{2}$") bars

WITH AN AUGUST BIRTHDAY, I've grown accustomed to a birthday cake made with zucchini from our garden. This bar recipe is an offshoot of that layer cake, something I created when short on time. It is easy to pull together for late-summer to fall weekend entertaining. And it begs to be baked ahead—the spices seem to improve in flavor when the cake sits and waits patiently to be served.

Baking with zucchini began right after carrot cake mania. It was the late 1970s, and cakes had gone through a renaissance of sorts, moving from butter cakes to easy-assemble cakes using oil. These cakes were moist, and they contained carrots, zucchini, sweet potatoes, pumpkin, and apples. And they are still popular.

PREP: 35 TO 40 MINUTES   BAKE: 20 TO 25 MINUTES

---

1. Place a rack in the center of the oven, and preheat the oven to 350°F. Mist an 18" × 12" half sheet (jelly roll) pan with vegetable oil and line the bottom with waxed or parchment paper.

2. Stir together the flour, cinnamon, nutmeg, baking soda, salt, baking powder, and ginger or cloves in a medium-size bowl.

3. Place the eggs and granulated sugar in a large mixing bowl and blend with an electric mixer on low speed until combined, 1 minute. Increase the speed to medium and blend until lemon colored, 2 minutes. Add the oil and vanilla and blend until combined, 1 minute. Fold in the flour mixture. Fold in the zucchini. Stir until the ingredients are well combined. Pour into the prepared pan, and place the pan in the oven.

4. Bake the cake until it springs back when you press the top lightly with your fingers, 20 to 25 minutes. Remove from the oven.

5. Meanwhile, for the glaze, place the cream cheese and butter in a medium-size bowl and beat with the mixer on low speed until creamy, 1 minute. Add the brown sugar and vanilla and beat until smooth, 1 minute. Spread the glaze over the top of the warm cake. Let the cake rest 30 minutes before slicing into 4 dozen bars (depending on how large you slice them.) Store the bars in the fridge for up to 1 week or the freezer for up to 3 months.

PECAN SURPRISE BARS

CRUST

1 package
(18.25 ounces) yellow
cake mix, divided use

½ cup (1 stick)
unsalted butter,
melted

1 large egg, lightly
beaten

FILLING

½ cup light brown
sugar, lightly packed

1½ cups dark corn
syrup

1 teaspoon vanilla
extract

3 large eggs

1½ cups roughly
chopped pecans

¼ teaspoon sea salt, if
desired

MAKES: About 3 dozen
(3¼" × 1") bars

BAKING TIP: *For a
Kentucky twist, add a
couple of teaspoons
bourbon and a
handful of miniature
chocolate chips to the
filling.*

WHEN OUR FAMILY STAGED a family reunion a few years ago, my cousin Mary Beth shared this bar recipe her mom used to bake in the 1960s and '70s in Wayne, Pennsylvania. It was a favorite recipe of Mary Beth's father because "anything with pecans was right up his alley," she said. And her mom, my Aunt Jane, knew this recipe was easy to pull together because it began with a cake mix! Thus the recipe's name—you will be surprised it begins with a mix. Ever since the 1950s, when cake mixes rose in popularity, busy cooks have used them to jump-start bar and cookie recipes. This recipe has lasted through the years because you would never guess it contains a mix and because it tastes just like pecan pie! If you don't have pecans, use walnuts.

PREP: 25 TO 30 MINUTES   BAKE: 40 TO 50 MINUTES

---

1. Measure out ⅔ cup of the mix and place in a large bowl for the filling. Set aside.

2. Place a rack in the center of the oven, and preheat oven to 350°F.

3. For the crust, place the remaining cake mix, the melted butter, and egg in a large bowl and stir with a fork until the mixture comes together into a ball, 1 minute. Turn the dough into a 13" × 9" metal baking pan. With your fingertips, press the dough to cover the bottom. Place the pan in the oven and bake until golden brown, 15 to 20 minutes. Remove the pan from the oven.

4. For the filling, place the brown sugar, corn syrup, vanilla, and eggs in the bowl with the ⅔ cup reserved cake mix. Beat with an electric mixer on low speed until the ingredients are combined, 20 seconds. Increase the speed to medium and beat until well combined, 2 minutes. Pour the filling over the top of the crust. Scatter the pecans on top of the filling. Sprinkle with the sea salt, if desired. Place the pan in the oven.

5. Bake until deeply brown and the filling has nearly set, 25 to 30 minutes. Remove the pan to a rack to cool 20 minutes, then cut into bars and serve. These bars keep covered at room temperature for up to 5 days.

OATMEAL JAM BARS

3 cups all-purpose
flour

3 cups quick-cooking
oats

2 cups light brown
sugar, lightly packed

2 teaspoons baking
powder

1 teaspoon salt

1½ cups (3 sticks)
unsalted butter,
melted

3 cups peach, apricot,
raspberry, or cherry
jam or preserves

MAKES: About 4 dozen
(3" × 1½") bars

ONE OF THE MORE popular recipes of the early 20th century, the jam bar combines the crunch of an oatmeal cookie and whatever jam or preserves are in your fridge. Economy, resourcefulness, speed, and comforting flavors—these were all factors playing into the success and staying power of this recipe through the years.

A friend, Missy Myers, passed along the Little St. Simons Apricot Oatmeal Bars recipe to me several years back. It was an old family recipe she made each year vacationing at the beach. I have since turned that recipe into a blueprint, because you can use whatever jam is on hand. And feel free to add cinnamon or chopped nuts to the oatmeal mixture, creating your own recipe.

PREP: 15 TO 20 MINUTES   BAKE: 35 TO 40 MINUTES

1. Place a rack in the center of the oven, and preheat the oven to 350°F.

2. Place the flour, oats, brown sugar, baking powder, and salt in a large bowl and stir to combine. Pour in the melted butter and stir with a wooden spoon to make a crumbly mixture. Press 5 cups of this mixture into the bottom of an 18" × 12" half sheet (jelly roll) pan. Spread the preserves evenly over the oats mixture, then crumble the remaining oat mixture randomly over the top of the preserves. Place the pan in the oven.

3. Bake the bars until bubbly around the edges and lightly browned, 35 to 40 minutes. Remove the pan to a rack to cool completely, at least 2 hours. Slice and serve. For easiest slicing, bake these bars ahead of time, let them come to room temperature, then chill for an hour before slicing. The bars keep at room temperature for up to 4 days or in the freezer for up to 4 months.

MAIDA HEATTER'S SANTA FE BROWNIES

CHOCOLATE LAYER

Soft butter for prepping the pan

1½ cups unbleached all-purpose flour

1½ teaspoons baking powder

¾ teaspoon salt

6 ounces unsweetened chocolate, chopped

6 ounces (1 cup) semisweet chocolate chips

1 cup (2 sticks) unsalted butter

5 large eggs

1¼ cups granulated sugar

1½ cups dark brown sugar, firmly packed

1 tablespoon vanilla extract

2¼ cups (8 ounces) chopped walnuts, divided use

MAKES: 32 (2¼" × 1½") brownies

(continued on next page)

DESSERT MAVEN AND AUTHOR Maida Heatter perfected power brownies in the 1980s. She has been one of the most important cookie and bar influencers in our country, and she found these particular brownies in a pastry shop on the historic Santa Fe Plaza decades ago and shared the recipe in her *Maida Heatter's Best Dessert Book Ever* book. There is nothing regionally "Santa Fe" about them, but when Heatter shared them, this was a turning point for brownie bakers. That's because these brownies are deep, dark, fudgy, and unapologetic. They contain a ribbon of cream cheese running through them and are outrageously delicious. They're fussy to make, and Maida was meticulous about her instructions. But you want these brownies, need these brownies, and so you put in the effort. And then, once you taste one, you understand in a mouthful the 1980s and how Maida changed our brownies forever.

PREP: 40 TO 45 MINUTES   BAKE: 1 HOUR 10 TO 15 MINUTES   COOL: 4 HOURS

1. Place a rack in the center of the oven, and preheat the oven to 350°F. Line a 13" × 9" pan with heavy-duty aluminum foil. (This is how Maida did it: She turned the pan upside down and centered an 18" length of foil over it, then pressed the foil around the corners and down the sides to fit the pan. Then she removed the foil, turned the pan over, filled it with water, emptied out the water to wet the pan, and placed the foil liner into the still-wet pan. It sticks better that way.) Place 1 teaspoon of butter in the pan, and place the pan in the oven for a few minutes to melt the butter. Blot the butter with paper towels and dab this on the sides of the pan so the bottom and sides are greased. Set the pan aside.

2. Sift together the flour, baking powder, and salt in a small bowl. Place the chocolates and the 1 cup butter in a heavy-bottomed saucepan over low heat, and stir until the chocolate and butter have melted and the mixture is smooth, 4 to 5 minutes.

3. Place the eggs in a large bowl and beat with an electric mixer on medium speed just to combine, 1 minute. Add the granulated sugar, brown sugar, and vanilla and beat until smooth, 30 seconds. Add the chocolate mixture to the bowl and beat on

(continued on next page)

12 ounces cream cheese, at room temperature

6 tablespoons (3 ounces) unsalted butter, at room temperature

1½ teaspoons vanilla extract

¾ cup granulated sugar

3 large eggs

low until just combined, 15 seconds. Add the flour mixture, beating until just combined, 30 seconds more. Scrape down the sides of the bowl with a rubber spatula, and stir until smooth. Set aside 2¼ cups of the mixture in a medium-size bowl. Add about 1⅔ cups of the walnuts to the chocolate mixture remaining in the large bowl. Stir to combine. Spread this chocolate and nut mixture in the prepared pan.

4. For the cream cheese layer, place the cream cheese and butter in a large bowl and beat with clean beaters on medium speed until smooth, 30 seconds. Add the vanilla and sugar and beat until smooth. Add the eggs, one at a time, beating until smooth, about 1 minute total. Scrape down the sides of the bowl and pour the cream cheese mixture on top of the chocolate mixture in the pan. Spread it to the edges of the pan. Stir the remaining chocolate mixture and dollop it in tablespoons over the cream cheese layer. It does not need to cover all the cheese layer or reach the edges of the pan. Cut through the top chocolate layer and cream cheese layer with a table knife to create a marble effect. Sprinkle the remaining walnuts over the top. Place the pan in the oven.

5. Bake the cake until a wooden pick inserted in the center comes out clean, between 1 hour 10 and 15 minutes. The chocolate layers should be barely clean and not runny. Do not overbake. You can tent the pan with foil during the last 10 minutes if needed to prevent overbrowning. Transfer the pan to a wire rack and let the brownies cool in the pan for 4 hours.

6. When ready to serve, cover the pan with a baking sheet or cutting board and turn the pan and board upside down. Remove the pan and the foil lining. Cover the cake with waxed paper and then another board or baking sheet and turn upside down, leaving the cake right side up. Mark the cake into quarters with a sharp knife, and cut each quarter into 8 brownies. Serve at once. Or chill for up to 1 week or freeze for up to 4 months.

ADD A SOUTHWEST TOUCH: Brush the cooling brownies with Kahlúa.

FLOURLESS CHOCOLATE BROWNIES

Vegetable oil spray for prepping the pan

$\frac{1}{2}$ cup (1 stick) unsalted butter

$\frac{1}{4}$ cup unsweetened cocoa powder

$\frac{1}{2}$ cup light brown sugar, firmly packed

$\frac{1}{2}$ cup granulated sugar

1 teaspoon vanilla extract

2 large eggs

$\frac{1}{4}$ cup cornstarch

$\frac{1}{2}$ teaspoon salt

$\frac{1}{2}$ cup semisweet chocolate chips or chopped semisweet chocolate

---

MAKES: 16 (2") brownies

SEVERAL YEARS BACK, I was asked by a reader to come up with a recipe for gluten-free brownies. At first I thought the task formidable, because how could you make a brownie without wheat flour—somehow, substituting the gritty rice flour just wouldn't do. But then I got to thinking about how flourless chocolate cakes rise and it isn't with flour—it's often the chocolate and eggs that allow that cake to rise up. I wondered if the same could be true for brownies. So as I usually do when developing recipes, I found a mixing bowl and a blank sheet of paper and began testing. And with a half-dozen tries, I settled on this gem of a recipe, made with cocoa and a little cornstarch. What you get is a super-fudgy brownie that everyone loves, gluten-free diet or not.

PREP: 10 TO 15 MINUTES   BAKE: 25 TO 30 MINUTES

---

1. Place a rack in the center of the oven, and preheat the oven to 350°F. Lightly mist an 8" square baking pan with the vegetable oil spray and set it aside.

2. Place the butter in a medium-size saucepan over low heat and stir until melted. Add the cocoa and stir until it thickens and smooth, about 20 seconds. Remove the pan from the heat and stir in the brown sugar, granulated sugar, and vanilla until smooth, 30 seconds. Break the eggs into the pan and stir to combine well. Add the cornstarch and salt and stir until smooth. Fold in the chocolate. Turn the batter into the prepared pan, and place the pan in the oven.

3. Bake the brownies until the edges are firm, the top is shiny, and the center is just set, 25 to 30 minutes. Remove the pan from the oven, and let the brownies cool at room temperature for 1 hour. For best slicing, place in the freezer for up to 1 hour. Slice and serve. Then store covered at room temperature up to 3 days, in the fridge for up to a week, or in the freezer for up to 6 months.

BAKING TIPS: *If you like gooey brownies, bake them for 25 minutes, and if you like chewy brownies, bake them for 30 minutes. Add a scattering of finely chopped pecans or walnuts to the top before baking, if desired.*

NANAIMO BARS

CRUST

Soft butter and parchment paper for prepping the pan

2 large eggs

1 cup (2 sticks) unsalted butter, melted

$\frac{2}{3}$ cup unsweetened cocoa powder

$\frac{1}{2}$ cup granulated sugar

3 cups graham cracker crumbs (from 18 crackers)

2 cups (about 6 ounces) sweetened shredded coconut

1 cup (about 7 ounces) finely chopped walnuts

FILLING

4 tablespoons unsalted butter

2 tablespoons whole milk

2 teaspoons vanilla extract

2 cups confectioners' sugar

MAKES: About 24 ($2\frac{1}{4}$") squares

IN A BEAUTIFUL AND remote part of western Canada, in the town of Nanaimo (pronounced "nuh-NIGH-moe") on Vancouver Island, comes this intensely rich, triple-layer chocolate bar recipe now associated with Seattle and the Pacific Northwest.

No one seems to know its origin, but when the *Seattle Times* found a local expert on the bars, a University of Victoria English professor and Nanaimo native, he said the recipe dates back to the 1950s. According to professor G. Kim Blank, the recipe was found in his mother's cookbook from the Women's Association of the Brechin United Church. That would fit with the ingredients, because the combination of graham cracker crumbs and coconut is right out of the '50s.

Yet it's really Seattle-based Starbucks that put Nanaimo Bars on our radar. Starbucks placed the bars in their pastry cases nationwide, and forever since we have associated them with Seattle and Washington State.

This is a three-layer recipe that's not tough to assemble, but it does take a little time because you've got to let the cakelike crust cool to room temperature before you can pour over the sweet buttercreamlike filling. And that has to chill until firm before you can pour over the melted chocolate glaze. And that in turn needs to chill before you can slice and serve. So build in some extra time when making this recipe.

And think about how you'd like to slice these chocolate treasures. Technically, the way I have the recipe sliced below, this is a "square" and not a "bar." Squares, as you may recall from geometry, have even sides. Bars, on the other hand, are rectangles, and one set of sides is longer than the other. So if you are particular about these being bars, slice them into pieces about 3" long × 1" wide. Whatever you do, cut small portions, as these are very rich and delicious!

This recipe is adapted slightly from one shared by the *Seattle Times* in 2010.

PREP: 25 TO 30 MINUTES   BAKE: 12 TO 15 MINUTES   COOL: 1 HOUR
CHILL: 1 HOUR 20 MINUTES

1. Place a rack in the center of the oven, and preheat the oven to 350°F. Lightly grease a 13" × 9" pan with soft butter and line it

GLAZE

4 tablespoons unsalted butter

8 ounces (about 1¼ cups) semisweet chocolate chips or chopped chocolate

with parchment paper, leaving 1" extended over the longer sides of the pan. Set aside.

2. For the crust, place the eggs in a very large bowl and whisk to break up the yolks. Add the melted butter, cocoa, and granulated sugar. Whisk until smooth, about 1 minute. Add the graham cracker crumbs, coconut, and walnuts and stir to combine using a large wooden spoon, 1 minute. When the ingredients are well incorporated, turn the mixture into the prepared pan, and place the pan in the oven.

3. Bake the cake until the top springs back when pressed with a finger, 12 to 15 minutes. Remove the pan from the oven and transfer to a wire rack to cool to room temperature, about 1 hour.

4. When the cake has cooled, prepare the filling. Place the butter in a large saucepan over low heat, stirring until melted, about 2 minutes. Add the milk and vanilla and stir to combine. Whisk in the confectioners' sugar until smooth, then pour the mixture over the cooled cake, spreading it to the edges. Place the pan, uncovered, in the fridge to set, about 1 hour.

5. For the glaze, place the butter and chocolate in a large glass bowl and heat in the microwave oven on medium power for 60 seconds. Stir. Heat until melted and smooth, about 30 seconds more. Stir again until smooth. Remove the pan from the refrigerator and pour the chocolate glaze over the top, spreading it evenly to the edges. Score the surface into 24 squares, about 2¼", or choose the size you like. Place the pan back in the fridge until the glaze has set, about 20 minutes. Remove, slice, and serve. You can store these at room temperature in a cool kitchen for up to 2 days, or keep them covered in the fridge for up to 1 week.

5

TEA CAKES, POLITICS & CONVERSATION

Talking politics in polite company isn't something that etiquette experts advise, but it's been going on in genteel circles in America for centuries. The conversation over tea and cakes, cookies, bars, and squares really depends on the place in time.

When you think about America's grassroots brand of democracy, it makes sense that before cable news and the Internet, hot-button issues like taxes, the right to vote, and entering war might need to be discussed in home parlors, at picnics, at church revivals, and in tearooms. As America's boundaries expanded beyond the 13 colonies, that frontier environment created an isolation and deep need to socialize with others.

One of the first gatherings over tea and cakes that we still have records of today was, in fact, a tea-less party in Edenton, North Carolina, in 1774. The colonists were enraged over British taxation, and a group of 51 ladies gathered for cake and to sign a petition that they would not bring expensive British tea into their homes. The meeting would be called the Edenton Tea Party, and I share that tea cake recipe in this chapter.

Post-Revolution, when political parties were beginning to take shape, social gatherings served as ways for people to meet candidates or honor elected officials. On the table were some of our first patriotic cakes, and I share the Webster Cakes and Jackson Jumble recipes in this chapter.

Dolley Madison Seed Cakes were baked to pay tribute to the wife of President James Madison, who had the forethought and moxie to pull the portrait of George Washington from the wall of the White House before she left and the British invaded the city at the onset of the War of 1812. And queen cakes, which pre-dated Washington Cakes, were so named for Queen Charlotte, the wife of George III, king during the American Revolutionary War.

After the end of the Civil War, many freed slaves left the South and took with them their recipes for tea cakes, which came to represent their diaspora. Tea cakes have a special meaning to African Americans whose ancestors migrated to other parts of the country.

Other memorable little cakes from our history and present include madeleines, whoopie pies, chocolate bouchons, ladyfingers, ginger cakes, black and white cookies, coconut cupcakes, marguerites, and pecan tassies—small sweets that have their own stories to tell.

As America changed, our conversations changed. Railroads drew people of different backgrounds and regions together. Immigrants relocated here. The little cakes baked and served were forever changed by new ideas, customs, and conversation.

QUEEN CHARLOTTE CAKES

Butter and flour for prepping the pan

1 cup (2 sticks) unsalted butter, at room temperature

1¼ cups granulated sugar

4 large eggs

1 medium lemon (see Baking Tip)

2 cups all-purpose flour

1 cup currants

MAKES: 12 to 16 servings

WHILE KING CAKES WERE popular in New Orleans, the cake of the day in the Colonies was the queen cake or smaller queen cakes. A pound cake batter flavored with lemon or nutmeg and loaded with currants, the queen cake was so-named to honor England's Queen Charlotte, wife of King George III. And it was first named when the cake was baked for the queen's visit, according to Nic Butler, Charleston food historian. The plural of the word *cake* usually implied small cakes, individual cakes baked in a round or heart-shaped tin, and early queen cakes were small cakes. Hannah Glasse, an English food writer whose cookbooks were much used in Colonial America, shares a recipe for the individual cakes in her book *The Art of Cookery, Made Plain and Easy* in 1760. But queen cakes share a lot in common with the later Washington Cakes and beg the question if after the Revolutionary War it was more patriotic to rename your recipe after George Washington rather than the British queen. If you don't have miniature muffin pans or molds, you can bake the batter in a loaf pan and cut the cake into squares or small slices. The following recipe is adapted from a Williamsburg recipe as featured in Mary Miley Theobald's book, *Recipes from the Raleigh Tavern Bake Shop*.

PREP: 20 MINUTES   BAKE: 70 TO 75 MINUTES

---

1. Place a rack in the center of the oven, and preheat the oven to 325°F. Grease and flour a 9" loaf pan with butter and flour, and shake out the excess flour.

2. Place the soft butter and sugar in a large mixing bowl and beat with an electric mixer on medium speed until light and creamy, about 2 minutes. Add the eggs, one at a time, beating well after each addition.

3. Grate the zest from the lemon to yield 2 teaspoons. Slice the lemon in half and juice the halves to yield 2 tablespoons. Fold the zest and juice into the butter and sugar mixture with a wooden spoon or rubber spatula.

4. Remove 1 tablespoon from the flour and toss with the currants. Fold the remaining flour into the batter, a little at a time. Fold in

(continued on next page)

the flour-dusted currants. Turn the batter into the prepared pan, and place the pan in the oven.

5. Bake the cake until golden brown and a toothpick inserted in the center comes out clean, 70 to 75 minutes. Transfer the pan to a wire rack to cool for 20 minutes. Run a knife around the edges of the pan, and give the pan a gentle shake. Invert the cake once and then again so it cools right side up on a rack for 45 minutes. Slice into small slices or squares and arrange on a platter. These cakes keep, lightly covered, at room temperature for up to 3 days or in the freezer for up to 1 month.

BAKING TIP: *You need 2 tablespoons lemon juice and 2 teaspoons grated lemon zest, which should come from a medium-size lemon.*

Prized Citrus Flavors in Early Cakes

Lemons were a much-loved flavoring in early American cakes and had to be imported for baking. The best lemons were said to be from Lisbon, Portugal, and lemon was reserved for special, commemorative desserts, such as these Queen Cakes. American author Eliza Leslie said queen cakes should be flavored only with lemon. The citrus was also used to flaunt wealth and would be placed as decoration in wreaths and in table arrangements. Oranges, while also prized as an ingredient and decoration, were cultivated by the Spanish in Florida. And the prized satsuma orange was grown in Louisiana and along the Gulf Coast.

WEBSTER CAKES

Soft butter and flour for prepping the pan

1 cup (4½ ounces) currants

2 tablespoons brandy or dark rum

1 cup (2 sticks) unsalted butter, at room temperature

1¼ cups granulated sugar

5 large eggs, at room temperature

1 tablespoon fresh lemon or orange juice

½ teaspoon grated lemon or orange zest

2 cups unbleached all-purpose flour

½ teaspoon salt

2 teaspoons confectioners' sugar, for garnish

MAKES: 36 (1½") cakes

LAWYER, ORATOR, AND POLITICIAN Daniel Webster was well known in America in the early 1800s. Born in New Hampshire, Webster lived in Boston most of his life and became a senator from Massachusetts. Being such a high-profile man, people baked cakes and named them after him.

These Webster Cakes were full of currants and brandy. They were scented with lemon and orange, and they were constructed of butter, sugar, flour, and eggs, much like a fancy pound cake. Except they were baked in a small pan, cut into squares, dusted with sugar, and served at tea. Perhaps a tea supporting the Whig Party, of which Webster was a staunch member?

Webster Cakes were different from the simple tea cakes known as Jackson Jumbles in much the same way that well-heeled Daniel Webster differed from the frontiersman and Democrat Andrew Jackson. America was a new country, and one way of expressing this new nationalism was getting behind a cause, a politician, a political party—and even naming recipes after them.

SOAK: 1 HOUR   PREP: 10 TO 15 MINUTES   BAKE: 21 TO 25 MINUTES
COOL: 20 MINUTES

---

1. Place the currants in a plastic container with lid, and pour the brandy or rum over them to coat. Close the container and set the currants aside to soak for 1 hour, or until the liquor is absorbed.

2. Meanwhile, place a rack in the center of the oven, and preheat the oven to 350°F. Lightly grease a 9" square pan with soft butter and dust with flour.

3. Place the butter and granulated sugar in a large mixing bowl and beat with an electric mixer on medium speed until light and creamy, 1 minute. Scrape down the sides of the bowl with a rubber spatula. Add the eggs, one at a time, and beat just until blended. Scrape down the sides of the bowl. Add the lemon or orange juice and zest, and beat just to combine. Add the flour and salt in three additions, beating until just combined after each addition. Fold in the soaked currants. Scrape down the

(continued on next page)

sides of the bowl, and turn the batter into the prepared pan. Place the pan in the oven.

4. Bake the cake until golden brown around the edges and the top springs back when lightly pressed with a finger, 21 to 25 minutes. Remove the pan from the oven, and place the pan on a wire rack to cool for 20 minutes. Dust with the confectioners' sugar. Cut into squares and serve. Store these cakes covered at room temperature for up to 5 days, or freeze them for up to 2 months.

Whig Cakes and a Little Explanation

Whig Cakes were originally British tea cakes, according to Mark Zanger in The American History Cookbook. *In fact, in England, Whig Cakes have nothing to do with politics and are wedges of cake. The word* whig *comes from the Middle English spelling of "wedge." Ironically, sweet, round breads cut into quarters were the tea cakes baked and served at parties for the American Whigs—Daniel Webster, Henry Clay, and Presidents Harrison, Taylor, Tyler, and Fillmore. The word* Whig, *when used to describe a political party, comes from the British Whig party. It was so named after the Presbyterian Scots, called "Whiggamors."*

DOLLEY MADISON SEED CAKES

Soft butter for greasing the pan

1 cup (2 sticks) unsalted butter, at room temperature

Generous ¾ cup (6 ounces) sifted granulated sugar (see Baking Tip)

3 large eggs

1½ cups plus 2 tablespoons all-purpose flour

½ teaspoon caraway seeds

¼ teaspoon ground mace

¼ teaspoon ground nutmeg

¼ teaspoon salt

1½ ounces brandy

MAKES: 36 (1½" × 1½") cakes

BAKING TIP: *Sift the granulated sugar into a bowl and measure ¾ cup.*

PRESIDENT JAMES MADISON'S WIFE, Dolley, was known for her hospitality, conversational skills, and this seed cake recipe. It is said that Dolley served these caraway seed cakes to visiting dignitaries, including the British minister David Erskine during his visit in 1809. But when times weren't so peaceful, Dolley was a symbol of American strength. She carried the portrait of George Washington, along with valuable documents and silver, out of the White House when the British were advancing on Washington, DC, in the War of 1812. How ironic, then, that the recipe most associated with Dolley is a British recipe. Pound cake batters studded with caraway, anise, cumin, or coriander seeds were beloved British cakes that made their way to America. They held a special fascination and symbolized religious holidays (Lent) as well as the change of seasons (sowing seeds in spring). Today they are brightly flavored cakes that symbolize a bygone day but are still perfect with a cup of tea or a sip of brandy.

PREP: 15 TO 20 MINUTES   BAKE: 33 TO 37 MINUTES

---

1. Place a rack in the center of the oven, and preheat the oven to 325°F. Lightly grease the bottom and sides of a 9" square pan.
2. Place the butter in a large mixing bowl and beat with an electric mixer on medium speed until creamy, about 1 minute. Add the sugar gradually, while the mixer is running, and beat until creamy and light, 1 minute more. Add the eggs, one at a time, beating well after each addition.
3. Whisk together the flour, caraway seeds, mace, nutmeg, and salt in a medium-size mixing bowl. Add the flour mixture to the butter and sugar mixture and mix on low speed until just combined, 30 seconds. Scrape down the sides of the bowl with a rubber spatula, and stir in the brandy until combined. Turn the batter into the prepared pan, and place the pan in the oven.
4. Bake the cake until very lightly golden brown around the edges, 33 to 37 minutes. Remove the pan from the oven, and place on a wire rack until cool enough to slice, about 20 minutes. Cut into squares and serve still a little warm. These cakes keep covered for up to 4 days at room temperature, or they freeze for up to 4 months.

THOMAS JEFFERSON SAVOY CAKES

6 large eggs, at room temperature

1¼ cups granulated sugar, divided use

1 medium-large orange, washed and patted dry

½ teaspoon salt

1½ cups sifted cake flour

1 cup confectioners' sugar

MAKES: 24 small cakes

OUR THIRD PRESIDENT, THOMAS Jefferson, was a man of many talents. He drafted the Declaration of Independence and composed its well-known preamble about "life, liberty, and the pursuit of happiness." He was Virginia governor, a gentleman farmer, US minister to France, and a complicated idealist noted for his keen intellect and life of contradictions. For example, Jefferson was a slave owner but a proponent of personal liberty. Yet it was Jefferson's love of fine food and wine that led him to record specific recipes while he lived in Paris from 1784 to 1789. In addition to macaroni and ice cream, he wrote down how to make these light sponge cakes called *biscuits de Savoy.* And he brought this French method of beating egg yolks with sugar, adding flour, and then folding in beaten egg whites back to America and to his state-of-the-art kitchen at Monticello, his Virginia home.

This orange-scented cake was the original ladyfinger. And according to Damon Lee Fowler, culinary historian who has studied the Jefferson papers and recipes, this recipe in Jefferson's handwriting is part of the Library of Congress collection. It was shared in later diaries and recipe books belonging to his granddaughters. Interestingly, the recipe is much like the "Spunge Cake" published later—in 1824—by Mary Randolph in *The Virginia House-wife.* Except Mary Randolph's version is flavored with lemon instead of Jefferson's orange and baked in round layers and spread with a warm custard sauce or lemon curd. Here is my modern adaptation of that original Jefferson recipe.

PREP: 25 TO 30 MINUTES   BAKE: 12 TO 14 MINUTES

---

1. Separate the eggs, placing the whites in a medium-size bowl and the yolks in a large mixing bowl. Set both aside. Place a rack in the center of the oven, and preheat the oven to 350°F. Line 24 muffin cups with paper liners, and set aside.

2. Beat the yolks with an electric mixer on medium-high speed until they are thick and lemon-colored, about 2 minutes. Gradually add 1 cup of the granulated sugar, beating until the mixture is smooth.

(continued on next page)

3. Grate the zest from the orange to yield 2 teaspoons. Cut the orange in half and juice it to yield 2$\frac{1}{2}$ tablespoons juice. Set aside 1$\frac{1}{2}$ tablespoons of the juice in a small bowl for the glaze. Add the zest and the remaining 1 tablespoon orange juice to the egg yolk and sugar mixture. Beat on low speed until combined, and set this mixture aside.

4. Beat the egg whites with clean beaters on high speed until soft peaks form, 2 to 3 minutes. Gradually add the remaining $\frac{1}{4}$ cup granulated sugar until stiff peaks form, 2 to 3 minutes longer. Turn the beaten egg whites on top of the yolk mixture. Sift the sifted flour on top of the whites. With a rubber spatula, fold the mixture together until it is well blended. Using a spoon or scoop, dollop the mixture into the lined muffin cups until nearly full. Place the pans in the oven.

5. Bake the cakes until the tops are golden brown, 12 to 14 minutes. Remove them from the oven, and carefully remove the liners from the cups. Place them on a wire rack to cool. The cakes will sink a little as they cool.

6. To make a glaze, place the confectioners' sugar in the bowl with the reserved orange juice. Whisk to combine. Drizzle the glaze over the top of the cooled cakes. Serve at once. These cakes keep, lightly covered, at room temperature for up to 5 days.

LADYFINGERS

4 large eggs, separated

$\frac{1}{2}$ cup granulated sugar

$\frac{1}{2}$ teaspoon vanilla extract

$\frac{1}{4}$ teaspoon salt

1 cup sifted cake flour, divided

2 teaspoons confectioners' sugar for dusting

MAKES: About 24 ladyfingers

MY 1960S MEMORIES OF ladyfingers come from my mother assembling a grand company dessert. She would make some fabulous and light orange charlotte or chocolate mousse and then pile it into a glass dish lined with ladyfingers and stick it in the refrigerator to chill. Once that moussey filling had time to soak into the spongy, delicate ladyfinger cakes, well, you spooned it into serving bowls, dolloped it with whipped cream, and wowed even the finickiest guest.

Today you don't see those refrigerated desserts. And you don't see ladyfingers either—not in desserts or commercially in packages or made at home. They seem to represent a bygone day and era of light and delicate treats, of angel cakes and shimmers of sauces. It was a day when a dessert was intended to be easy on your palate. It was ladylike, sensible, never more than the size of a finger. And other recipe names had similar titles—"date nut fingers" and "finger sandwiches," for example.

If this concept interests you, then you should try your hand at making ladyfingers. They were originally just a stiff sponge cake batter spooned onto the pan in 3" lengths. In fact, the French call them *biscuits à la cuillère* (*cuiller* is the word for spoon). You can still use a spoon to shape them, but you might prefer the uniformity and precision of a pastry bag. Later Americanized versions of the recipe contained butter and fewer egg whites and enough flour to bake a stiff batter. In the *Congressional Club Cook Book* of 1927, the stiff dough is cut into little strips and rolled in sugar before baking.

Here is an old method adapted for today's kitchen. It calls for just the basics—eggs, sugar, flour, vanilla, and a little salt. Bake and enjoy with tea, or serve with your favorite ice cream or chocolate mousse.

PREP: 15 TO 20 MINUTES   BAKE: 6 TO 8 MINUTES

---

1. Place a rack in the center of the oven, and preheat the oven to 400°F. Line 2 baking sheets with parchment or waxed paper.

2. Separate the eggs, placing the yolks in a large bowl and the whites in another large bowl. Beat the egg yolks with an electric mixer on medium-high speed until they are light and lemon-colored, 2 to 3 minutes. Gradually add half of the granulated sugar while you continue to beat until the mixture is thick and

(continued on next page)

lemon-colored and has increased in volume, 2 minutes. Add the vanilla and salt and beat just to combine. Beat the egg whites with clean beaters on high speed until soft peaks form, $1\frac{1}{2}$ to 2 minutes, then gradually add the remaining granulated sugar and beat until stiff peaks form, another 1 to 2 minutes. Sift half of the flour over the egg yolk mixture and fold in lightly. Turn the beaten egg whites on top, and fold them in with a rubber spatula until nearly smooth. Sift the remaining flour over the top of the mixture and fold it until smooth.

3. Gently spoon the batter into a pastry bag fitted with a $\frac{3}{4}$" plain tip and pipe the batter onto the prepared baking sheets into strips 3" to $3\frac{1}{2}$" long. Sprinkle the tops with confectioners' sugar. Place one pan at a time into the oven, and bake until they are lightly browned, 6 to 8 minutes. Remove the pan from the oven, and let the ladyfingers rest on the pan 1 minute. Transfer them with a metal spatula to a wire rack to cool completely. The ladyfingers keep, lightly covered, for up to 5 days at room temperature or for up to 1 month in the freezer.

The Congressional Club Cook Book

In 1908 the Congressional Club in Washington, DC, opened as a social club for wives of the US Senate and House of Representatives. The members collaborated on a fund-raising cookbook in 1927, and have continued to do so, as the cookbook has been revised and is in its 14th edition.

Looking through that first cookbook, in which Mrs. Herbert Hoover wrote the introduction, and in which ambassadors and dignitaries from other countries shared recipes like gnocchi, chocolate mousse, and "gaspacho," you have an open window into the tastes of the time.

Of the cookies and small cake recipes assembled here, the clear favorite baked in 1927 was brownies, followed by icebox cookies, oatmeal cookies, macaroons, ladyfingers, and rocks. In fact the array of these small sweet bites is exhaustive, covering all genres from hard-times bread crumbs cookies—a holdover from World War I—to various cookies and cakes that reflect the melting pot of the changing America. You find German, Scottish, Finnish, Moravian, English, and French influences in the names of the recipes or the stories behind the recipes and why they are still baked. Although the Great Depression was just 2 years away, the 1927 *Congressional Club Cook Book* was clearly written with the 1930s in mind—automobile transportation, toting of food, baking ahead with icebox and "overnight" cookies, and an infatuation for new products on the shelf. Recipe include dates, cornflakes cereal, and even a quick version of an old marguerite cookie where a meringue is piled atop saltine crackers and run under the broiler.

MARGUERITES

½ cup (1 stick) lightly salted butter, at room temperature (see Baking Tip)

½ cup plus 2 teaspoons granulated sugar

3 large eggs, at room temperature, separated

1 scant cup (4 ounces) all-purpose flour, plus more flour for rolling the dough

⅛ teaspoon ground nutmeg

⅓ cup confectioners' sugar

½ to ¾ cup fruit jam (strawberry, blueberry or fig, or lemon curd)

MAKES: About 18 (3") cookies

IF YOU TOP A nutmeg-scented sugar cookie with a dab of fruit jam, then pile on meringue and bake until lightly browned, you have a marguerite. Now, most people will say that's a lot of trouble to go to just for a cookie. But this early-1800s cookie isn't a cookie like we know cookies today.

Marguerites were baked in wealthy households where sugar was available and jam was put up from summer fruit. They were served with tea. And their recipe is found in old Quaker cookbooks and in *The Carolina Housewife*, by Sarah Rutledge, published in 1847. The following recipe is adapted from Rutledge's recipe. It's remarkable that nearly 200 years later, her method can still be followed in today's kitchen. Even though no one bakes marguerites anymore, they should. Marguerites were thought to be named for the French word for a white daisy. Maybe that's how they appeared coming out of the 19th-century oven, something beautiful and white and like no other.

PREP: 40 TO 45 MINUTES   CHILL: 2 HOURS   BAKE: 15 TO 18 MINUTES

1. Place the soft butter and granulated sugar in a large mixing bowl and beat with an electric mixer on medium-high speed until light and creamy, about 1 minute. Add the egg yolks, one at a time, beating well after each addition. Scrape down the bowl with a rubber spatula.

2. Whisk together the flour and nutmeg in a small bowl. Add the flour mixture to the butter and sugar mixture, beating on low speed until just combined, 30 seconds. Scrape down the sides of the bowl, and turn the dough onto a sheet of plastic wrap and wrap tightly. Place in the refrigerator to chill until firm, at least 2 hours.

3. When ready to bake, remove the dough from the refrigerator. Place a rack in the center of the oven, and preheat the oven to 375°F. Scatter a couple of tablespoons flour on a clean working surface, and turn the chilled dough onto the flour. Generously flour a rolling pin. Roll dough out to ¼" thickness. Using a 2½" cookie cutter, cut rounds and place on 2 ungreased baking

(continued on next page)

sheets about 2" apart. Place a pan in the oven. Bake the cookies until lightly browned around the edges, 8 to 10 minutes. Remove the pans from the oven, and transfer the cookies to a wire rack to cool. Repeat with the remaining dough.

4. Increase the oven temperature to 400°F to bake the meringues. Line 2 baking pans with foil, and set them aside.

5. Place the egg whites in a large mixing bowl and beat with clean beaters on high speed until soft peaks form, about 2 minutes. Add the confectioners' sugar a little at a time while the egg whites are beating, and beat on high speed until stiff and glossy peaks form, about 1 minute longer.

6. Arrange the cooled cookies on the lined baking pans. Dollop 1 to $1\frac{1}{2}$ teaspoons jam in the center of each cookie. Dollop about 2 heaping tablespoons of beaten egg whites on top of the jam. Using a small metal spatula, spread the egg whites to the edges of the cookie (to seal the meringue to the cookie so it doesn't shrink when the cookies cool). Place one pan at a time in the oven.

7. Bake the cookies until the meringue is lightly browned, 7 to 8 minutes. Remove the pan from the oven and repeat with the other pan. Using a spatula, carefully go under the warm cookies to transfer them to a wire rack to cool. Serve at once. These keep uncovered at room temperature for 2 days.

BAKING TIP: *If you want to use unsalted butter, add $\frac{1}{8}$ teaspoon salt to the recipe when you add the flour.*

JACKSON JUMBLES

2½ cups unbleached all-purpose flour

¼ teaspoon salt

½ cup (1 stick) unsalted butter, at room temperature

1¼ cups granulated sugar

1 large egg, at room temperature

½ cup plus 2 tablespoons buttermilk

½ teaspoon baking soda

½ teaspoon grated lemon zest or 1 tablespoon brandy, if desired (see Lemon Jumbles on next page)

MAKES: 18 to 24 (3") cakes

WHEN BAKING SODA AND baking powder came into the American pantry in the mid-1800s, the British ring-shaped biscuit (cookie) known as a "jumble" morphed into what we call a tea cake today. It became soft and light, and it often contained buttermilk to work its leavening magic with the soda.

Named after the Battle of New Orleans hero and seventh American president, Jackson Jumbles were like their namesake. They weren't afraid of bucking tradition. Their method of assembly didn't require rolling and cutting—you just dropped the batter onto cast-iron or tin pans and baked. Anyone could do it.

This recipe has also been called Democratic Tea Cakes, and it is edible proof how old-school British recipes evolved once they were baked in America. In the early 1800s and throughout the 19th century, America was moving west, expanding, changing—just like these small cookies and cakes. The following recipe is adapted from a Quaker cookbook called *Domestic Cookery* by Elizabeth Ellicott Lea and published in 1869—24 years after Jackson died. You can flavor them with either "the peel of a fresh lemon grated" or a splash of brandy, as Lea suggests, but Jackson would probably think those flourishes wouldn't be necessary.

PREP: 10 TO 15 MINUTES   BAKE: 11 TO 15 MINUTES

---

1. Place a rack in the center of the oven, and preheat the oven to 375°F.
2. Place the flour and salt in a large bowl and whisk to combine. Cut the butter into tablespoon-size pieces and add to the center of the bowl. Add the sugar and egg on top. Measure the buttermilk into a small bowl and stir in the baking soda to dissolve. Add the buttermilk mixture to the mixing bowl. Add the lemon zest or brandy, if desired. Blend with an electric mixer on low speed (or by hand with a wooden spoon) until the ingredients come together and are smooth, 1 to 1½ minutes.
3. Scoop or spoon a generous ¼ cup of dough onto ungreased baking sheets, spacing them about 2" apart. Place a pan in the oven.

(continued on next page)

4. Bake the cakes until the edges are golden brown and the tops are pale in color but spring back when lightly touched, 11 to 15 minutes. Remove the pan from the oven, let the cakes cool on the pan for 1 minute, then transfer the cakes with a metal spatula to a wire rack to cool completely. Repeat with the remaining dough. These tea cakes keep, lightly covered, at room temperature for up to 4 days.

LEMON JUMBLES

Add $\frac{1}{2}$ teaspoon grated lemon zest (from 1 small lemon) to the dough. Once the jumbles have baked and cooled, drizzle with a lemon glaze made by whisking together $\frac{1}{2}$ cup confectioners' sugar and 1 tablespoon fresh lemon juice from the small lemon. If you need more liquid, add more lemon juice or a little milk to thin the glaze to the right consistency. Stick a butter knife into the glaze and, holding it above the jumbles and moving it in a zigzag fashion, let the glaze fall onto the cookies. It will set as it cools.

WHOOPIE PIES

CAKE

2 cups all-purpose flour

1/2 cup unsweetened cocoa powder

1 1/2 teaspoons baking soda

1/2 teaspoon salt

1/2 cup vegetable shortening

1 cup granulated sugar

1 large egg, at room temperature

1 teaspoon vanilla extract

1 cup buttermilk, at room temperature

FILLING

1/2 cup vegetable shortening

1/2 cup (1 stick) unsalted butter, at room temperature

2 cups confectioners' sugar

2 cups marshmallow creme

2 teaspoons vanilla extract

MAKES: 10 to 12 (3 1/2") cakes

CAKES THAT MASQUERADE AS pies? There's the Boston cream and the shoofly, and also the adorable whoopie—or whoopee—pie. Which isn't a pie at all, but two pillowy chocolate cakes sandwiched together with fluffy marshmallow creme (such as Marshmallow Fluff) filling. It's the stuff of dreams if you are a child or from the Northeast. And if you talk with Mainers and Pennsylvanians as to who was the first to bake a whoopie pie, each will claim the rights. Maine hasn't gone so far as to claim the whoopie pie as its state dessert—that's reserved for the blueberry pie. But its residents do count the Whoopie Pie as their "state snack." And you'll find annual whoopie pie festivals in both states.

Plus, there are differing stories as to how the name of this pie/cake originated. The most believable is that it was named for the 1928 hit song called "Makin' Whoopee!" by Gus Kahn and Walter Donaldson. But this was 3 years after a Lewiston, Maine, bakery called Labadie's baked and advertised their chocolate Whoopie Pies. So it might very well be a bakery confection that baked its way into the home kitchen. Berwick's bakery in Boston was also known for its "Whoopee Pies."

Regardless of how you spell it or where it came from, whoopie pie is an American classic snack cake. It oddly resembles the Moon Pie of the South. It would not have graced the Victorian tables—far too large, way too messy. But it delights children and anyone with a sense of humor and history. And if you don't want to fill your pies with the soft creamy filling, add peppermint or vanilla ice cream instead and store these in the freezer. Whoopie!

PREP: 40 TO 45 MINUTES   BAKE: 11 TO 13 MINUTES

---

1. Place a rack in the center of the oven, and preheat the oven to 350°F. Line 2 baking sheets with parchment paper.

2. Sift the flour and cocoa into a medium-size bowl. Stir in the baking soda and salt until well combined. Set aside.

3. Place the shortening and granulated sugar in a large bowl and beat with an electric mixer on medium-high speed until creamed, about 2 minutes. Add the egg and vanilla, beating until combined. Scrape down the sides of the bowl with a rubber

(continued on next page)

spatula. On low speed, alternately add the flour mixture and the buttermilk, beginning and ending with the flour mixture. Scrape down the sides of the bowl. Dollop scant $\frac{1}{4}$ cups of batter about $2\frac{1}{2}$" apart on the prepared pans. With the back of a spoon, shape the batter into circles about $2\frac{1}{2}$" in diameter. Place one pan in the oven.

4. Bake the cakes until the tops are puffy and a toothpick inserted in the center comes out clean, 11 to 13 minutes. Pull the parchment with the cakes attached off the baking pan and slide it onto a wire rack to cool. When the cakes are cool, run a metal spatula underneath them and transfer the cakes to a serving platter. Repeat with the remaining batter.

5. For the filling, place the shortening, butter, confectioners' sugar, marshmallow creme, and vanilla in a large bowl. Beat with the electric mixer on medium-high speed until the mixture is smooth and well blended, $1\frac{1}{2}$ to 2 minutes. Spread the flat side of half of the cookies with about $\frac{1}{4}$ cup filling. Place the flat side of the remaining cookies on top. Wrap each cookie in plastic wrap until ready to serve. The pies keep up to 5 days at room temperature.

OLD-FASHIONED TEA CAKES

2 cups granulated
sugar

1 cup unsalted butter
(2 sticks), vegetable
shortening, or lard (or
a combination), melted

3 large eggs

1 teaspoon vanilla
extract

4¼ cups all-purpose
flour, divided use

1 tablespoon baking
powder

¼ teaspoon salt

¼ teaspoon ground
nutmeg, if desired

4 tablespoons milk
(see Baking Tip)

MAKES: 3 to 4 dozen
(3") cakes

BAKING TIP: *Notice
that with the baking
powder, you use
regular milk instead of
buttermilk in this
recipe. But many cooks
insist on buttermilk, so
use it if you like for a
more acidic and tangy
flavor. Or use
evaporated milk. If
your oven bakes hot,
turn the temperature
down to 350°F to bake
these more slowly.*

OF ALL THE LITTLE cakes in America's history, the one recipe that creates the most chatter is the "tea cake." You might go so far as to say it is the Southern version of the French madeleine. It is and was a small cake of childhood and one powerful enough to bring back memories.

But tea cakes can't be lumped into one group like the madeleine. They are different in their ingredients and preparation. Some are crisp and golden around the edges. Others are salty from lard. Some are cut into rounds like a cookie, and others are dropped onto the pan before baking. Some are soft and pillowy from the vegetable shortening, and other tea cakes are buttery like shortbread. It really depends on your tastes, because you can customize a tea cake to suit it!

If we go back to the South in 1872, when Annabella P. Hill wrote her book *Mrs. Hill's New Cook Book*, tea cakes were leavened with a little baking soda, rolled thinly, and baked in a hot oven. So you could say they were offshoots of British tea "biscuits" or cookies, except they had been Americanized with the addition of this new leavening.

Flash forward to *The Blue Grass Cook Book* of 1904, and you will find the tea cakes look like pound cake or contain hard-cooked egg yolks and a little baking powder, or they are made with lard and brown sugar. And it is the last variation that is telling about the tea cake story in the South. They evolved from being the small cake baked by enslaved people for their masters to a small cake that was representative of their struggle and adapted by their own families for generations. This did not change after the Civil War as African Americans relocated outside the South and brought their tea cake recipes with them.

Which is what interested Elbert Mackey in creating his Tea Cake Project more than a decade ago. He wanted to preserve the lore of the tea cake, which he said was an important part of the African American recipe collection. "Tea cakes are just part of our history that's gradually fading away."

Athens, Georgia, historian and archivist Valerie J. Frey said rural whites also have been drawn to tea cakes. They might have originally been baked with cornmeal—you baked with corn unless you were rich and could afford wheat flour. The fact that these recipes called for flour tells Frey that these cakes "were not quite everyday. They are a food for company." When wheat flour became more available after the Civil War, their popularity rose.

Testing a dozen or more variations of tea cakes, I settled on a recipe that received the most applause. It has a soft and cakey texture in the center, but the edges are crisp. It contains butter, but you could just as well use vegetable shortening or lard. It doesn't have a glaze, but if you want to add a glaze after baking, stir 2 tablespoons milk into 1 cup confectioners' sugar, and add a little vanilla or almond extract for flavor. Because tea cakes, like people, come in all shapes and sizes.

PREP: 30 TO 35 MINUTES   BAKE: 7 TO 9 MINUTES

---

1. Place a rack in the center of the oven, and preheat the oven to 375°F.

2. Place the sugar in a large mixing bowl. Add the melted butter, shortening, or lard. Blend with an electric mixer on medium speed or a wooden spoon until well incorporated, 1 minute. Add the eggs and vanilla and blend to combine. Set aside.

3. Place $3\frac{1}{4}$ cups of the flour in a medium-size bowl and whisk in the baking powder, salt, and nutmeg, if desired, to combine. Dump the flour mixture into the butter and sugar mixture. Add the milk. Stir with a spoon or mix with the electric mixer on low speed until the mixture comes together and is smooth, 1 minute.

4. Place the remaining 1 cup flour in the middle of a clean work surface and scatter it out loosely with your fingers. With a small 1" scoop or spoon, scoop 1" balls of batter into the flour, and toss them with your fingers to lightly coat. Transfer the balls to an ungreased baking sheet, pressing down slightly to form a circle. Place about 8 circles on each pan, allowing them plenty of room to spread as they bake. Place the pan in the oven.

5. Bake the cakes until the edges are turning light brown but the tops are still pale, 7 to 9 minutes. Remove the pan from the oven and transfer the tea cakes to a wire rack to cool completely. Repeat with the remaining dough. Store the tea cakes in an airtight container at room temperature for up to 1 week or in the freezer for up to 2 months.

EDENTON TEA PARTY CAKES

¾ cup (12 tablespoons) unsalted butter or vegetable shortening (see Baking Tip)

2 cups dark brown sugar, lightly packed

3 large eggs

1 teaspoon baking soda

1 tablespoon warm water

½ teaspoon salt

1 teaspoon vanilla extract

3¾ cups all-purpose flour, plus flour for rolling out the cakes

---

MAKES: 7 to 8 dozen (2") cakes

ON OCTOBER 25, 1774, Penelope Barker invited 51 women from five counties in eastern North Carolina to come to the Edenton home of Elizabeth King for a party. There would be tea cakes, but no tea, because the ladies were protesting the British Tea Act of 1773. They signed a petition to say "in proof of their patriotism" they would not bring British tea or cloth into their homes "until such time that all acts which tend to enslave our Native country shall be repealed."

It was a silent protest that was eventually heard across the Atlantic when a London cartoonist poked fun of the protesting, "uncontrollable" ladies. And yet in America it served as the first recorded organized political event for women. They were praised for initiating this bold boycott, and other such boycotts of British goods followed.

The recipe for those tea cakes has evolved through the years, transforming from crisp tea cookies into little cakes.

PREP: 20 TO 25 MINUTES   BAKE: 8 TO 10 MINUTES

---

1. Place a rack in the center of the oven, and preheat the oven to 375°F.
2. Place the butter and sugar in a large mixing bowl and beat with an electric mixer on medium speed until the mixture is creamy, 1 minute. Add the eggs, one at a time, beating well after each addition. In a small bowl, dissolve the baking soda in the warm water and spoon into the sugar and butter mixture. Add the salt and vanilla. Blend until incorporated, 30 seconds. Add up to 3¾ cups flour, and beat on low speed until the mixture comes together into a stiff dough.
3. Sprinkle some extra flour onto a work surface, and turn the dough onto the flour. Roll until it is ¼" thick, then cut into 2" circles and place on ungreased baking sheets. Place one pan at a time in the oven.

4. Bake the cakes until lightly browned around the edges and still a little soft in the center, 8 to 10 minutes. Remove the cakes immediately from the pan and place on a wire rack to cool completely. Store in a tightly covered container for up to 1 week.

BAKING TIP: *You can use lard instead of the shortening.*

Vegetable Shortening in Tea Cakes

The Edenton ladies of 1774 would not have baked with vegetable shortening, because it wasn't invented until the early 1900s. But vegetable shortening is often seen in tea cake recipes today, and many cooks use shortening because it prevents the cakes from spreading as they bake. When shortening first appeared on grocery shelves, nutritionists thought this new ingredient was more digestible and better tasting than lard. It was cheaper to buy, and vegetarians welcomed a fat that wasn't animal-based.

FOLLOWING PAGE, LEFT TO RIGHT: *Edenton Tea Party Cakes, Victorian Ginger Drop Cakes, and Old-Fashioned Tea Cakes*

VICTORIAN GINGER DROP CAKES

½ cup butter (1 stick) or vegetable shortening, plus a little for greasing the pans

½ cup light brown sugar, firmly packed

1 large egg

⅓ cup molasses

1½ cups all-purpose flour

½ teaspoon ground cinnamon

½ teaspoon ground ginger

¼ teaspoon ground nutmeg

½ teaspoon baking soda

¼ teaspoon salt

½ cup chopped nuts, coconut, or currants for topping, if desired

---

MAKES: 36 drop cakes

DROPPING BATTER INTO PANS before baking was one of the first ways to create tea cakes. The batters were made with white sugar and flavored with lemon, or they were sweetened with molasses and redolent of spices.

In America and England, the period between 1837 and 1901 when Queen Victoria ruled is called the Victorian era. Say the word *Victorian* and your mind wanders to beautiful parlors and ladies sipping tea and nibbling small cakes.

The following tea cake recipe is adapted from a collection of recipes called *Victorian Cakes* by Caroline B. King. First published in 1941, the book is a collection of recipes and stories of Victorian home life in Chicago in the 1880s and 1890s. The author, who wrote for women's magazines and was the lead US Army dietitian in France during World War I, was a remarkable lady. Like Robin Hood, she would steal oranges at night from the officer's quarters and then quarter the oranges and squeeze juice into the mouths of wounded soldiers in hospital beds.

King died in 1948, but this book is a glimpse into her Victorian childhood. These drop cakes, as she remembered and wrote, "were always different and always good." They varied depending on what ingredients her mother had at hand, "a few raisins or currants or chopped nut meats, or perhaps a few spoonfuls of jam or marmalade." And long before ice cream scoops were used to portion out dough, this cookie batter was dropped from a spoon onto baking pans, thus the name "drop cakes." For a treat, King's eldest sister, Emily, iced the cakes with a confectioners' sugar and milk icing. The author says icing cakes created instant currency—"we could have traded them for anything we wanted, from any lunch basket or pail in the school, for they were certainly at a premium."

PREP: 15 TO 20 MINUTES   BAKE: 10 TO 12 MINUTES

---

1. Place a rack in the center of the oven, and preheat the oven to 350°F. Lightly grease 2 baking sheets with butter or vegetable shortening.

2. Place the butter or shortening and brown sugar in a large bowl and beat with an electric mixer on medium-high speed until

light and fluffy, about 2 minutes. Add the egg and beat well to combine. Stop the mixer and scrape down the sides of the bowl with a rubber spatula. Add the molasses and beat until just blended, 30 seconds. Scrape down the bowl.

3. Whisk together the flour, cinnamon, ginger, nutmeg, baking soda, and salt in a medium-size bowl. Add to the brown sugar mixture in three batches, beating on low speed after each addition. Scrape down the sides of the bowl.

4. Dollop the batter by teaspoonfuls onto the prepared baking sheets, spacing them about 2½" apart. Sprinkle the tops with nuts, coconut, or currants, if desired. Place one pan at a time in the oven.

5. Bake the cookies until they spring back when pressed lightly, 10 to 12 minutes. They will spread out as they bake. Remove the pan from the oven and let the cakes rest 1 minute. Then transfer the cakes with a metal spatula to a wire rack to cool. Repeat with the remaining batter. Store in a tightly covered container at room temperature for up to 1 week.

BLACK AND WHITE COOKIES

COOKIES

7 tablespoons unsalted butter, at room temperature

$\frac{1}{2}$ cup granulated sugar

1 teaspoon vanilla extract

2 large eggs, at room temperature

2 cups cake flour

1 teaspoon baking powder

$\frac{1}{2}$ teaspoon salt

6 tablespoons whole milk, at room temperature

GLAZE

3 cups confectioners' sugar

$2\frac{1}{2}$ to 3 tablespoons water, plus 1 teaspoon

$2\frac{1}{2}$ tablespoons unsweetened cocoa powder

MAKES: About 14 ($3\frac{1}{2}$") cookies

JEWISH IMMIGRANTS IN NEW York have given us the beloved cheesecake and also the black and white cookies. According to Jewish foodways expert Joan Nathan, the first black and whites were baked at Ratchets Bakery in Brooklyn at the turn of the 20th century. But what many people don't know is that the cookies baked in this deli and later in Glaser's Bake Shop in the Yorkville neighborhood of Manhattan had German roots.

In Germany that cookie is called an *Amerikaner* and is a lemon-glazed round cake. But in New York, it has always been glazed with a half circle of white confectioners' glaze next to a half circle of dark chocolate glaze. And that cookie says Jewish culture, pure and simple. It is wrapped and found on deli counters nationwide.

In the following recipe, cake flour yields a cookie that is tender and soft, lightweight, and much more enjoyable than black and white cookies I have sampled in New York delis. But the downside of using cake flour is the loss of structure, and so these cookies are not as perfectly rounded as you might get if you use all-purpose flour instead of cake flour. You've got to choose between perfectly shaped or perfectly soft and delicious—up to you. And you can also choose to forgo the black and white glaze and just add a little lemon zest to the glaze and turn these into German *Amerikaners*.

PREP: 1 HOUR   BAKE: 11 TO 13 MINUTES

---

1. Place a rack in the center of the oven, and preheat the oven to 350°F. Line 2 baking sheets with parchment paper.

2. Place the soft butter and sugar in a large bowl and beat with an electric mixer on medium-high speed until the mixture is light and fluffy, 2 minutes. Beat in the vanilla. Scrape down the sides of the bowl with a rubber spatula. Add the eggs, one at a time, beating well after each addition. Scrape down the sides of the bowl.

3. Whisk together the flour, baking powder, and salt in a small bowl. Add this mixture to the butter and sugar mixture

(continued on next page)

alternately with the milk, blending just until combined and smooth. Scrape down the sides of the bowl.

4. Dollop 14 equal portions of batter onto the prepared baking pans. Using the back of a spoon, shape the dough into rounds. Place one pan in the oven.

5. Bake the cakes until they spring back to the touch but there is no browning around the edges, 11 to 13 minutes. Remove the pan from the oven. Gently pull the parchment sheet off the pan and slide it onto a wire rack to cool. Repeat with the second pan of cookies. When the cookies have cooled completely, slide a metal spatula under them and transfer to a rack.

6. For the glaze, sift the confectioners' sugar into a large bowl. Add $2\frac{1}{2}$ tablespoons of the water and whisk until smooth. Add another $\frac{1}{2}$ tablespoon water, if needed—you want the glaze to be smooth. Place half of the glaze into a small bowl, and into this bowl whisk in the cocoa and the 1 teaspoon of water until smooth.

7. Frost half of each cookie with the white glaze using a small metal spatula. Let the glaze set for 15 to 20 minutes. Spread the chocolate glaze on the other half of the cookies, just touching the white border. Let the glaze set for about 30 minutes. Serve, or store in an airtight container for up to 3 days.

CORNMEAL AND LEMON MADELEINES

Soft butter and flour
for prepping the pan

$1/2$ cup cake flour

2 tablespoons white
cornmeal

$1/2$ teaspoon baking
powder

Pinch of salt

1 large egg

$1/3$ cup granulated
sugar

1 small lemon

4 tablespoons unsalted
butter, melted and
cooled

Confectioners' sugar
for dusting

MAKES: 12 madeleines

MORE THAN A CENTURY ago, French novelist Marcel Proust was writing about little almond-flavored cakes dipped in tea that his aunt Leonie fed him as a child. Proust recalled these cakes as if it were yesterday in his *Remembrance of Things Past.* The old gray house, the gardens, and the village people of his youth "sprang into being," just by having that cup of tea.

Proust believed it was a longing for what he left behind in childhood that allowed memories to resurface: "taste and smell alone . . . remain poised a long time, like souls, remembering, waiting, hoping, amid the ruin of all the rest, and beat unflinchingly, in the tiny and almost impalpable drop of their essence, the vast structure of recollection." To have a "Proustian" memory today means you allow cues to take you back in time.

Madeleines—or petite madeleines, as they are often called—are small sponge cakes baked in a scallop-shaped pan. They originated in the French town of Commercy and came to America when the late Chuck Williams of Williams-Sonoma fame turned a Sonoma, California, hardware store into the region's first French cookware shop. Williams-Sonoma offered cookware and bakeware not seen before in America at a time when Julia Child would soon become the French Chef on television and just before the Kennedys hired a French chef in the White House.

A few years ago, when Williams celebrated his 100th birthday, the company shared Williams's madeleines recipe. His was a little different than the one I baked in French cooking school in the 1980s. I bought my first madeleine pan, called a *plaque*, in Paris. It is beautiful and shiny. I have varied from the traditional French method of making madeleines through the years, adding almond, cornmeal, often lemon or orange zest. The cornmeal adds texture and is a delicious crossroads between the classic madeleine and Southern cornbread of my youth.

Classic madeleines do not call for baking powder, but it does help the structure of the cakes and allows the small cakes to rise. These are perfect for tea. They would have been welcomed at the Victorian tea table. Today, dipped in tea, they just might trigger a childhood memory waiting to be summoned.

PREP: 30 TO 35 MINUTES   BAKE: 12 TO 15 MINUTES

(continued on next page)

1. Place a rack in the middle of the oven, and preheat the oven to 375°F. Grease a 12-mold madeleine pan with soft butter. Dust with flour, and shake out the excess.

2. Sift the flour and cornmeal into a medium-size bowl and whisk in the baking powder and salt.

3. Place the egg and sugar in a large mixing bowl and beat with an electric mixer on medium speed until combined, 30 seconds. Increase the speed to high and beat until thickened and the mixture has increased in volume, 5 to 6 minutes. Turn the flour mixture into the egg and sugar mixture using a rubber spatula until nearly combined.

4. Zest and juice the lemon, and add up to $1/2$ teaspoon grated zest and no more than 1 teaspoon of the juice to the mixture. Fold in the cooled, melted butter until smooth. Spoon a generous tablespoon of batter into each of the prepared molds, filling each three-quarters of the way. Place the pan in the oven.

5. Bake the madeleines until golden brown around the edges, 12 to 15 minutes. Darker pans bake more quickly than shiny pans, so keep the oven light on as these bake so you can see their doneness. Remove the pan from the oven and turn out the madeleines shell side up onto a wire rack. Dust with confectioners' sugar and serve warm. Serve at once. These madeleines keep lightly covered at room temperature for up to 5 days, or they can be frozen for up to 1 month.

BAKING TIP: *The number of wells in a madeleine pan varies. If you have 8 wells, you will need to cool down, wipe clean, and regrease the pan between baking another round.*

CHOCOLATE BOUCHONS

Melted butter for
prepping the molds

1 cup unsweetened
cocoa powder

¾ cup all-purpose
flour

½ teaspoon salt

3 large eggs

1 cup granulated sugar

1 teaspoon vanilla
extract

12 ounces (3 sticks)
unsalted butter,
melted

1 cup (6 ounces) good
quality bittersweet or
semisweet chocolate
chips

Confectioners' sugar
for dusting

_____

MAKES: 24 (2- or
3-ounce) bouchons

_____

I'LL NEVER FORGET WALKING into the Pearl Bakery in Portland, Oregon, 10 years ago and spying chocolate corklike cakes on a plate. Forget that I was hungry for lunch, because lunch could wait. I had to try these dark, fat thimbles of what appeared to be chocolate cake. And after just one bite, I was hooked. Bouchons became my new obsession. They were and still are the perfect accompaniment to coffee, more fashionable than a cupcake, and intensely, fearlessly chocolate.

Super-chef Thomas Keller is supposedly the one who put bouchons on the American culinary map. He named his Yountville, California, bistro Bouchon—meaning "cork" in French. And what could be more suitable on the dessert menu of a bistro located smack-dab in the middle of the California wine country than a chocolate corklike cake for dessert?

Comparing the flavor of the Pearl Bakery bouchon to the Keller bouchon, there are some differences. Pearl's is less intensely chocolate but pleasantly flavored overall. Keller's is deep and dark but too salty for my taste. So when I tested a recipe for this book, I created something of a hybrid. These bouchons are chocolatey and dark but have the right balance of sugar and salt. You can make these in 2- or 3-ounce mini popover pans or use French stainless steel timbales about that size or buy special bouchon pans. Or just bake them as cupcakes! They won't look like corks, but they are still delicious warm with a dusting of powdered sugar. And regardless of the pan, they are delicious even on the second day.

_____

PREP: 30 TO 35 MINUTES   BAKE: 14 TO 22 MINUTES

_____

1. Place a rack in the center of the oven, and preheat the oven to 350°F. Brush the inside of 2- or 3-ounce small popover or timbale pans with melted butter.

2. Whisk together the cocoa, flour, and salt in a medium-size bowl.

3. Place the eggs and sugar in a large mixing bowl and beat with an electric mixer on medium speed until the mixture is well combined and lightens in color, 3 to 4 minutes. Beat in the vanilla. Turn off the mixer and add a third of the cocoa mixture to the egg mixture. Turn the mixer back on and beat on low

(continued on next page)

speed until combined. Add half of the melted butter and beat briefly. Turn off the mixer and add another third of the cocoa mixture, the last half of the butter, and the remaining cocoa mixture. Beat until smooth. Fold in the chocolate chips.

4. If using individual timbales, place these on a baking sheet before filling. Fill the molds to your liking—two-thirds full for flat tops, higher if you want tops that rise above the pan. Place the pan in the oven.

5. Bake the bouchons until the center is still soft but the edges are set when pressed with a finger, 14 to 17 minutes for a 2-ounce mold, or 18 to 22 minutes for a 3-ounce mold. Remove the pan from the oven let the bouchons rest in the pan for 3 to 4 minutes, then run a knife around the edges and unmold them onto a wire rack to cool completely. When the pan cools down after about 15 minutes, repeat the process with the remaining batter. You do not need to grease the molds for the second round of baking.

6. To serve, line the bouchons on a serving tray and dust the tops with confectioners' sugar. Or individually plate them, dust with sugar, and serve a scoop of ice cream on the side.

BAKING TIP: *How to tell the size of your bouchon mold? Fill a well with water and pour this water into a liquid measuring cup.*

Filling the Pan Determines the Look

Fill the pans two-thirds full of batter and the bouchons will be flat on top. Fill higher and to the top of popover or timbale pans and the batter will rise above the top and look like champagne corks instead of wine corks. It's really up to you. Let them rest in the pan for 3 to 4 minutes before unmolding on a wire rack.

KATE'S PECAN TASSIES

CRUST

$\frac{1}{2}$ cup (1 stick) unsalted butter

1 cup all-purpose flour

3 ounces cream cheese, chilled (see Baking Tips)

FILLING

1 large egg, at room temperature

$\frac{1}{2}$ cup light brown sugar, firmly packed

1 tablespoon unsalted butter, melted

1 teaspoon vanilla extract

Pinch of salt

$\frac{2}{3}$ cup finely chopped pecans, divided use (about 2.75 ounces, see Baking Tips)

MAKES: About 30 tassies

IN THE MOVIE *Steel Magnolias* Clairee (Olympia Dukakis) marches proudly into the beauty shop with a plate of her pecan tassies. These are the small bites of pecan pie—heaven—that have been served at Southern parties and barbecue for decades.

Tassies were first mentioned in newspapers in the 1950s and seem to be a recipe that came out of a food editor conference, as in a food company developed the recipe to promote its product and passed it along to the editors to share with their readers. It might have been Philadelphia Cream Cheese or the pecan growers association behind those efforts. The pecan growers of Texas have been sharing a tassie recipe since the 1970s. But surely in the last 30 years, well-known cookbook author and personality Nathalie Dupree gets credit for tassies' fame because she has been sharing their recipe in her books about that long. Dupree, now of Charleston, ran the famous Rich's Cooking School in Atlanta for many years and her right-hand assistant during that time was the late Kate Almand, whom Dupree credits with passing along a number of fabulous recipes including these pecan tassies.

"I do love them," Dupree says. "And I love teaching them for the same reason." They are joy in a bite—a warm gooey pecan pie filling in flaky crust baked in a mini muffin pan.

PREP: 30 TO 35 MINUTES   FREEZE AND CHILL: 45 TO 50 MINUTES, OR UP TO 5 DAYS   BAKE: 28 TO 32 MINUTES

---

1. For the crust, cut the butter into $\frac{1}{2}$" cubes and place them in a bowl in the freezer until firm, 15 to 20 minutes.

2. Place the flour in a food processor fitted with a steel blade. Add the frozen butter cubes and pulse 30 to 40 times, or until it is the texture of oatmeal. Cut the cream cheese into 4 pieces and distribute these on top of the butter and flour. Pulse about 15 times, until the dough begins to pull together. With your hands, gather the dough and press it together into a ball. It may seem dry at first, but keep pressing. Wrap the dough in plastic wrap and place it in the fridge to chill for at least 30 minutes and up to 5 days.

3. When ready to bake, place a rack in the center of the oven, and preheat the oven to 325°F. Remove the dough from the fridge.

(continued on next page)

This recipe was developed back when 3-ounce packages of cream cheese were easy to find. If you have an 8-ounce block of cream cheese, the amount needed for this recipe will be slightly less than half. Or use a kitchen scale to weigh out the exact 3 ounces. The pecans should be well chopped so that there aren't large pieces of pecan, but not so finely chopped that they are minced. Striking that balance will be up to you and your chopping knife.

Pinch off pieces of dough that are about $\frac{1}{2}$ tablespoon in size. Press these into the ungreased 2" wells of a mini muffin or cupcake pan. You will fill about 30 wells with dough. Press the dough so that it covers the bottom and sides of the well to form a miniature crust. Place the pans in the fridge while you prepare the filling.

4. For the filling, whisk together the egg, brown sugar, melted butter, vanilla, and salt in a medium-size bowl until smooth.

5. Remove the crusts from the refrigerator. Scatter half of the pecans evenly into the bottom of the crusts, using about $\frac{1}{2}$ teaspoon each in each crust. Using a small spoon, portion the egg and sugar mixture over the nuts, evenly filling the crusts a little more than halfway and not allowing the filling to get between the pan and the shell. Sprinkle the remaining pecans on top of the filling. Wipe any drops of filling off the pan, and place the pan in the oven.

6. Bake the tassies until the crust is lightly golden brown, 28 to 32 minutes. Let the tassies cool in the pan for about 10 minutes, then run a knife around each crust. Transfer them to a wire rack to finish cooling or to a plate to serve slightly warm. These keep well in an airtight container at room temperature for up to 5 days, or you can freeze them in that container for up to 1 month.

Pecans: A Native Nut

An essential ingredient in this recipe, pecans are native to the southern tier of the United States and are harvested in late fall. Plenty of online companies ship right to your doorstep, and for holiday baking there is nothing like fresh pecans to pick up the flavor of cookies, pies and cakes. Store them in your freezer. The Spanish explorers found them in what is now Louisiana, Texas, and Mississippi. And we know now that pecans were a important foodstuff that sustained early Native Americans through the winter.

How to Make Petits Fours

One of the first mentions of petits fours was at a New York dinner for Randolph Guggenheim in 1894. While Americans tend to think of petits fours as small squares of cakes that have been covered in icing and decorated, they are a larger category of small cakes or cookies. The earliest were French, and their name comes from the small brick ovens in which they were baked at a low temperature—a "petit four."

The easiest way to bake petits fours today is to bake your favorite cake recipe on a jelly-roll or half sheet pan, then cut into squares when cooled.

You can also bake a loaf of cake, such as a pound cake, then trim the loaf of its crusts, and slice it into strips and then squares.

To ice your petits fours, use a confectioners' sugar and water or milk recipe—about 1 to 2 tablespoons liquid per cup of sugar. Flavor as you like with vanilla, almond, lemon, rose water, or orange. Place the cakes on a wire rack, ladle the glaze over each cake to cover, and let them set before serving. While the glaze is still a little sticky, add a small edible flower or other garnish on top.

A Suffrage Cookbook and Tea Cakes

Cookbooks containing recipes for tea cakes were often fund-raising tools for cultural change. An example is *The Woman Suffrage Cook Book*, published in 1886 and assembled by Hattie A. Burr. Here are 88 recipes for cakes and cookies in addition to the usual veg, meat, pickles, breads, etc., plus housekeeping advice at the back of the book and quotes from prominent figures on their thoughts on giving women the right to vote. *Suffrage* meant the right to vote in public elections. While these early advocate feminists were painted as neglectful mothers, cookbooks with recipes and household and domestic advice promoted the health and happiness of a home. The sale of these books helped women not only raise funds for their cause but also network. Thirty-four years later, when Hattie Burr was 79, the 19th Amendment to the US Constitution was ratified on August 18, 1920, and it granted American women the right to vote.

COCONUT CUPCAKES WITH LIME BUTTERCREAM FROSTING

CUPCAKES

2½ cups cake flour

¾ teaspoon baking powder

½ teaspoon baking soda

½ teaspoon salt

1 cup (2 sticks) unsalted butter, at room temperature

1½ cups granulated sugar

4 large eggs

1 teaspoon vanilla extract

½ teaspoon coconut extract

⅔ cup whole milk, at room temperature

1 cup unsweetened shredded coconut, very finely chopped

LIME BUTTERCREAM FROSTING

½ cup (1 stick) lightly salted butter, at room temperature

3 to 3½ cups confectioners' sugar

1 medium lime

2 to 3 tablespoons milk, as needed

MAKES: 24 (2½") cupcakes

EVERY RECIPE COLLECTION NEEDS a good cupcake recipe. I'll bet you could have said that same thing 60 years ago, or possibly earlier, as cupcakes have been baked in America for quite a while. The word *cupcake* originally meant cake recipes that were measured by the cup—as in 2 cups flour, 1 cup sugar, etc. Who baked the first cupcake as we know it isn't clear, but we do know that cupcakes were baked during World War II as a snack cake to take to work to share with others.

Ever since 1998, when the TV series *Sex and the City* introduced America to vanilla and chocolate cupcakes heavily frosted and sprinkled, we've been crazy about them. And one of my favorite cupcakes to bake—and I am sure it rates right up there with a lot of you—is the coconut.

Coconut in America has an interesting history. It has always been a frugal substitute for nuts in baking, and coconut cake is a regional favorite of the South, but packaged, shredded coconut came to the store shelves completely by accident. In 1895 Philadelphia's Franklin Baker flour company received a shipload of coconut as payment for flour it sent to Cuba. Unable to sell the coconuts, the company invested in a way to crack them, then shred and dry them. Within 10 years, Baker's coconut was on grocer's shelves, and coconut cake and cupcakes became part of our baking lexicon.

This recipe is a modern adaptation of a coconut cake. I like the fresh flavor that lime adds in the buttercream frosting. To gild the lily, go ahead and toast some coconut and sprinkle on top as a garnish.

PREP: 25 TO 30 MINUTES   BAKE: 15 TO 20 MINUTES

---

1. Place a rack in the center of the oven, and preheat the oven to 350°F. Place paper liners in 24 wells of cupcake pans.

2. For the cupcakes, whisk together the flour, baking powder, baking soda, and salt in a medium-size bowl.

3. Place the soft butter and granulated sugar in a large mixing bowl and beat with an electric mixer on medium speed until creamy, about 1 minute. Add the eggs, one at a time, beating after each addition, just until combined. Add the vanilla and the

(continued on next page)

coconut extract. Add the flour mixture alternately with the milk, beginning and ending with the flour mixture and beat until just smooth. Scrape down the sides of the bowl with a rubber spatula.

4. Fold the coconut into the batter. Scoop the batter into the prepared pans, filling each liner two-thirds to three-quarters full. Place the pans in the oven.

5. Bake the cupcakes until lightly golden brown and the tops spring back when lightly pressed with a finger, 15 to 20 minutes. Remove the pans from the oven and let the cupcakes rest in the pan 1 minute. Run a small metal spatula underneath the cupcake liners and transfer the cupcakes to a wire rack to cool completely, about 30 minutes.

6. Meanwhile, for the frosting, place the soft butter in a large mixing bowl and beat on medium speed until creamy, about 1 minute. Add 2 cups of the confectioners' sugar and beat to combine. Stop the mixer. Zest and juice the lime. Add both to the butter and sugar mixture. Add the rest of the sugar and the milk, 1 tablespoon at a time, beating until smooth and adding as much milk as needed to pull together a spreadable consistency. Increase the mixer speed to medium-high and beat until fluffy, about 1 minute. Frost the cupcakes. Serve at once. These cupcakes can be lightly covered and stored at room temperature for up to 2 days. They can be frozen *unfrosted* for up to 1 month. Thaw and frost.

6

CANDY, FRIED CAKES & CULINARY ARTISTRY

Fritters, fudge, doughnuts, brittle, and beignets are not cookies, but they reflect the skill of worn hands and availability of ingredients in a changing America. A key ingredient was sugar. Refined white sugar yielded white divinity and candied fruit such as grapefruit. Less expensive molasses, raw sugar, cane syrup, or sorghum resulted in pralines, brittles, and the fragrant spice doughnuts we still love today.

Candied and fried cakes were treats. Their preparation was labor intensive. And they were often street foods—pralines and calas, for example—made and sold by vendors to support their families. When Mass was over and parishioners filed out of church, there was no better way to assuage hunger than by biting into a hot rice cala—soft and creamy in the center and crispy on the sugar-glazed exterior.

In port cities such as Philadelphia, streets were lined with French-inspired chocolate and candy shops. Candy making was both a prized skill and a growing business. Likewise in Charleston, candies of all types were sold on Market Street by African-American street vendors. Benne brittle, caramels, groundnut cakes, and something called "monkey meat," a mixture of molasses and coconut, were America's first street candy. And in New Orleans, the tradition of women dressed in mammy outfits and selling pralines goes way back.

Candy and fried foods might seem like unlikely recipes to group into one chapter, but when you think about it, they share something in common. They take simple ingredients and elevate them to an art form. Not just anyone can turn white sugar into divinity. And not just anyone can turn flour, water, and yeast into a doughnut. You have to be somewhat fearless to cook at such high heats. We should be thankful there were so many brave and resourceful cooks who prepared these recipes and handed down their methods so that we can continue to make all the sweet treats that are part of our American culinary story.

Groundnut Cakes and Street Candy

Before shrimp and grits became associated with Charleston, there was a sweet iconic food known as groundnut cakes that everyone wanted to sample. Sold by African Americans on Market Street in Charleston, these peanut brittle–like candies were flavored with lemon peel. The vendor was an older woman with a turban, and when the weather was nice, she sat on a stool holding a platter of groundnut cakes in her lap.

The recipe was found in later editions of *The Carolina Housewife* and resembled a rich peanut taffy. In 1895 they cost a penny each.

Two decades later, health inspectors would crack down on street vendors and the groundnut cakes were no more. The peanut used in these cakes was the 'Carolina African' runner peanut, which was the original peanut of the Low Country until the early 1900s. It was small and oily and flavorful. In his book *Classical Southern Cooking*, Damon Lee Fowler writes that groundnut or groundpeas were old names for what we know today as peanuts.

The groundnut wasn't confined to Charleston. When Philadelphia hosted the US Centennial in 1876, and a cookbook of national dishes was assembled, the only peanut recipe shared was one for a Ground Nut Cake. It was supposedly introduced to Philadelphia by refugees of the Haitian revolution in 1792. And that recipe mirrors peanut brittle recipes today—a syrup of brown sugar and water that when cooked enough turns brittlelike. According to historian Andrew F. Smith, in his book *Peanuts: The Illustrious History of the Goober Pea,* Haitian women sold these cakes on street corners.

ELLA BRENNAN'S PRALINES

4 cups (1 quart) heavy cream

3 cups granulated sugar

1 to 2 tablespoons lemon juice (from 1 lemon)

1 pound pecans, chopped (about 4 cups)

MAKES: About 40 (2") pralines

A VISIT TO NEW Orleans is incomplete without tasting pralines, the creamy caramel and pecan candy that has deep roots in this city. They are French in origin, coming with French settlers to New Orleans. The word *praline* originated in 17th-century France and is named for the Maréchal du Plessis-Pralin, an aristocrat who suffered from indigestion and ate sugar-coated almonds to alleviate the pain, according to Chanda M. Nunez in her graduate thesis at the University of New Orleans in 2011. But some historians believe the milk or cream in the praline recipe is the result of the Spanish influence on the cuisine of New Orleans.

When New Orleans historian Rien Fertel researched the history of pralines, he knew well the story of the French "casket girls" who arrived in the 1720s with just one bag—the *casquette*—and how they had been credited with introducing pralines to New Orleans. But what he didn't know was how the African American women who made those pralines and sold them on the street are responsible for their lasting success. Through their creativity, the recipe for pralines evolved to use local pecans. And their selling of pralines created demand.

After the Civil War, freed slaves dressed up in mammy costumes and sold pralines out of baskets, said Fertel. They used this money to support their families. "It was brilliant advertising." Before the war these women had made the pralines "in the kitchens of the fancy houses, but as free people they now had the recipes and they sold pralines." Fertel said pralines were popular to make because sugar was available and cheap.

New Orleans historian and author Elizabeth Williams said there was such an abundance of raw sugar in New Orleans and Louisiana that it was natural for people to cook with it. It was cheaper than refined white sugar. And the natural tan color of raw sugar lent itself to the caramel color of pralines. "Pralines were born out of poverty," she said. "People used what they could afford."

Today, praline is a flavor all its own. It is not just a candy but also a topping and an add-in to Baskin-Robbins ice cream, and it lead to those praline cheesecakes so in vogue in the 1990s. Praline vendors have all but disappeared in New Orleans. But you can find homemade pralines wrapped in waxed paper on the counter at some of the neighborhood po'boy shops. Or you can try your hand at making them at home.

Here is a recipe from the matriarch of the Brennan restaurant family,

(continued on next page)

Ella Brennan. She shared it in a 1983 cookbook called *Gifts from the Christmas Kitchen*, which benefited Meals on Wheels, and it was one of the first praline recipes that I attempted. It is a little different from other praline recipes because it calls for a quart of cream that you slowly boil down with sugar until it caramelizes and thickens. But these are delicious and decadent treats. Always store pralines at room temperature. If you refrigerate them, they will get hard and grainy.

PREP: 1½ HOURS   COOL: 2 HOURS

---

1. Place the cream and sugar in a deep 6-quart heavy saucepot and place over low heat. Stir and cook until the mixture reaches 238°F on a candy thermometer, the soft ball stage. This will take 35 to 40 minutes. The mixture will foam up, then it will settle back down and begin to reduce in volume and take on a light, golden brown color.

2. Add the lemon juice and pecans. If you are using a stainless steel pan, place it back over the heat, briefly, until the mixture comes back to 238°F. (If you are using a cast-iron pan that retains heat, do not place it back over the heat. Check the thermometer and see if the mixture will reach 238°F again off the heat—to prevent overlooking.) Once the mixture is at 238°F, remove it from the heat for 30 seconds, then stir vigorously for 1 minute.

3. Work quickly and drop tablespoons of candy onto a marble surface or a board covered with lightly greased waxed paper. Let cool about 2 hours, then wrap completely in waxed paper and store in airtight containers at room temperature for up to 3 weeks.

UNDERSTANDING THE ART OF PRALINES: Stirring vigorously is a critical step in creating creamy-textured pralines. You want to shake up all the sugar molecules, in the words of food chemist superstar Shirley Corriher.

LADY BIRD JOHNSON'S PEANUT BRITTLE

1½ cups granulated sugar

½ cup water

½ cup light corn syrup

1½ cups unsalted, shelled peanuts

1½ tablespoons unsalted butter

½ teaspoon salt

¼ teaspoon baking soda

MAKES: About 1¼ pounds

MARY FAULK KOOCK WAS an Austin, Texas, caterer extraordinaire in the 1940s through the 1960s who orchestrated parties for dignitaries. She often helped President Lyndon B. Johnson and his wife, Lady Bird, stage these gatherings at their LBJ Ranch. During the Johnson presidency, there was talk of the need for a definitive Texas cookbook, something to explain the way Johnson ate and entertained. So Little, Brown Publishing sent James Beard to Austin to help Koock write *The Texas Cookbook,* published in 1965. It was a fascinating collection of Koock's recipes as well as behind-the-scenes stories of what it took to stage these grand gatherings, a real "snapshot of mid-20th century Texas," according to the *Austin Chronicle.*

A period-perfect recipe of that time was peanut brittle, and Koock shared Lady Bird Johnson's recipe in her book. Although the *Los Angeles Times* declared that peanut brittle was the new candy in town in 1892, it wasn't made at home until 5 years later when the first recipes started appearing. Old recipes called for sugar and water to be cooked until a hard crack, and then peanuts folded in. Later recipes called for the addition of baking soda, which causes the candy to foam and slightly soften, as well as the addition of corn syrup—either light or dark—to prevent the candy from crystallizing.

The Lady Bird Johnson recipe calls for light corn syrup. Use dark if you prefer a darker color and deeper flavor. Following this recipe will take you back in time, to the LBJ Ranch, located about 50 miles west of Austin, in the Hill Country. It was a time when the ranch was the scene of grand parties, where the kitchen was the center of the home, and where Mary Faulk Koock sat at the Johnsons' dining room table and planned parties for dignitaries. Here the staff learned on November 22, 1963, that President John F. Kennedy, who was expected at the ranch that evening for dinner and pecan pie, had been shot in Dallas. Today the LBJ Ranch is the Lyndon B. Johnson National Historical Park.

PREP: 20 TO 25 MINUTES   COOK: 15 TO 20 MINUTES   COOL: 1 HOUR

---

1. Place the sugar, water, and corn syrup in a large, heavy saucepan. Stir over medium-high heat until the sugar has

(continued on next page)

dissolved and the mixture comes to a boil. Reduce the heat to medium, but keep the mixture at a brisk simmer. Stir and cook until the mixture comes to 238°F on a candy thermometer, 4 to 5 minutes.

2. Add the peanuts and continue cooking and stirring until the mixture rises to 302°F, which is a hard crack. This will take 3 to 4 minutes. Do not let the peanuts burn. Gently lower the heat if needed to prevent them from burning. And keep stirring, being careful not to scrape the sides of the pan. Once the mixture hits 302°F, add the butter, salt, and baking soda and stir to combine. Turn out onto a greased marble slab or baking pan.

3. Let the brittle cool at least 1 hour, then break up with your hands or a mallet into serving-size pieces. Store peanut brittle in an airtight container to keep it crisp. It keeps for up to 3 weeks at room temperature.

UNDERSTANDING THE ART OF PEANUT BRITTLE: Be careful once you add the peanuts that the brittle doesn't burn. The temperature rises really quickly from 280° to 302°F, so watch it closely, and stir constantly.

Three Essentials to Perfect Candy

To make crisp peanut brittle and other homemade candies, you need:

1. Candy thermometer.
2. Heavy pans, preferably copper. They need to be thick and wide enough to cover the burner and protect the candy from burning. Copper heats up quickly, which is good in candy making, and it also cools down quickly, also important. Cast iron is heavy, but because it retains heat you need to get the candy out of the cast-iron pan as quickly as possible.
3. Clear skies. It's true that you don't want to make candy on rainy or humid days. The moisture in the air can prevent many candies from hardening.

Candy and Medicine

Some of our earliest candies were actually medicines. Flavored with the silvery herb called horehound, the "horehound" or "hoarhound" candy was made by cooking sugar with the herb-infused water until the mixture cracked. The lozenge was said to soothe sore throats and treat the common cold. And it tasted good, too.

If you have a patch of horehound in your herb garden, here is how to turn it into a simple and pure cough medicine.

HOREHOUND CANDY

1 quart (4 cups) horehound leaves and stems, rinsed and dried	2½ cups water
	3 cups granulated or brown sugar

1. Place the horehound in a large saucepan and cover with the water. Cook over medium heat until the water is infused, about 30 minutes. Strain the leaves from the water, and leave the water in the pan.

2. Add the sugar. Stir and cook over medium-high heat until the mixture comes to a boil. Place a candy thermometer on the side of the pan. Stir and cook until the syrup reaches the hard ball stage—265°F.

3. Pour the syrup onto a lightly buttered pan, and when the mixture is cool enough to handle, scoop it up with a small spoon into small balls. Roll them between your palms to shape them, and wrap each in a square of waxed paper.

POPCORN AND PISTACHIO BRITTLE

Soft butter for prepping the pan

1½ cups shelled pistachios

1 cup popcorn, coarsely crumbled

1½ cups granulated sugar

½ cup light corn syrup

⅓ cup water

3 tablespoons unsalted butter

½ teaspoon salt

¼ teaspoon baking soda

1 teaspoon vanilla extract

MAKES: About 1½ pounds

IF YOU COMBINED THE flavors and textures that cause the average person to weaken, you would create a sweet, salty, and crunchy candy. Thus the popularity of old-fashioned popcorn balls and caramel corn. And the following recipe.

This is a method I tried years ago after I spied it in Helen Witty's book called *Fancy Pantry*. Here old-fashioned brittle meets popcorn ball. You choose a combination of nuts and popcorn—I like pistachios, but you might prefer toasted almonds or dry-roasted peanuts. And the brittle part—the sugar syrup—is straightforward. You are creating the same sort of candied sugar syrup as when making peanut brittle. Once it is cool, you break it into pieces and give as gifts. Or keep for yourself!

PREP: 30 TO 35 MINUTES   COOK: ABOUT 10 MINUTES   COOL: 2 HOURS

---

1. Place a rack in the center of the oven, and preheat the oven to 250°F. Lightly grease a large baking sheet with soft butter.

2. Place the pistachios and crumbled popped popcorn on the baking sheet. Place the pan in the oven to warm the nuts and popcorn, 4 to 5 minutes. Turn off the oven, leaving the pan in the oven.

3. Place the sugar, corn syrup, and water in a large heavy saucepan over medium-high heat. Stir until the sugar dissolves, 2 to 3 minutes. As the sugar heats, wipe down any sugar crystals that form on the sides of the pan with a pastry brush dipped in water. When the mixture comes to a boil, add the butter and stir until the mixture registers 310°F on a candy thermometer. This will take 6 to 8 minutes.

4. Remove the pan from the heat and immediately stir in the salt, baking soda, and vanilla. Stir in the warm nuts and popcorn, and turn out onto the baking sheet. Let it cool completely, about 2 hours. Break into pieces and serve, or store in an airtight container for up to 2 weeks.

UNDERSTANDING THE ART OF NUT AND POPCORN BRITTLE: The sugar syrup is the tricky part. The nuts and popcorn combination is up to you. Use freshly popped popcorn that is as free of flavoring as possible.

Easy as Fudge

THE FIRST BATCH OF fudge was supposedly made in Baltimore in the 1880s. It was the confection of candy shops in big cities and in small towns. And for some reason, fudge has always attracted tourists.

Jennifer Lewis, Chicago author and midwestern candy historian, says fudge has been loved in and around the Upper Peninsula of Michigan. Today, tourists pile off ferries and onto Mackinac Island, where the streets are lined with fudge shops. It's not fancy stuff—just chocolate, sugar, corn syrup, some flavorings, often nuts, cooked and then poured onto marble. But the aroma of that fudge drives tourists crazy, and they flock to these shops like flies. It is said electric fans were used in the 1920s to push the irresistible fudge perfume out onto the street to attract shoppers.

Not too far south from Mackinac Island is the lake town of Charlevoix, which has an old and interesting history and obviously shares the love of fudge. The *Charlevoix Cook Book*, published in 1907, contains four chocolate fudge recipes plus one just made of brown sugar called "pinoche."

The word *fudge* has been used in early America since Colonial times and is English. In old newspaper political commentary, it was used to refer to something other than the truth and usually in the context of unscrupulous politicians. In the 1920s, Wellesley College and other girls' colleges in the Northeast became associated with fudge. The students would cook chocolate fudge in their dorm rooms, and the Wellesley Fudge Cake—which has a cooked fudgelike frosting—rose in popularity. Through the years, most fudge recipes are chocolate. But we find peanut butter, Mexican milk fudge using sweetened condensed milk, and pumpkin fudge in the Southwest today.

Through the years, the recipes for fudge changed from cooking down granulated sugar to adding corn syrup and other convenience items like sweetened condensed milk or marshmallow creme (Marshmallow Fluff) to make the process easier. The fudge is creamy, but what it lacks is the old-fashioned chocolate flavor you get by cooking down granulated sugar, chocolate, and butter. So I am sharing three recipes that together tell the American fudge story.

The first is an old-fashioned fudge recipe, coming from a *Philadelphia Inquirer* food article in 1896. It yields a thin fudge with enormous flavor. The second is mid-20th century and has been updated a bit to decrease the sugar and increase the chocolate flavor. In order to cut it into squares, you need to place it in the freezer until it sets. And the third recipe is the most recent, calling for semisweet chocolate chips and evaporated milk. It's creamy like old-fashioned fudge, benefits from freezing first before slicing, and is truly as easy as fudge!

OLD-FASHIONED CHOCOLATE FUDGE

Soft butter for prepping the pan

2 cups confectioners' sugar

½ cup whole milk

2 ounces unsweetened chocolate, chopped

Pinch of salt

2 tablespoons unsalted butter

½ teaspoon vanilla extract

MAKES: About 8 ounces (16 pieces)

PREP: 15 TO 20 MINUTES   COOK: 7 TO 8 MINUTES   CHILL: 30 MINUTES TO 2 HOURS

1. Rub an 8" or smaller baking pan with butter and set aside.

2. Place the confectioners' sugar, milk, chocolate, salt, and butter in a large, heavy saucepan over medium-high heat. Cook and stir until the chocolate and butter melt, then reduce the heat slightly and let simmer until it thickens, 7 to 8 minutes. Stir in the vanilla.

3. With a wire whisk or electric mixer on medium speed, beat the fudge in the pan until it is glossy and thick, about 5 minutes. Turn the fudge into the prepared pan, and let it set in a cool place for 2 hours or in the fridge for 30 minutes. Cut into squares and serve.

FOLLOWING PAGE, LEFT TO RIGHT: *Easy Freezer Fudge, Simple Chocolate Fudge, and Old-Fashioned Chocolate Fudge*

EASY FREEZER FUDGE

Soft butter for prepping the pan

1 jar (7 ounces) marshmallow creme

1⅓ cups granulated sugar

⅔ cup evaporated milk

4 tablespoons unsalted butter

½ teaspoon salt

2 cups semisweet chocolate chips

2 tablespoons unsweetened cocoa powder

1 teaspoon vanilla extract

½ cup toasted chopped pecans or walnuts (see Note)

MAKES: About 1 pound (16 to 24 pieces)

1. Rub an 8" baking pan with butter and set aside.
2. Place the marshmallow creme, sugar, evaporated milk, butter, and salt in a 3-quart heavy saucepan over medium heat. Stir and cook until the butter and marshmallow have melted and the mixture thickens and is smooth, about 5 minutes.
3. Fold in the chocolate chips, cocoa, and vanilla. Stir until smooth. Fold in the nuts.
4. Pour the fudge into the prepared pan and smooth the top with a rubber spatula. Place the pan, uncovered, in the freezer to set, about 2 hours. Cut into squares while cold, then transfer to a serving plate or store in an airtight container in the fridge for up to 1 week. You may freeze this fudge for up to 1 month.

NOTE: The addition of unsweetened cocoa is new. Also, toasting the nuts is new. They get buried in all that fudge, but they have more flavor if they go into the fudge toasted first. Place the nuts in a 350°F oven while you are prepping everything. Then pull the pan from the oven, turn the nuts out onto a cutting board and chop if needed, and fold into the warm fudge.

SIMPLE CHOCOLATE FUDGE

Soft butter for prepping the pan

3 cups semisweet or bittersweet chocolate chips

1 cup (2 sticks) lightly salted butter, at room temperature

1 can (12 ounces) evaporated milk

4¼ cups granulated sugar

Dash of salt

1 teaspoon vanilla extract

2 cups chopped pecans or black walnuts

MAKES: About 48 squares (3 pounds)

PREP: 15 TO 20 MINUTES   COOK: 5 TO 6 MINUTES   CHILL: 2 TO 3 HOURS, OR FREEZE FOR 1 HOUR

---

1. Rub a 13" × 9" glass baking pan with butter and set aside.
2. Place the chocolate chips and soft butter in a large heatproof mixing bowl.
3. Place the milk and sugar in a large saucepan over medium-high heat, stirring continually. When the mixture comes to a boil, reduce the heat slightly so that it continues to simmer until thickened, 5 to 6 minutes. Pour this mixture over the chocolate and butter and stir with a wooden spoon until the chocolate and butter have melted and the mixture is smooth. Fold in the salt, vanilla, and nuts.
4. Turn the mixture into the prepared pan, and place in the fridge to chill 2 to 3 hours or into the freezer for 1 hour, or until set. Cut into squares and serve.

The Magic of Fudge

Back when people routinely made fudge for gifts and treats, there was a recipe called "magic" fudge. The mystery behind it was that it set almost instantly. You placed 1 cup sugar, ¼ cup water, and a can of sweetened condensed milk in a large heavy saucepan and cooked and stirred until the soft ball stage, about 238°F. Then you folded in unsweetened chocolate—about 2 ounces—and ½ cup chopped nuts. Once you poured this mixture into a buttered pan, it took 20 minutes or less in the fridge to set. The year was 1940, and the recipe was from Borden's Eagle Brand. The mascot, Elsie, proclaimed in advertising, "Here's fudge that'll bring you fame!" But through the years, this recipe wasn't so magical because people didn't own candy thermometers or know what the soft ball stage was. So the new quick fudge from Eagle Brand today melts 3 cups semisweet chocolate chips with a can of sweetened condensed milk and a pinch of salt. You add vanilla and nuts, pour in a pan, chill for 2 hours, and you've got fudge. Now that's magic!

DOUBLE DIVINITY

IF YOU THINK THE only people who have been obsessed with divinity candy have been old matrons sharing tea and conversation, then you're mistaken. This soft and creamy egg white and sugar candy—named because of its pillowy, cloudlike, ethereal, divine quality—was at one time a national favorite.

That was the early 1900s, and the candy's popularity likely benefited from the marketing efforts of Karo corn syrup in 1910. Adding white corn syrup to the old divinity recipe made the result creamier and the process easier. Divinity was also called "white candy," not to be confused with "sea foam" candy when the recipe was made with brown sugar. And there were all variations of divinity. Some were tinted with food coloring, others contained grated chocolate and cherries, some were layered in a pan with chocolate fudge. In a 1922 Flint, Michigan, cookbook compiled by the Daughters of the American Revolution, Grape-Nuts cereal was added to divinity. Clearly, divinity was a blank canvas. And it was a time when people made candy themselves and thought homemade candy was superior to that they purchased at the store. Corn syrup manufacturers reminded customers that their children were going to eat candy anyway, why not be a better parent and make the candy yourself?

The recipe that follows isn't your average divinity. It is called "double" divinity because you cook two sugar syrups, one a little lower and one a little higher, and add them to the beaten egg whites one after the other to create an incredibly creamy-textured candy that must have been the inspiration for today's Marshmallow Fluff. (Spread this on a graham cracker, add a piece of milk chocolate, top with another graham cracker, and you have the most exceptional s'more you have ever tasted.)

The method comes from *America's Cook Book,* which was compiled by the "Home Institute of *The New York Herald Tribune*" in 1938—strong divinity years. But it takes some equipment—a candy thermometer and two heavy pans. And it takes some bravery—candy temperatures get hot, so you've got to use oven mitts and be careful of splatters and spills. Oh, and did I mention the stand mixer on high power beating egg whites to stiff peaks before you continue to beat while pouring in the hot sugar syrups?

Purists will call this confection divine. *America's Cook Book* lauds this as the divinity to beat all divinities. I think it's a lot of trouble to make. But I'm glad I mastered it while writing this book, because now I can understand a time in our history when making beautiful soft and spongy white candy was an art and anyone who tasted it appreciated the effort.

(continued on next page)

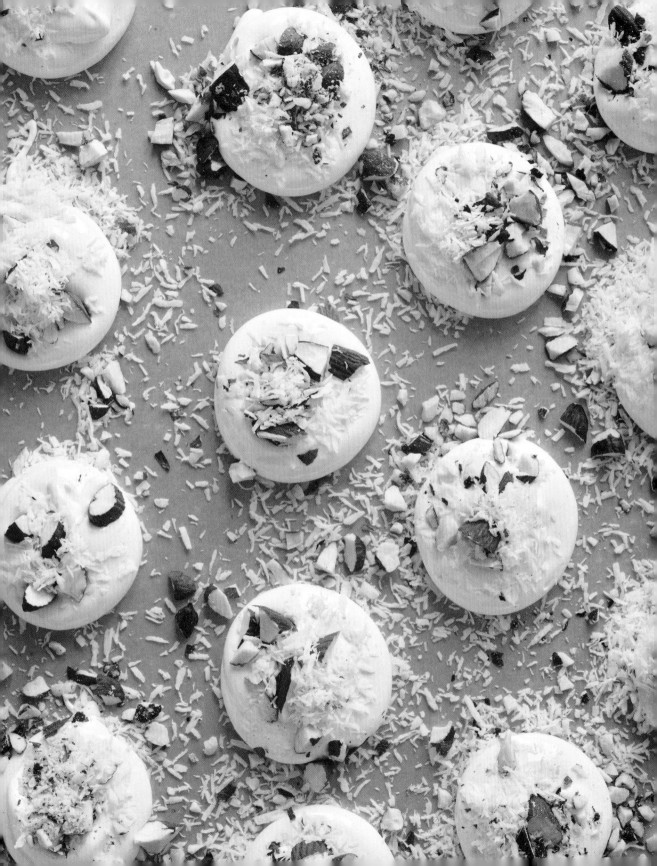

2 cups granulated sugar, divided use

²⁄₃ cup water, divided use

½ cup light corn syrup

2 egg whites, stiffly beaten

2 tablespoons toasted almonds

1 teaspoon vanilla extract

Pinch of salt

2 tablespoons shredded unsweetened coconut

MAKES: 24 to 36 pieces

PREP: 35 TO 40 MINUTES   CHILL: 1 HOUR

---

1. Place ½ cup of the sugar and ⅓ cup of the water in a small heavy saucepan and stir over medium heat until the sugar dissolves. Attach a candy thermometer to the side of the pan, and stir and cook over medium to medium-high heat until the mixture comes to 240°F. Remove from the heat and let the syrup cool slightly.

2. Place the remaining 1½ cups sugar, the remaining ⅓ cup water, and the corn syrup in a medium-size heavy saucepan and stir over medium heat to dissolve the sugar. Attach a candy thermometer to the side of the pan, and stir and cook over medium to medium-high heat until the mixture comes to 255°F.

3. While the second syrup is cooking, and using an electric stand mixer, slowly dribble the first cooled syrup into the beaten egg whites while the mixer is running on high speed. Be careful not to scrape the sides of the syrup pan. Beat until the egg whites lose their gloss, 1½ to 2 minutes. Turn off the mixer.

4. When the second syrup has come to 255°F, remove the pan from the heat. Let it rest while you finely chop the toasted almonds. Set aside. Turn on the mixer and pour the second syrup into the egg whites mixture until combined and the egg whites lose their gloss, about 1½ minutes. Briefly beat in the vanilla and salt.

5. Line a sheet pan or baking sheet with waxed paper. Dollop the mixture by teaspoons onto the waxed paper, being careful not to scrape the sides of the pan. Scatter the chopped almonds and coconut on top. Place the pan in the refrigerator to set, about 1 hour. Serve at once. If desired, you can pour the divinity into a buttered 12" × 8" glass pan instead.

UNDERSTANDING THE ART OF DIVINITY: Divinity masters carefully swab away sugar crystals that form while the sugar syrup cooks so the spoon doesn't scrape down back into the pan. If you don't want to wipe the crystals with a damp cloth, just make sure you don't scrape the sides of the pan with the spoon when you are pouring syrup into the egg whites or when you are transferring the finished divinity to the pan. And make this on days with clear skies—moisture in the air from rain prevents divinity from setting up.

Seven Tips for Successful Homemade Candies

I have gleaned these tips from my own candy-making experience and include the good suggestions of food chemist Shirley Corriher as well. These might help demystify candy making and bring you success with these classic American recipes.

1. You want to prevent sugar from crystallizing in your candy, and there are specific ways to go about this. First of all, follow the recipe exactly. Some recipes call for the mixture to be stirred vigorously before pouring—pralines. It is important that you do this.

2. Use a candy thermometer or at least these eye tests as to what happens when the candy syrup is dropped in cold water:

    234° to 236°F—Forms a soft ball. For fudge

    242° to 248°F—Forms a firm ball. Divinity and caramels

    250° to 265°F—Forms a hard ball. Taffy

    And when the candy is dropped from a spoon onto a plate:

    270° to 290°F—Makes a soft crack. Soft crunchy candies

    300° to 315°F—Makes a hard crack. Peanut brittle and toffee

3. Don't scrape the sides of the pan as you cook candy. Scraping pulls uncooked sugar crystals into the pan and they will multiply, turning your candy grainy.

4. When making fudge, stir vigorously once the mixture has cooked to the right temperature. This makes a creamy fudge.

5. Add different sugars to the mixture to prevent the candy from getting grainy. That's why recipes call for granulated sugar plus corn syrup.

6. Add a mild acidic ingredient like lemon juice or vinegar to alter the sucrose and turn it into a different sugar like glucose or fructose. This process is an old trick that still works and keeps candy smooth.

7. Add just 1 tablespoon of corn syrup to old candy recipes like pralines so they don't get grainy when cooling.

KENTUCKY BOURBON BALLS

1 cup finely chopped pecans

⅓ cup bourbon

½ cup (1 stick) lightly salted butter, at room temperature

3¼ cups confectioners' sugar

1 pound semisweet chocolate, chopped

About 60 small pecan halves, for garnish, if desired

MAKES: About 5 dozen (1") balls

MY FATHER USED TO drive from Tennessee to Kentucky to buy a box of Rebecca Ruth's bourbon balls. He was pretty crazy about that candy, and it was back in the day when local products stayed local and often didn't cross state lines. I wondered if all the bourbon in that candy was the reason my dad liked them so much and why they seemed like sweet contraband. We children didn't like the strong alcoholic flavor, but it's funny how as you age, that distinctive and delicious bourbon flavor grows on you!

Rebecca Ruth candies began in Frankfort, Kentucky, in 1919. Two schoolteachers, Ruth Hanly Booe and Rebecca Gooch, had been making chocolate candies—without bourbon—to give as Christmas gifts and decided they would earn more money making candy than teaching. They rented the bar of the Frankfort Hotel, which was closed due to Prohibition, and made chocolates on a marble-topped table.

The years passed, Rebecca sold her half of the business to Ruth, the Depression came, Ruth's house and factory were destroyed by fire, and chocolate sales nearly dried up. Until 1936, when Ruth came up with the genius idea of pairing chocolate with Kentucky's finest ingredient—bourbon. Sales boomed.

The family still operates the business, and it has become a revered taste of Kentucky. Many cooks and cookbooks have shared their homemade version of these famous candies. And compared to more complicated pralines and peanut brittle, bourbon balls are pretty easy to make at home.

PREP: 1 TO 1½ HOURS   CHILL: 1 TO 2 HOURS   REST: 2 HOURS

---

1. Place the chopped pecans in a small bowl. Stir in the bourbon to combine. Cover the bowl with waxed paper or plastic wrap and let the pecans soak in the bourbon for about 30 minutes.

2. Place the butter and confectioners' sugar in a large bowl and beat with an electric mixer on medium speed until the mixture is stiff, 1 to 2 minutes. Add the pecans and bourbon and beat on low speed until just combined. Roll the mixture into small ¾" balls, and place in the fridge to chill until firm, 1 to 2 hours.

(continued on next page)

3. Meanwhile, place the chocolate in a medium-size heavy saucepan over low heat. Stir the chocolate until it begins to melt, then pull the pan off the heat and stir until the chocolate melts completely, 5 to 7 minutes.

4. Remove the bourbon balls from the fridge. Stick a toothpick or fork in each ball and dunk on all sides in the chocolate. Transfer to a sheet of waxed paper to cool. Repeat with the remaining bourbon balls. While the chocolate is soft, press a pecan half into the top of each candy, if desired. Let the chocolate set about 2 hours before placing in a covered container to keep at room temperature for up to 2 weeks.

UNDERSTANDING THE ART OF BOURBON BALLS: The chocolate coats best if the filling has been chilled first. An easy way to coat the candies is to use melted semisweet chocolate chips.

CANDIED GRAPEFRUIT

4 large grapefruit

2 teaspoons salt

2 cups granulated sugar, plus more for coating

1 cup water

___

MAKES: 8 ounces

___

STRIPS OF GRAPEFRUIT PEEL candied and rolled in sugar were a delicacy in the early 1900s. They were called "candied" or "crystallized" grapefruit and appeared at the end of banquet menus, after the dessert and before the coffee. Sugar was more accessible and inexpensive then. People candied their own fruit at home.

In fact, a 1915 St. Louis newspaper columnist suggested that women who wanted to stay at home could generate income if they candied grapefruit peel and sold it. That peel sold for 60 to 80 cents a pound. Clearly there was more profit if you were living in a citrus-producing region of the country.

The peel of grapefruit is thicker and tougher than that of the orange, which makes it a pain to peel but perfect to candy. Each grapefruit yields about 1 cup of peel, so you'll need about 4 grapefruit for this recipe. A 1912 *Chicago Tribune* reader wrote in to say she used scissors to cut her grapefruit peel into strips.

But because grapefruit peel is bitter, you need to boil it three times to remove the bitterness before you can candy it. Look for grapefruit that are "thin-skinned," meaning they don't have a lot of white pith under the skin. And while older recipes used to call for tinting the grapefruit with food coloring, today the natural look of grapefruit peel is beautiful. Roll it in granulated sugar before drying and serve as a chewy and moist candy alongside dark chocolate and salted almonds.

___

PREP: ABOUT 2 HOURS   COOK: 30 MINUTES   COOL: 3 HOURS

___

1. With a small, sharp paring knife, cut the peel away from the flesh of the grapefruit. Place in a large, nonreactive (not aluminum) pan and cover with water. Stir in the salt. Bring to a boil over medium-high heat, then reduce the heat to medium and boil for 20 minutes. Drain off the water. Cover with fresh water (no salt), and boil again 20 minutes. Drain, and repeat the boiling one more time with fresh water to cover (no salt). After 20 minutes, drain the water from the pan.

2. Cut the white pith away from the peel. With clean kitchen shears, cut the peel into strips about $1/4$" wide and $2^1/2$" long.

(continued on next page)

3. For the sugar syrup, place 2 cups granulated sugar and 1 cup water in a medium-size saucepan over medium-high heat. Bring to a boil, stirring to dissolve the sugar. Reduce the heat slightly and continue to simmer until the syrup comes to 232°F. Add the reserved strips to the syrup and stir. Let simmer gently until the peel is translucent and the syrup is nearly gone, about 30 minutes. Drain and turn out onto a wire rack. Working with a handful of peel at a time, dredge them in granulated sugar, then shake to remove the excess sugar. Place back on the rack to let dry, about 3 hours. Store lightly covered at room temperature for up to 2 weeks.

UNDERSTANDING THE ART OF CANDIED GRAPEFRUIT: Thin-skinned grapefruit, which are better for using in this recipe, tend to be heavier than other grapefruit because they contain more fruit than rind.

NEW ORLEANS BEIGNETS

1 package (0.25 ounce) active dry yeast

¹⁄₄ cup warm water

¹⁄₄ cup granulated sugar

¹⁄₂ teaspoon salt

1 large egg, beaten

³⁄₄ cup evaporated milk

2 tablespoons melted and cooled butter or vegetable oil

3 to 3¹⁄₂ cups all-purpose flour

Peanut oil for frying

¹⁄₂ cup confectioners' sugar for dusting

MAKES: About 36

A COUSIN OF THE sopaipillas of the Southwest, beignets are rectangular, yeasty, and pillow-like. They were made famous at the Café du Monde in New Orleans, dunked in French-roast chicory coffee. And they often contain that ingredient found in few other fried things— canned evaporated milk, an ingredient that has been well received in warm climates, especially before refrigeration.

The first recipe for beignets was French, and it was by reading French cookbooks such as the popular *La Petite Cuisinier Habile* (*The Clever Little Cook*), published in 1840, that New Orleans cooks learned to make them. Interestingly, the word *beignet* means "rounded lump" in Old French, which is a pretty good descriptor of their appearance.

But it does not do their flavor justice, as this simple dough, this "rounded lump," when fried is sheer bliss. And if you've ever eaten beignets at Café du Monde, you know how much confectioners' sugar falls onto your clothes because those beignets are covered in sugar. So when you make these at home, toss them in a brown paper bag with the sugar while still warm. It clings to the beignets better this way.

PREP: 40 TO 45 MINUTES   RISE: 1 HOUR 20 MINUTES   COOK: 3 MINUTES

1. Place the yeast and warm water in a large bowl and stir with a fork to dissolve. Add the sugar and salt and stir to combine. Add the beaten egg, evaporated milk, and butter or oil. Beat with a wooden spoon until smooth, 1 to 2 minutes. Add 3 cups of the flour, and beat until well incorporated. Add another ¹⁄₂ cup of the flour as needed to pull the dough together. It should no longer be sticky. Cover the bowl with plastic wrap and place it in a warm place to rise until doubled, about 1 hour.

2. Punch down the dough and turn it out to a lightly floured surface. Knead it with your hands a few times and roll it into an 18" × 12" rectangle about ¹⁄₈" thick. Cut into rectangles measuring about 2" × 3" and cover them with waxed paper or plastic wrap and let rise again, about 20 minutes.

3. Pour 3" of oil into a heavy deep pot and heat over medium-high heat until it reaches 365°F. Drop 2 or 3 dough rectangles into the oil and fry until they are golden brown on one side (about 1½ minutes), then turn them over to cook on the other side, about 1½ minutes longer. Remove the beignets with a slotted spoon and transfer to a wire rack set over brown paper to drain. Repeat with the remaining batter.

4. Place the confectioners' sugar in a paper bag and add the warm, drained beignets a few at a time. Toss until well coated. Serve warm.

UNDERSTANDING THE ART OF THE BEIGNET: Just like cooking sopaipillas, you need to turn the beignets in the oil as they cook so they develop the pillowy shape and crisp texture.

FOLLOWING PAGE, LEFT TO RIGHT: *New Orleans Beignets and Funnel Cakes*

FUNNEL CAKES

1²⁄₃ cups whole milk

2 large eggs

2²⁄₃ cups all-purpose flour

4 tablespoons granulated sugar

1 teaspoon baking soda

1 teaspoon baking powder

¹⁄₂ teaspoon salt

Peanut oil for frying

¹⁄₂ cup confectioners' sugar for dusting

MAKES: About 12 funnel cakes

THE FOOD OF STATE fairs, funnel cakes didn't always have such humble roots. In fact, they were originally a 19th-century Christmas and New Year's treat sold at church bazaars and holiday markets, according to Pennsylvania Dutch food authority William Woys Weaver. And because they called for eggs when eggs were scarce in winter months, they were a luxury, afforded only by those with means.

And yet the story goes that once they were made at the 1950 Pennsylvania Dutch Folk Festival in Kutztown, Pennsylvania, they became an instant hit. The women who made and sold the funnel cakes realized they had a success on their hands, and kept frying. Those first funnel cakes were fried in hot lard.

You can form the cakes any size or shape you like, according to Ruth Hutchison, who wrote *The Pennsylvania Dutch Cook Book* in 1977. Then "frying becomes quite an art because all sorts of shapes can be achieved by quick twists and turns of the funnel and covering and uncovering the opening."

The batter is pretty basic—just flour, eggs, milk, and a little sugar. You must have a funnel with a big enough opening for dropping the pancakelike batter into hot oil. They cook in no time. Remove to brown paper or a wire rack to drain and dust with powdered sugar. This recipe is a hybrid of several recipes—it uses baking powder and a little baking soda for lots of crispiness. That seems to be the secret behind these fried cakes—if they don't rely on yeast for lightness, you've got to use plenty of leavening to make them crisp.

PREP: 20 TO 25 MINUTES   COOK: 3 MINUTES

---

1. Place the milk and eggs in a large bowl and whisk to combine.

2. Whisk together the flour, granulated sugar, baking soda, baking powder, and salt in a medium-size bowl. Turn the flour mixture on top of the milk and egg mixture and whisk until smooth, about 1 minute.

3. Pour 2" oil into a large, deep skillet or pot and heat over medium-high heat until it reaches 375°F. When the oil is nearly hot enough, pick up a funnel (with at least a ⁵⁄₈" opening) with one

hand and hold one finger over the bottom of the funnel to close it. Pour or ladle batter into the funnel. Move your hand over to the hot oil, and release your finger to let the batter drop enough. Move the funnel in circles to create a spiral, beginning at the center and moving outward. You can make these as large or small as you like. About 6" in diameter is a good size. Fry for about $1\frac{1}{2}$ minutes per side, turning once, until deeply browned. With tongs, remove the cakes to brown paper or a wire rack to drain. Dust with confectioners' sugar and serve hot. Repeat with the remaining batter.

UNDERSTANDING THE ART OF FUNNEL CAKES: The batter needs to be thin enough to come out of the funnel. Add more milk if needed to thin it.

Frying Cakes—What You Need to Know

"People tell me they don't like fried food," says culinary historian John Martin Taylor. "They are either lying or they haven't done it properly."

To fry cakes well, you need:

1. A deep, heavy pot, such as a 6-quart Dutch oven for frying
2. Peanut oil, which has a higher smoke point than regular vegetable oil so it is less likely to burn and imparts no off flavors to the food
3. A slotted spoon or sieve for removing fried cakes from the oil
4. A wire rack set above brown paper to drain the fried goodies and keep them crisp and not soggy
5. Plenty of confectioners' sugar for dusting or dredging the cakes!

CALAS

1/3 cup long-grain rice

1 1/2 cups whole milk

1/2 teaspoon salt, divided use

2 tablespoons unsalted butter, at room temperature

1 1/2 tablespoons warm water (110° to 115°F)

3/4 teaspoon active dry yeast

1 tablespoon granulated sugar

2 large eggs, lightly beaten, at room temperature

1/8 teaspoon ground nutmeg

1 teaspoon vanilla extract

1 cup all-purpose flour

Peanut oil for frying

1/2 cup confectioners' sugar for dusting

MAKES: 25 calas

THE HUMBLE FRITTER KNOWN as the cala is more than just a fried ball of rice. It was once sold on the streets of the French Quarter of New Orleans, and it was made in fine homes in South Carolina—except that in Carolina, the cala was called a *beignet de riz.*

The New Orleans freed slaves who hawked hot calas used the money to support their families. The calas sold outside Catholic Churches in the city broke fasts. And the children raised on calas in Creole homes remember them for First Communion breakfasts, wedding breakfasts, and the first Sunday in Lent.

The cala's heritage is French but also rooted in Africa. Early-American rice production was dependent on slaves. According to the late historian Karen Hess, who researched and wrote *The Carolina Rice Kitchen: The African Connection*, the word *cala* itself is African in origin. And the way it was sold in New Orleans reflected how it was sold in Africa. The 1901 *Picayune's Creole Cook Book* in New Orleans described the call of the street vendors: *"Belle cala! Tout chaud!"* (Beautiful calas, piping hot!) The batter was mixed and allowed to sit overnight, then the next morning it was fried, dusted with powdered sugar, and sold hot outside churches and homes.

Whether you call these delicate fritters calas or beignets de riz or croquettes as they did in Maryland and Kentucky, they are a vanishing foodstuff. The people who fried them are gone. Their descendants became more concerned with employment, education, and livelihood. But if you take the time to make calas, you will not be disappointed. They are creamy but light, filling, and yet not so. They are redolent of yeast, but they are so much less time consuming to make than traditional doughnuts. They are a treat, and yet you wish you had them every day. Calas, like other fritters, are a foodstuff we need to keep alive. The following recipe is adapted from one created by Anson Mills of South Carolina.

PREP: 40 TO 45 MINUTES   SOAK: OVERNIGHT   RISE: 2 HOURS
COOK: ABOUT 3 MINUTES

---

1. Place the rice in a medium-size bowl. Pour enough water over the rice to cover by 1". Cover the bowl with plastic wrap and place in the fridge overnight.

(continued on next page)

2. The next day, drain the rice. Place it in a medium-size saucepan with the milk and $\frac{1}{4}$ teaspoon of the salt. Bring to a boil, cover, then reduce the heat and simmer until tender, about 20 minutes. Remove the lid from the pan. All the milk should be absorbed. Add the butter. Press on the rice and butter until the rice is broken up and cottage cheese–like in texture. Transfer the mixture to a mixing bowl, and let cool 5 minutes.

3. Place the warm water in a small bowl and stir in the yeast. Let the mixture stand until the yeast has dissolved, about 5 minutes. Spoon the yeast mixture into the rice. Add the granulated sugar. Stir and combine. Cover the bowl with plastic wrap and let it rise at room temperature until doubled, about 1 hour.

4. When the rice mixture has risen, add the eggs, nutmeg, vanilla, and the remaining $\frac{1}{4}$ teaspoon salt. Combine well. Add the flour and stir until just combined. Turn the mixture into a clean mixing bowl, cover, and let the mixture rise until doubled, about 1 hour.

5. When you are ready to fry, pour $1\frac{1}{4}$" oil into a large heavy pot and heat over medium-high until it reaches 365°F. Spoon big tablespoons of the rice batter into the oil and cook until they are deep golden brown, about 3 minutes. Remove the calas with a slotted spoon to a wire rack set on top of brown paper to drain. Repeat with the remaining batter. While the calas are still warm, toss them with the confectioners' sugar. Serve warm.

UNDERSTANDING THE ART OF THE CALA: The first calas got their flavor from yeast spores in the air. The batter was left at room temperature to rise overnight. Today, we are so concerned with food safety, we would never do this. And thus, the flavor of today's calas is bound to be different from those of yesteryear.

BANANA FRITTERS

3/4 cup plus
2 tablespoons
whole milk

1 large egg

1 1/3 cups all-purpose
flour

1 1/2 tablespoons
granulated sugar

1/2 teaspoon baking
soda

1/2 teaspoon baking
powder

1/4 teaspoon salt

4 bananas

Peanut oil for frying

1/4 cup confectioners'
sugar

1/4 teaspoon ground
cinnamon

MAKES: 12 servings

FRITTERS ARE THOSE INDESCRIBABLY delicious fried puffs of crispness encasing something wonderful—a piece of fruit, but possibly vegetables and fruit. You know they are French when you bite into them, because the French are so good at isolating one flavor, really lifting it up to be the star. The word *fritter* comes from the French word *friture*, a generic term used for foods fried in deep fat. In America, you find fritter recipes on menus and in cookbooks of cities with French ancestry.

If there was a heyday for fritters, it would have been sometime between the 1830s and 1880s. According to David Shields in his book *Southern Provisions*, fritters were originally from Southern Europe and West Africa, dusted in sugar, and drenched in syrup. The batter could be of wheat, corn, buckwheat, or rice flour, and the fritters could be fried in rendered lard or vegetable oil. Being able to fry in deep oil was a West African technique, according to culinary historian Jessica B. Harris.

In fritters of fruit, the best selections are soft fruit—banana, a strawberry, or possibly a small fig inside. And while Mary Randolph soaked apple slices in sugar and wine and spices before frying them into fritters, the softer fruits are much nicer and their textures seem to complement the crunchy coating of the fritter. To prepare these fruits, use firm bananas, not too ripe. Cut figs lengthwise three times, not cutting through, leaving the stem intact, and fan them out by gently pressing down on them. Do the same with strawberries, except remove the cap first before frying.

PREP: 30 TO 35 MINUTES   COOK: 2 TO 3 MINUTES

---

1. Place the milk and egg in a large bowl and whisk to combine.
2. Whisk together the flour, granulated sugar, baking soda, baking powder, and salt in a medium-size bowl. Turn the flour mixture on top of the milk and egg mixture and whisk until smooth, about 1 minute. Set aside while you prepare the bananas.
3. Peel the bananas and cut each one crosswise into 3 equal sections. Cut each section lengthwise into 4 strips. You should have about 48 pieces of banana.

4. Pour 1½" oil into a large heavy pot or Dutch oven and. heat over medium-high heat until it reaches 365°F. Line a baking sheet with a wire rack set over brown paper. Combine the confectioners' sugar and cinnamon in a small bowl and set aside.

5. Piece by piece, dunk the fruit into the batter, using your fingers or a fork or small tongs. Once coated, drop about 6 pieces at a time into the hot oil. Fry until well browned on one side, 1 to 1½ minutes, then turn with a slotted spoon or spatula to brown on the other side, 1 to 1½ minutes longer. With a slotted spoon, transfer the fritters from the oil to the prepared rack to drain. Repeat with the remaining pieces of banana. Dust with the cinnamon sugar while the fritters are warm. Serve at once.

UNDERSTANDING THE ART OF THE FRITTER: Test to make sure the oil is hot enough for frying by dropping a teaspoon of batter into the oil as it heats. It should sizzle and brown when ready for frying.

FOLLOWING PAGE, CLOCKWISE FROM TOP: *Banana Fritters, Sopaipillas, and Orange and Ricotta Fritters*

ORANGE AND RICOTTA FRITTERS

1 cup whole milk ricotta cheese

2 large eggs, lightly beaten

$\frac{1}{3}$ cup whole milk

$\frac{1}{2}$ teaspoon vanilla extract

1 tablespoon fresh orange zest

1 cup unbleached all-purpose flour

$\frac{3}{4}$ cup confectioners' sugar, divided use

2 teaspoons baking powder

$\frac{1}{4}$ teaspoon salt

Peanut oil for frying

MAKES: 2 dozen (1$\frac{1}{2}$" to 2") fritters

A MODERN ADAPTATION OF the classic Sicilian *sfingi*, this ricotta-filled doughnut can be baked on weekends or for special days. Ricotta doughnuts were traditionally fried and served on St. Joseph's Day in Italian American communities throughout America.

In fact, immigrant communities have traditionally been the place where you will find the best doughnut and fritter recipes. These confections are tied to religious holidays and therefore made on the same day each year. The traditional Sicilian sfingi has two forms—either a yeast-based dough like a beignet, which is filled with ricotta cheese, chocolate, and cinnamon; or it is a doughnut with ricotta in the dough. These are often flavored with orange and dipped in honey.

The following recipe is a blend of old and new. The secret to keeping these fritters light is the generous amount of baking powder that lightens the ricotta cheese.

PREP: 15 TO 20 MINUTES   REST: 30 MINUTES   COOK: 2 TO 3 MINUTES

1. Place the ricotta, eggs, milk, vanilla, and orange zest in a large mixing bowl and whisk to combine well.

2. Place the flour, $\frac{1}{4}$ cup of the confectioners' sugar, the baking powder, and salt in a small bowl and stir to combine well. Add the flour mixture to the ricotta mixture and stir until smooth. Set the batter aside to rest for 30 minutes.

3. Pour 2" oil into a large, deep heavy pot or Dutch oven and heat over medium-high heat until it reaches 365°F. Line a baking sheet with a wire rack set over brown paper.

4. When the oil is hot, drop the dough by tablespoons or small scoops into the oil, frying 4 at a time. Make sure the oil stays between 350° and 365°F. Cook until deeply brown, 1 to 1$\frac{1}{2}$ minutes on one side, and then turn with a spatula to cook 1 to 1$\frac{1}{2}$ minutes on the other side. Remove with a spatula or strainer to the rack to drain. Repeat with the remaining batter. Dust while warm with the remaining $\frac{1}{2}$ cup confectioners' sugar and serve warm.

UNDERSTANDING THE ART OF FRITTERS: Sugar causes fritter and doughnut batters to burn while frying. That's why sugar is used to coat them after frying.

SOPAIPILLAS

2 cups all-purpose flour

1½ teaspoons granulated sugar

1 teaspoon baking powder

½ teaspoon salt

½ cup lukewarm water (95°F)

¼ cup milk, at room temperature

1½ teaspoons vegetable oil

Peanut oil for frying

1 cup honey

MAKES: 12 sopaipillas

THE INGREDIENTS OF AMERICA'S best-loved fried sweets were pretty simple—flour, sugar, oil, a little leavening, some milk or water, that's about it. What differed region to region was how the dough was prepared and fried, as well as when the fried sweet was served. In New Mexico, the doughnut of choice is the sopaipilla, a fried pocket often filled with honey.

It is nearly the same recipe as the beignet of New Orleans, but the sopaipilla contains no yeast and is leavened by baking powder. When frying sopaipillas, you must continue to turn them as they fry in order to create the pillow shape and crispy crust that shatters when you bite into it. Pour honey into the hollow cavity for an incredible treat!

In fact, it is the honey served with sopaipillas that makes them cool down the chiles and spices of Mexican and New Mexican cooking. This recipe is adapted from one shared in *Saveur* magazine and is similar to one prepared by southwestern food authority Cheryl Alters Jamison.

PREP: 20 TO 25 MINUTES   REST: 45 MINUTES   COOK: 2 MINUTES

1. Whisk together the flour, sugar, baking powder, and salt in a large bowl. Add the water, milk, and vegetable oil and stir until a sticky dough forms. Turn the dough out onto a floured surface. Knead until the dough is no longer sticky, about 1 minute. Cover the dough with a damp kitchen towel and let it rest for 15 minutes.

2. Divide the dough into 3 balls. Cover the balls with the towel and let rest for 30 minutes. Pour 2" peanut oil into a heavy 6-quart pan and heat over medium-high heat until it reaches 380° to 385°F.

3. Using a rolling pin, roll the balls on the floured surface to 8" rounds. Cut into wedges with a pizza cutter and carefully drop these wedges into the hot oil, one at a time. Cook until the dough rises back to the top, then turn it over. Continue to turn and cook the dough until it forms a pillow and turns golden brown, about 2 minutes total cooking time. Remove to paper towels or a wire rack set over brown paper to drain, and repeat with the remaining dough. Serve at once, drizzled with honey.

UNDERSTANDING THE ART OF SOPAIPILLAS: Let the dough rest before rolling it out. This makes it easier to work with. And fry these at a slightly higher heat than fritters.

ALBANY OLICOOKS (DOUGHNUTS)

¼ cup warm water
(110° to 115°F)

3 packages (0.25 ounce
each) active dry yeast

¼ teaspoon
granulated sugar

½ cup (1 stick)
unsalted butter, at
room temperature

¾ cup granulated
sugar

3 large eggs, at room
temperature

1 cup whole milk, at
room temperature

4 cups all-purpose
flour

Peanut oil for frying

COATING

¾ cup granulated
sugar

2½ teaspoons ground
cinnamon

¼ teaspoon ground
nutmeg, if desired

MAKES: 42 to 45 (2")
balls

ONCE AGAIN, THE NAME of the recipe tells the story. The original doughnuts were "nuts" of dough, not rings with holes in them. Thus the word *doughnuts*. The English Pilgrims, en route to America, made a long stop in Holland, and along the way they learned to make what we call doughnuts from the Dutch.

Yes, there has always been a connection between doughnuts and the sea. Yes, whalers ate them and fried the doughnuts in whale fat. But the Dutch who settled in America had been making doughnuts, called olykoeks or olicoocks, depending on where you lived, in their homeland.

You can read about these doughnuts in Washington Irving's *Knickerbocker's History of New York*—"balls of sweetened dough, fried in hog's fat, and called doughnuts or olykoeks (oil cakes)—a delicious kind of cake." For the record, the Germans had been frying doughnuts in Europe as far back as the Dutch, and for that reason we also have doughnuts present in the culinary history of the Pennsylvania Dutch, who were German and kept up the tradition of frying doughnuts on Shrove Tuesday. According to John Mariani in *The Dictionary of American Food & Drink*, the Pennsylvania Dutch were the first ones to make the doughnuts with holes—to dunk in their coffee. Plus, it sped up the cooking time.

Here is an old Dutch doughnut recipe from historian Peter G. Rose. It appeared in her book *The Sensible Cook: Dutch Foodways in the Old and the New World*. She says this recipe would have been made by the Dutch in Albany, New York.

PREP: 30 TO 35 MINUTES   RISE: 1 HOUR 15 MINUTES   COOK: 4½ TO 5 MINUTES

1. Place the water in a measuring cup and sprinkle the yeast on top. Add the granulated sugar. Stir to dissolve the yeast and sugar, and place in a warm spot in the kitchen to let the mixture slightly thicken, about 5 minutes.

2. Place the butter and sugar in a large bowl and beat with an electric mixer on medium speed until blended, about 1 minute. Add the eggs, one at a time, beating after each addition, and scrape down the sides of the bowl with a rubber spatula. Beat in the milk and the yeast mixture until smooth, 1 to 2 minutes.

(continued on next page)

Slowly stir in the flour, 1 cup at a time. Scrape the dough from the mixing bowl into a large glass bowl. Cover with plastic wrap and place in a warm place to rise until doubled, about 1 hour 15 minutes.

3. When the dough has doubled in size, punch it down with your fist. Pour 2" to 3" oil into a large, deep heavy pan and heat over medium-high heat until it reaches 365°F. When the oil is hot, drop tablespoons of dough into the oil and fry until deep golden brown on one side, about 2 minutes, then flip with a slotted spoon to the other side and fry for 2 minutes longer. Remove with the spoon to a wire rack over brown paper to drain. Repeat with the remaining dough.

4. For the coating, stir together the sugar, cinnamon, and nutmeg, if desired, in a small bowl. Toss the warm olicooks with the cinnamon-sugar mixture and place on a serving platter. Repeat until all the warm doughnuts are coated. Serve at once. You can keep these warm in a low oven.

The Sea and Doughnuts

The original Krispy Kreme doughnut recipe supposedly came from a riverboat captain. There has always been this connection between the river, the sea, and the doughnut. Because to fry a doughnut, you need oil. That oil was lard in the mid-1800s. But if you were at sea, that oil might have been whale blubber. According to historians, doughnuts were a reward for sailors. Far from home, the oil collected from catching whales allowed the ship's cook to make bread dough and all on board to fry up doughnuts.

Good Things to Remember When Making Homemade Doughnuts

1. Don't add too much flour. The dough needs to be sticky. Let it rest in the refrigerator for at least 30 minutes to make it easier to handle.

2. Don't overbeat the dough.

3. Use fresh oil for frying. I found peanut oil to be the best. Keep the oil at about 365°F. And use at least 2" to 3" oil in the pot.

4. Fry a few doughnuts at a time. Too many brings down the temperature of the oil. Turn them often during frying.

APPLE CIDER DOUGHNUTS

2 large eggs

$1/2$ cup apple cider

$1/2$ cup whole milk

2 tablespoons butter, melted

1 teaspoon vanilla extract

$1/2$ cup granulated sugar

2 cups self-rising flour, divided use

1 teaspoon ground cinnamon

$1/2$ teaspoon ground nutmeg

$2^1/2$ cups finely chopped apples (about 4 medium apples, peeled and cored)

Peanut oil for frying

$1/2$ cup confectioners' sugar for dusting

MAKES: About 20

ONE OF THE FIRST ways to cook apple doughnuts in America was to fry slices as fritters. These recipes appeared in all sorts of cookbooks, and they made good use of the local crop of apples when it came into season each fall. In fact, fall is the time of year when we think of apple fritters and doughnuts.

This more modern recipe combines two favorite autumn flavors—local apples and cider. It is easy to make because of the self-rising flour. No yeast is needed. The only trick is to make sure the doughnuts are small because the batter is dense and needs to cook through before the outside of the doughnuts browns.

Toss these while hot with confectioners' sugar, and serve with a mug of hot cider.

PREP: 35 TO 40 MINUTES   COOK: 3 TO 4 MINUTES

---

1. Place the eggs, apple cider, milk, melted butter, and vanilla in large bowl and whisk to combine. Whisk in the granulated sugar.

2. Measure $1^1/2$ cups of the flour into a small bowl. Stir in the cinnamon and nutmeg. Toss the apples with the remaining $1/2$ cup flour. Place the flour mixture in the bowl with the egg mixture and whisk until it is combined and smooth, about 1 minute. Fold in the floured apples until combined.

3. Pour 2" oil into a large, deep cast-iron skillet or Dutch oven and heat over medium-high heat until it reaches 350° to 365°F. When the oil is hot, drop generous tablespoons of the batter into the pan, frying about 4 doughnuts at a time. Let the doughnuts fry $1^1/2$ to 2 minutes per side, turn, and continue cooking $1^1/2$ to 2 minutes on the other side. Remove with a slotted spoon to a wire rack set on top of brown paper to drain. Repeat with the remaining batter, giving the oil time to reheat to 350° to 365°F before frying. With a slotted spoon or sieve, clean up the oil between batches, removing any burned bits from the oil. Dust the warm, drained doughnuts with confectioners' sugar and serve.

UNDERSTANDING THE ART OF THE DOUGHNUT: If these doughnuts begin to brown too quickly while frying, reduce the heat slightly.

Acknowledgments

In life, the small things *are often so much sweeter and more interesting than the big stuff. In the world of food, that's true—think caviar, a truffle shaving, Maine blueberries. And think the small, sweet bites in our recipe boxes—the pralines, calas, jumbles, brownies, and snickerdoodles that we pop into our mouths without thinking twice. They may be small but speak volumes.*

When I set out 4 years ago to write the history of American cake, I wanted to know the true stories behind our great cakes. But once I was deep in pound cake batter and had interviewed a dozen food historians, I realized the book was more than a collection of favorite recipes. It was a way to revisit American history and use cake as the lens. Each cake of our past tells a story and gives us clues as to what was happening when it was first baked. If you let them, the ingredients and methods take you back in time.

Along the way, I uncovered stories and recipes for little cakes and cookies that had something to say, too. They weren't the grand Lady Baltimore, red velvet, or coconut layer cakes, but they were recipes we love every day—Katharine Hepburn Brownies, Hello Dollies, peanut brittle, tea cakes, beignets, and more. And I wondered if examining these small bites might tell me about their history, just as the big cakes did.

So I took on this project. I baked peanut butter cookies and found out who first baked them. (Kudos to the lunchroom ladies!) And I baked my own Girl Scout cookies just like the Scouts did nearly 100 years ago when they were in charge of not only selling cookies but baking them, too. I discovered recipes that I had not heard of—marguerites, apisas, rocks, ground nut cakes, Jackson Jumbles, and Dolley Madison Seed Cakes. And I uncovered beautifully regional recipes I had not been raised on in the South—hermits, fig bars, bizcochitos, Joe Froggers, Nanaimo Bars, and peppernuts.

Just as in my last book project, I am thankful for the people who took the time to explain a regional difference, discuss an ingredient, detail a method, and explore a period of time or a people that were important to the recipe stories in my book. I would like to especially thank:

Peter G. Rose, for her knowledge of the Dutch in America

William Woys Weaver, for his writings about the Pennsylvania Dutch

Connie Carter of the Library of Congress, for sharing family recipes and her in-depth knowledge of old books and cookbook authors

Beatrice Ojakangas, for her calm explanation of Scandinavian baking

Joan Nathan, for explaining Jewish foodways

Damon Lee Fowler, for interpreting old Southern cookbooks and for his research on the recipes of President Thomas Jefferson

Nathalie Dupree, for connecting the dots to people and recipes of the past

Betty Fussell, for explaining gingersnaps and their unique history

In New Orleans: Liz Williams, Rien Fertel, Poppy Tooker, and Judy Walker, who know their city and its food so well

Charles A. Tingley, the senior research librarian at St. Augustine Historical Society, who brought that area of Florida to life for me

Jennifer Lewis, who suggested midwestern candies to make

Patty Erd, for giving background on spices in early American baking

Sharon Joyce, for talking about the foods of Maine

David Shields, who explained the connection of Southern baking and the land

Nic Butler, a wise interpreter of Charleston's food history

Alyssa Stribling, for researching the fascinating history of petits fours

Martha Bowden, for her dedication to testing old recipes

Greater Midways Food Alliance, for sharing the stories of the Midwest

Karen Haram, for telling me about the Mexican wedding cookie

Jennie Hytken, for sharing a family matzo cookie

Joanne Lamb Hayes, for all things wartime baking

John Martin Taylor, for his knowledge of coastal Southern food and frying

Stephanie Golding, for telling me about her Grandma Hartman and the molasses cookie

Sara Franco, a college friend, who has mastered thumbprint cookies in Atlanta

Shellie Unger, a longtime Philadelphia friend and talented baker

Alice Randall, for friendship and explaining the Neiman Marcus cookie as only she can

Emily Frith, for baking chocolate mocha cookies for me

Valerie Frey, for talking tea cakes and persimmon cookies

Julia Blakely, a Smithsonian researcher, who unlocked the Joe Frogger mystery

Again, I'd like to thank my family for giving me up, once again, to this project. If you couldn't tell from my blank stare, the stack of dirty dishes in the sink, and the books and papers strewn on top of the dining room table, Mom was deep in a book project again. I was back in the 1880s or the 1930s or the 1770s, depending on the day. So thank you, John, Litton, John, Kathleen, Hugh, and Ella for understanding.

And thanks to my agent, David Black, and his fine team, especially Jennifer Herrera and Matt Belford, for guiding me through this process so I could focus on reading and baking. Thanks again to my super editor, Dervla Kelly, who was patient with me turning in this manuscript the same year my daughter married and two other children went off to college and med school. It was a crazy, busy year, so thanks to Dervla and all of Rodale for understanding. Thanks to Marilyn Hauptly, Sara Cox, and Anna

Cooperberg of the editorial department for checking everything I wrote. And thanks, always to the creative genius Amy King, who must eat, sleep, and dream her projects because everything she does is fresh and brilliant. Bringing these recipes to life in photos was possible thanks to the accomplished team of photographer Tina Rupp, food stylist Paul Grimes, and prop stylist Stephanie Hanes. You have never seen so many cookies in one place in your life!

Finally, I am grateful to the librarians and libraries who opened their collections to me as they did with *American Cake*. And thanks to these online sources who are out there for you to use, as well. People ask me how I wrote *American Cake* and now *American Cookie*— where did I access these old recipes? Through the years, I have weakened and purchased some old rare books because I've read about them and wanted to own a copy. But you can spend a lot of money doing that. It's more cost effective to look at these old books through trusted online sources. The Library of Congress (loc.gov) is a first great place to start if you are looking for an old cookbook. And here are my other suggestions for old books and newspaper stories: Gutenberg .org, Archive.org, Newspapers.com, and Accessible.com. The latter two are subscription services. I also took advantage of the online research resources of Brittanica.com, NPR.org, NPS.org, NYTimes.org, Foodtimeline.org, Theoldfoodie.com, and Wikipedia. Thanks to all!

Bibliography

America's Cook Book: Compiled by the Home Institute of the *New York Herald*. New York: Charles Scribner's, 1938. Print.

Anderson, Jean. *The American Century Cookbook*. New York: Clarkson Potter, 1997. Print.

Andrews, Glenn. *Food from the Heartland: The Cooking of America's Midwest*. New York: Prentice Hall, 1991. Print.

Baird, Sarah C. Kentucky Sweets: *Bourbon Balls, Spoonbread, and Mile High Pie*. Charleston, SC: History, 2014. Print.

Bienvenu, Marcelle, and Judy Walker, eds. *Cooking Up a Storm*. San Francisco: Chronicle Books, 2008. Print.

Boatner, Mark. *Landmarks of the American Revolution*. New York: Hawthorn Books, 1975. Print.

Booth, Letha. *The Williamsburg Cookbook: Traditional and Contemporary Recipes*. Williamsburg, VA: Colonial Williamsburg Foundation, 1975. Print.

Bryan, Lettice. *The Kentucky Housewife*. (Cincinnati: Shepard & Stearns, 1839); Columbia, SC: University of South Carolina Press, 1991. Print.

Byrn, Anne. *American Cake*. New York: Rodale, 2016. Print.

Cannon, Poppy, and Patricia Brooks. *The Presidents' Cookbook; Practical Recipes from George Washington to the Present*. New York: Funk & Wagnalls, 1968. Print.

Clark, Marian. *The Route 66 Cookbook*. Tulsa, OK: Council Oak, 1993. Print.

Corbitt, Helen. *Helen Corbitt's Cookbook*. Boston: Houghton Mifflin, 1957. Print.

Corriher, Shirley. *BakeWise*. New York: Scribner, 2008. Print.

Dallas Junior League Cookbook, The. Dallas: Junior League of Dallas, 1976. Print.

Dull, Mrs. S. R. *Southern Cooking*. New York: Grosset & Dunlap, 1941. Print.

Dupree, Nathalie, and Cynthia Stevens Graubart. *Mastering the Art of Southern Cooking*. Salt Lake City: Gibbs Smith, 2012. Print.

Egerton, John. *Side Orders: Small Helpings of Southern Cookery & Culture*. Atlanta: Peachtree, 1990. Print.

Egerton, John, Ann Bleidt Egerton, and Al Clayton. *Southern Food: At Home, on the Road, in History*. New York: Knopf, 1987. Print.

Emily Dickinson: Profile of the Poet as Cook with Selected Recipes. Amherst, MA: Dickinson Homestead, 1976. Print.

Ferris, Marcie Cohen. *Matzoh Ball Gumbo: Culinary Tales of the Jewish South*. Chapel Hill, NC: University of

North Carolina, 2005. Print.

Fowler, Damon Lee. *Classical Southern Cooking.* New York: Crown Publishers, 1995. Print.

——.*Dining at Monticello: In Good Taste and Abundance.* Charlottesville, VA: Thomas Jefferson Foundation, 2005. Print.

Fox, Minnie C. *The Blue Grass Cook Book.* (New York: Duffield & Company, 1904) Bedford, MA: Applewood Books, 2008. Print.

Frey, Valerie J. *Preserving Family Recipes: How to Save and Celebrate Your Food Traditions.* Athens, GA: University of Georgia Press, 2015. Print.

Fussell, Betty Harper. *I Hear America Cooking.* New York: Viking, 1986. Print.

Gifts from the Christmas Kitchen. New York: Irena Chalmers Cookbooks, 1983. Print.

Gourmet's America. New York: Random House, 1994. Print.

Haber, Barbara. *From Hardtack to Home Fries: An Uncommon History of American Cooks & Meals.* New York: Penguin, 2003. Print.

Hachten, Harva, and Terese Allen. *The Flavor of Wisconsin: An Informal History of Food and Eating in the Badger State.* Madison, WI: Wisconsin Historical Society, 2009. Print.

Harbury, Katharine E. *Colonial Virginia's Cooking Dynasty.* Columbia, SC: University of South Carolina, 2004. Print.

Hayes, Joanne Lamb. *Grandma's Wartime Baking Book: World War II and the Way We Baked.* New York: St. Martin's Press, 2003. Print.

Heatter, Maida. *Maida Heatter's Best Dessert Book Ever.* New York: Random House, 1990. Print.

——.*Maida Heatter's Book of Great Chocolate Desserts.* New York: Knopf, 1980. Print.

——.*Maida Heatter's Book of Great Cookies.* New York: Alfred A. Knopf, 1977. Print.

——.*Maida Heatter's Cakes.* Kansas City, MO: Andrews McMeel, 1997. Print.

Heller, Edna Eby. *The Art of Pennsylvania Dutch Cooking.* Garden City, NY: Doubleday, 1968. Print.

Hess, John L., and Karen Hess. *The Taste of America.* New York: Grossman, 1977. Print.

Hess, Karen. *The Carolina Rice Kitchen: The African Connection.* Columbia, SC: University of South Carolina Press, 1992. Print.

Hill, Annabella P. *Mrs. Hill's Southern Practical Cookery and Receipt Book.* Columbia, SC: University of South Carolina Press, 1995. Originally published as *Mrs. Hill's New Cook Book* (New York: G.W. Dillingham Co.,1872). Print.

Hornblower, Malabar. *The Plimoth Plantation New England Cookery Book.* Boston: Harvard Common Press, 1990. Print.

Horry, Harriott Pinckney, and Richard J. Hooker. *A Colonial Plantation Cookbook: The Receipt Book of Harriott Pinckney Horry, 1770.* Columbia, SC: University of South Carolina, 1984. Print.

Hutchison, Ruth. *The Pennsylvania Dutch Cook Book*. New York: Harper, 1977. Print.

Jackson Cookbook, The. Jackson, MS: Symphony League of Jackson, 1971. Print.

Jamison, Cheryl Alters, and Bill Jamison. *Tasting New Mexico: Recipes Celebrating One Hundred Years of Distinctive Home Cooking*. Albuquerque: New Mexico Press, 2012. Print.

Jones, Evan. *American Food: The Gastronomic Story*. New York: Random House, 1981. Print.

Kander, Mrs. Simon, and Mrs. Henry Schoenfeld. *The Settlement Cookbook, 1903: The Way to a Man's Heart*. Carlisle, MA: Applewood, 1996. Print.

Kimball, Marie Goebel. *Thomas Jefferson's Cook Book*. Charlottesville, VA: University of Virginia, 1976. Print.

King, Caroline B., and Thelma Wise. *Victorian Cakes: A Reminiscence with Recipes*. Berkeley, CA: Aris, 1986. Print.

Kirlin, Katherine S., and Thomas M. Kirlin. *Smithsonian Folklife Cookbook*. Washington, DC: Smithsonian Institution, 1991. Print.

Klapthor, Margaret Brown, and Helen Claire Duprey Bullock. *The First Ladies Cook Book: Favorite Recipes of All the Presidents of the United States*. New York: Parents Magazine Enterprises, 1982. Print.

Koock, Mary Faulk. *The Texas Cookbook: From Barbecue to Banquet, an Informal View of Dining and Entertaining the Texas Way*. Denton, TX: University of North Texas, 1965. Print.

Lea, Elizabeth Ellicott. *Domestic Cookery, Useful Receipts, and Hints to Young Housekeepers*. Baltimore: Cushing and Bailey, 1869.

LeClercq, Anne Sinkler Whaley. *An Antebellum Plantation Household: Including the South Carolina Low Country Receipts and Remedies of Emily Wharton Sinkler*. Columbia, SC: University of South Carolina, 2006. Print.

Lewis, Jenny. *Midwest Sweet Baking History: Delectable Classics Around Lake Michigan*. Charleston, SC: History Press, 2011. Print.

Mariani, John F. *The Dictionary of American Food and Drink*. New York: Ticknor & Fields, 1983. Print.

Metcalfe, Gayden, and Charlotte Hays. *Being Dead Is No Excuse: The Official Southern Ladies Guide to Hosting the Perfect Funeral*. New York: Miramax, 2005. Print.

Neal, Bill. *Bill Neal's Southern Cooking*. Chapel Hill, NC: University of North Carolina, 1985. Print.

——. *Biscuits Spoonbread & Sweet Potato Pie*. Chapel Hill, NC: University of North Carolina Press, 2003.

Nesbitt, Henrietta. *The Presidential Cookbook*. Garden City, NJ: Doubleday & Co., 1951. Print.

——. *White House Diary*. Garden City, NJ: Doubleday & Co., 1948. Print.

Old Salem Museums & Gardens Cookbook, The. Winston-Salem, NC: Old Salem Museums & Gardens, 2008. Print.

Ojakangas, Beatrice A. *Great Old-fashioned American Recipes*. Minneapolis: University of Minnesota, 2005. Print.

Picayune's Creole Cook Book, The. New York: Random House, 1989. Print.

Puckett, Susan. *Eat Drink Delta: A Hungry Traveler's Journey through the Soul of the South*. Athens, GA: University of Georgia, 2013. Print.

Quaker Lady's Cookbook: Recipes from the Parry Mansion, A. New Hope, PA: New Hope Historical Society, 1998. Print.

Randolph, Mary. *The Virginia Housewife*. Birmingham, AL: Oxmoor House, 1988. Print.

Rawlings, Marjorie Kinnan. *Cross Creek Cookery*. New York: C. Scribner's Sons, 1942. Print.

Recipes from Old Virginia. Richmond, VA: Dietz, 1958. Print.

Recipes from the Raleigh Tavern Bakery. Williamsburg, VA: Colonial Williamsburg Foundation, 2014. Print.

Rhett, Blanche S. *200 Years of Charleston Cooking: Recipes Gathered by Blanche S. Rhett*. New York: Random House, 1934. Print.

River Road Recipes. Baton Rouge, LA: Junior League of Baton Rouge, 1959. Print.

Rombauer, Irma S. *The Joy of Cooking*. New York: Scribner, 1959. Print.

Russell, Malinda, and Janice Bluestein Longone. *A Domestic Cook Book: Containing a Careful Selection of Useful Receipts for the Kitchen*. Ann Arbor, MI: Longone Center for American Culinary Research, William L. Clements Library, University of Michigan, 2007. Print.

Rutledge, Sarah. *The Carolina Housewife*. (Charleston, SC: John Russell, 1855) Columbia, SC: University of South Carolina Press, 1979. Print.

Sax, Richard. *Classic Home Desserts: A Treasury of Heirloom and Contemporary Recipes from around the World*. New York: Houghton Mifflin, 1994. Print.

Scaggs, Deirdre A., and Andrew W. McGraw. *The Historic Kentucky Kitchen: Traditional Recipes for Today's Cook*. Lexington, KY: University Press of Kentucky, 2013. Print.

Sewell, Ernestine P., and Joyce Gibson. Roach. *Eats: A Folk History of Texas Foods*. Fort Worth, TX: Texas Christian University Press, 1989. Print.

Shields, David S. *Southern Provisions: The Creation & Revival of a Cuisine*. Chicago: University of Chicago, 2015. Print.

Simmons, Amelia, and Mary Tolford Wilson. *The First American Cookbook: A Facsimile of "American Cookery," 1796*. New York: Dover Publications, 1984. Print.

Smith, Andrew F. *The Oxford Companion to American Food and Drink*. New York: Oxford University Press, 2007. Print.

Sohn, Mark F. *Appalachian Home Cooking: History, Culture, and Recipes*. Lexington, KY: University of Kentucky, 2005. Print.

Sokolov, Raymond A. *Why We Eat What We Eat*. New York: Simon & Schuster, 1991. Print.

Staib, Walter, and Paul Bauer. *The City Tavern Cookbook: Recipes from the Birthplace of American Cuisine*. Philadelphia, PA: Running Press, 2009. Print.

Stallworth, Lyn, and Rod Kennedy, Jr. *The County Fair Cookbook*. New York: Hyperion, 1994. Print.

Sugar Spoon Recipes from the Domino Sugar Bowl Kitchen. New York: American Sugar Refining Company, 1962. Print.

Swell, Barbara. *The 1st American Cookie Lady: Recipes from a 1917 Cookie Diary*. Asheville, NC: Native Ground Music, 2005. Print.

Taylor, John Martin. *The Fearless Frying Cookbook*. New York: Workman Publishing, 1997. Print.

——. *The New Southern Cook: Two Hundred Recipes from the South's Best Chefs and Home Cooks*. New York: Bantam, 1995. Print.

Theobald, Mary Miley. *Recipes from the Raleigh Tavern Bake Shop*. Williamsburg, VA: Colonial Williamsburg Foundation, 1984. Print.

Thurman, Sue Bailey, and Anne Bower. *The Historical Cookbook of the American Negro*. Boston: Beacon, 2000. Print.

Tillery, Carolyn Quick. *The African-American Heritage Cookbook: Traditional Recipes and Fond Remembrances from Alabama's Renowned Tuskegee Institute*. Secaucus, NJ: Carol Group, 1996. Print.

Trager, James. *The Food Chronology: A Food Lover's Compendium of Events and Anecdotes from Prehistory to the Present*. New York: Henry Holt, 1995. Print.

Villas, James, and Martha Pearl Villas. *My Mother's Southern Kitchen*. New York: Macmillan, 1994. Print.

Wakefield, Ruth Graves. *Ruth Wakefield's Toll House Tried and True Recipes*. New York: M. Barrows & Company, 1938.

Wallace, Lily Haxworth. *The Rumford Complete Cook Book*. Providence, RI: Department of Home Economics of The Rumford, 1948. Print.

Weaver, William Woys. *A Quaker Woman's Cookbook*. Mechanicsburg, PA: Stackpole Books, 2004. Print.

——. *As American as Shoofly Pie: The Foodlore and Fakelore of Pennsylvania Dutch Cuisine*. Philadelphia: University of Pennsylvania, 2013. Print.

Weiss, Luisa. *Classic German Baking*. Berkeley, CA: Ten Speed Press, 2016. Print.

Whaley, Emily. *Mrs. Whaley's Charleston Kitchen: Advice, Opinions, and 100 Recipes from a Southern Legend*. New York: Simon & Schuster, 1998. Print.

Williams, Elizabeth M. *New Orleans: A Food Biography*. Lanham, MD: AltaMira, 2013. Print.

Zanger, Mark. *The American History Cookbook*. Westport, CT: Greenwood, 2003. Print.

Index

Boldface page numbers indicate photographs or illustrations. Underscored references indicate boxed text, charts, and graphs.